Settler Colonial City

Settler Colonial City

Racism and Inequity in Postwar Minneapolis

DAVID HUGILL

University of Minnesota Press
Minneapolis
London

Maps on pages x and xi by Brad Herried

Published by the University of Minnesota Press
111 Third Avenue South, Suite 290
Minneapolis, MN 55401-2520
http://www.upress.umn.edu

ISBN 978-1-5179-0479-1 (hc)
ISBN 978-1-5179-0480-7 (pb)
Library of Congress record available at https://lccn.loc.gov/2021025906.

Printed in the United States of America on acid-free paper

The University of Minnesota is an equal-opportunity educator and employer.

28 27 26 25 24 23 22 21   10 9 8 7 6 5 4 3 2 1

Contents

Preface

The final edits to this text were made in a hastily assembled home office during the first months of the Covid-19 crisis in North America. As I write these words, my three-year-old daughter—whose daycare is shuttered—is scampering back and forth on the other side of the drywall. The pitter-patter of Audrey's tiny feet is now a familiar workday rhythm.

The pandemic has produced enormous vulnerability, but the distribution of that vulnerability is uneven. The fantasy that "we are all in this together" belies the fact that the real burdens of exposure fall on some and not others. At this moment, I am working from the relative isolation of a desk in the corner of Audrey's bedroom. At the other end of my street, a group of underhoused people is sitting in close proximity to one another waiting for a local church to start its daily lunch distribution. In my neighborhood as elsewhere, these distinctions are racialized. Ruth Wilson Gilmore's now-famous definition of racism as "the state sanctioned and/or extralegal production and exploitation of group-differentiated vulnerability to premature death" is particularly apt in this moment.[1] Indigenous people and people of color share disproportionately in the millions of years of potential life that have already been lost to the pandemic in the United States.[2]

And yet while such inequities are entrenched in North American societies, their endurance is not inevitable. Rather, that endurance is contingent on the sustained reproduction of a set of material, social, and political relations. One decade ago, it was possible for Neil Smith to lament that in the dominant discourses of the Global North the very idea of transformative political action had been banished to "the infinite horizon of never never land" and "erased from the memory banks of future social possibility."[3] Today, however, the confidence in a flat and predictable future that Smith scorned seems more misplaced than ever. For better and worse, tectonic shifts are under way. And the pandemic is only part of the story. Some changes bode ill: the rise of new authoritarianisms, the deepening of the climate emergency, the mainstreaming of overt forms of white supremacy. Others bode well: the rebirth of an institutional left in the United States, the growing strength of social movements demanding ecological and "racial" justice, and the mainstreaming of demands to transform (and even abolish) existing models of criminal punishment. All of these shifts are reminders that the contemporary order of things is contingent, interruptible, and up for grabs.

As I write, the city of Minneapolis, which is the subject of this book, has emerged as a global symbol of the fight for a different kind of world. On Monday, May 25, 2020, Minneapolis police suffocated George Floyd in broad daylight after he was accused of passing a counterfeit bill at a local food store. Videos of the killing were shared widely and demonstrations against racialized police violence were quickly organized, first in Minneapolis but soon across the United States and around the world. Subsequent reporting suggests that these protests may well be the largest in American history, with an estimated fifteen to twenty-five million people participating in some form during the spring and summer of 2020.[4]

In the days that followed Floyd's murder, demonstrations in Minnesota's Twin Cities grew to a massive scale. Momentum was palpable. Minneapolis-based geographer Kate Derickson described it as the kind of moment where "the previously unthinkable becomes thought." By early June, the movement's demands had become so persuasive that even city council members were declaring themselves prepared to defund the city's police department.[5]

These developments were neither a spontaneous reaction to popular revolt nor the product of enlightened governance. They were, rather, the fruit of a long history of careful organizing against racialized inequity and the violence of the criminal justice system. "All credit to the abolitionists—women of color in particular—who have been chopping the wood, arranging the kindling, and tending to every single spark," wrote Derickson. "I only hope the rest of us can give this fire the space and time it needs to burn."[6]

The revolt provoked by Floyd's murder is unique in its scale and intensity, but it is not without precedent. Racialized police repression has often been vigorously contested in Minneapolis. For generations, Black and Indigenous organizers have deployed creative strategies to counter and challenge Minneapolis Police Department (MPD) targeting. The successes of recent demonstrations speak to the efficacy of this long struggle.

But why has this long history of organizing been necessary? How should we make sense of the fact that some people are served and protected by police, while others are menaced and killed? What historical contexts shape contemporary inequities?

Settler Colonial City aims to help answer some of these questions by shedding light on how diverse forms of racialized inequity have structured life in inner-city Minneapolis. Specifically, this book seeks to understand how the hierarchical politics of settler colonization—which have been at the center of social relations in the place now called Minnesota since at least the nineteenth century—had a decisive impact on life in South Minneapolis during the second half of the twentieth century. In the chapters that follow, it argues that settler colonists and their descendants (people who are almost always white) have reproduced and reaped advantage from a racialized economy of power that has funneled advantages and immunities to themselves, almost always at the expense of others. In short, this book is a study of how people like me, that is, the descendants of Europeans and Euro-Americans who "settled" in western North America, have been unduly advantaged by the establishment of a society that operates to promote and defend the "interests" of non-Indigenous settlers (including their territorial ambitions, economic well-being, political commitments, and interpretive frames) over and above the interests of Indigenous people(s). Of course, this is not strictly a historical matter and one of the key contentions of this book is that the settler colonial relation endures as a constitutive dimension in the organization of collective life in the United States, whether this fact is acknowledged or not.

These considerations are not wholly separate from Floyd's murder and the revolt that it provoked. Of course, racism experienced by

African Americans has a particular history in the United States, and that history should not be simply conflated with settler colonization. With that said, the form that white supremacy has taken in Minnesota's largest city—the specific ways, that is, that a racialized economy of power has operated to distribute advantage and immunity—demands that we take seriously the common ways that Black and Indigenous people have been disproportionately excluded from the benefits of the city's considerable prosperity and targeted by the coercive arm of the state, even if the context of that targeting differs.

Cities and Indigenous Communities of Minnesota.

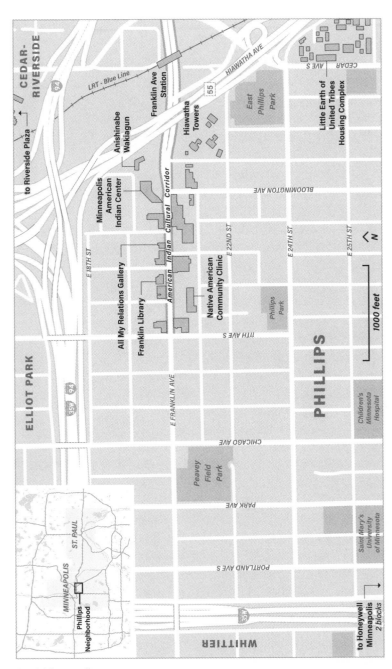

South Minneapolis.

Minneapolis as a Settler Colonial City

In late May 2017, the Walker Art Center announced that it would delay the opening of a renovation to its sculpture garden after objections were raised about the inclusion of a replica gallows by artist Sam Durant. The new installation, titled *Scaffold,* featured design elements from a range of historic hanging platforms, including those used to execute the abolitionist John Brown, the Haymarket Square martyrs, Saddam Hussein, and, most provocatively, thirty-eight Dakota men in Mankato, Minnesota, some eighty miles from the Walker's front door. Euro-American settlement in the woodlands of the Upper Mississippi was extraordinarily brutal and Dakota people were forced to contend with bad faith treaty making, geographical containment, mass incarceration, and territorial expulsion, among other indignities. Indeed, the 1862 executions at Mankato are merely the most famous episode in a broad pattern of revanchist colonial violence. Given this context, it is no stretch to say that *Scaffold* was a bold addition to a collection hitherto known for a Pop Art sculpture of a cherry balancing on a spoon.

Not surprisingly, the inclusion of *Scaffold* was vigorously contested. As the reopening of the sculpture garden approached, large protests were organized and matched by a torrent of online criticism. In these initial days, the situation shifted rapidly. Dakota elders held a meeting to get community feedback and plot the way forward. A delegation of Indigenous leaders met with Walker officials and city staff. Statements were issued. Press conferences were held. An agreement was reached. The sculpture was removed.

Importantly, though, the *Scaffold* incident is about more than a public relations blunder. Critics observed that the failure of Walker officials to consult with Dakota people about Durant's sculpture was indicative of a broader failure of Minnesota institutions to emerge from the long shadow that colonization and dispossession have cast on life in the region.[1]

The relationship between Minnesota's leading institutions and colonial dispossession is anything but abstract. In fact, the Walker Art Center is itself an explicit product of settler territorial expropriation. Thomas Barlow Walker, the gallery's namesake, was a Gilded Age timber baron who reaped enormous personal benefit from the American colonization of what is now the Upper Midwest. Walker's life was the stuff of a Horatio Alger Jr. novel. He arrived in Minneapolis as a man of decidedly modest means in 1862. By the turn of the twentieth century, he had completed a meteoric ascent to the very heights of the plutocracy.[2] Building on the spoils of initial good fortune, Walker transformed modest timberland holdings into a sprawling set of interests in extraction, processing, milling, and stumpage. Lumber was big business in nineteenth-century Minnesota and Walker amassed a fortune so large that he was reputed to be the richest man in the state, with an estimated personal worth of ten to sixteen million dollars.[3]

As Walker's fortune grew, so too did his urban investments, which soon included interests in industrial, commercial, and residential real estate. He took personal pride in endowing Minneapolis's intellectual and cultural life. Walker amassed one of the most impressive private art collections in the country. His personal holdings provided the foundation on which the Walker Art Center would be built.

Yet Walker's life is more than a story of acumen, philanthropy, and élan. His capacity to generate wealth and endow institutions is inseparable from the sweeping transformation of social and political life that was accomplished as large swaths of western North America were incorporated into the territorial ambit of the United States. "Rugged individualists" like Walker did not venture to the "frontier"

The installation of Sam Durant's *Scaffold* in the Minneapolis Sculpture Garden in 2017 was met with vigorous opposition. Photograph by Lorie Shaull.

of westward Euro-American expansion alone but were accompanied by "banks, railways, the state and other collective sources of capital."[4] Walker's accumulations cannot, in other words, be decoupled from the predatory violence of settler colonization and its valorization of the territorial and social claims of Euro-Americans over and above those of the people they sought to replace as the rightful users and occupiers of the land. Neither do those accumulations belong to the past. Advantages acquired through dispossession endure as a dynamic force of economic and cultural power, even to this day.

This fact is rarely interrogated. In the United States—like other settler colonial societies—the structured advantages enjoyed by the beneficiaries of colonization and racial capitalism are obscured by a pervasive culture of "organized forgetting."[5] While many acknowledge that American *history* is replete with monstrous injustice and routinized racial violence, far fewer accept that these foundational inequities continue as ordinary features of contemporary American life. Colonial inequity, in particular, is almost always relegated to the province of the regrettable past. Rarely is it conceptualized as a problem to be considered, confronted, and dismantled in the politics of the present.

This is particularly true in urban contexts. Although Indigenous people have always lived in North American cities, they have often been ideologically evacuated from the dominant urban imaginary.[6] From an urban vantage, the colonial encounter is usually imagined as something that happens *back then* and *out there*, insofar as it is imagined at all.[7]

Settler Colonial City challenges this culture of organized forgetting by arguing that the life of Minnesota's largest city is enduringly bound up with the hierarchical politics of settler colonization. It makes the case that historically inaugurated modes of being together persist as structural features of shared contemporary experience, functioning as a "relatively secure or sedimented" set of relations that continue to enforce racialized forms of inequity, albeit in always changing forms.[8] It contends, in other words, that a racialized economy of power continues to funnel advantages and immunities to some groups and not others, often while rendering that inequitable distribution opaque.[9] By using Minneapolis as a case study, this book offers an empirical counterpoint to analyses that draw sharp lines of distinction between the modern lives of North American cities and the settler colonial process. It seeks to make plain that Minneapolis is actively produced by the politics of settler colonization.

North American urban centers were not brought to life by spontaneous acts of settler creation. They were produced in a context of predatory territorial redefinition.[10] In Minnesota, as elsewhere, the emergence of cities of regional significance has often been imagined as a consequence of the vision, courage, and commitment of "big-minded" men who impressed their wills on an "unimproved" wilderness. Consider, for example, the architectural critic Montgomery Schulyer's description of fin-de-siècle Minneapolis as a city that had risen like an "exhalation," a sudden creation that sprung forth "from the heads of its projectors full-panoplied in bricks and mortar."[11] Urban genesis myths like this one trade in crude hagiography and obscure the immense violence that animates settler colonial projects of invasion and expropriation.[12] Minnesota's "great" cities did not spring from the "heads" of their "projectors." They were (and are) produced on the strength of a massive transfer of territory, resources, and control from Indigenous people to settlers.

Critically, settler colonial city building does not occur at a distance from the broader process of dispossessing Indigenous people of their lands. Urban centers are pivotal to the project of racialized geographic engineering that settler colonization entails. They are both sites of dispossession themselves *and* key hubs for the organization, financing, and outfitting of broader regional transformations.[13]

But this book is not about the founding of Minneapolis. Rather, it considers events that transpired in the five decades that followed the end of the Second World War and examines a series of distinct "sites" in which the enduring potency of the settler colonial relation is observable. Above all else, it is concerned with tracking how the settler colonial relation was articulated, refashioned, and reborn at a moment when the Twin Cities Indigenous community was growing substantially, and new geographies of racialized advantage and privation were emerging. Accordingly, the four chapters at the center of the book draw on empirical evidence to track (in a nonlinear way) how settler colonial inequities were reproduced in (1) the processes of metropolitan reorganization that remade the urban geography of the Twin Cities in the period after 1945, (2) various forms of liberal community organizing and "Indian affairs advocacy" undertaken by non-Indigenous researchers in the 1960s and 1970s, (3) a culture of racialized police targeting that was pervasive from the 1960s through the 1990s, and (4) the entanglements of Cold War forms of American imperialism with longer patterns of settler colonization, especially in events that transpired in the inner-city during the 1980s.

Clearly, these are not the only realms in which the settler colonial relation is observable. This book makes no claim to comprehensiveness. Nevertheless, it is my view that analyses of these disparate "sites" offer a more-or-less representative sense of how the actions, assumptions, and practices of non-Indigenous Minneapolitans (the vast majority of whom were white) operated to produce and enforce a racialized economy of power across a diverse field of experience.

When read together, these chapters demonstrate that phenomena that might otherwise appear to be distinct from one another are, in fact, elements of a distinct pattern of group-differentiated inequity.

What do I mean by "settler colonial relation"? I use this term to describe the inequitable relationship that exists between Indigenous and settler constituencies in Minnesota. Specifically, I am concerned with understanding the persistent effect of practices and mentalities that operate to promote the economic interests, social forms, political commitments, territorial ambitions, and interpretive frames of Euro-American settlers and their descendants, over and above those of Indigenous peoples and their descendants. Of course, it is analytically perilous to suggest that a distinct sort of relationship persists between groups as broadly defined as "Indigenous" and "settler" and it should go without saying that there is an immense degree of internal differentiation within and among these groups, in Minnesota as elsewhere. Those that might reasonably be included in these categorizations come from a huge range of cultural traditions, backgrounds, class positions, and geographic locations. This book's intention is not to assign singular or static identities to any group. Neither is it to suggest that the forms of inequity that are considered in the chapters that follow have uniform effects. Rather, it starts from the premise that all of us negotiate our lives within shared political contexts, however divergent our individual experiences of them might be. And these contexts are not neutral. They are shaped by the interaction of myriad social relations, including those that sustain and render legitimate the economic, social, and political power of certain groups.[14] The analyses that follow are concerned with this aggregate effect and especially the ways in which certain practices and mentalities operate to privilege the putative interests of Euro-American settlers, over and above those of Indigenous people.

For all this talk of relations, readers will notice that the analyses that follow engage more thoroughly with the actions and attitudes of settlers than they do with the actions and attitudes of Indigenous people. This focus is a function of design rather than omission. Indigenous researchers and commentators continue to produce a rich literature on Indigenous social, political, and cultural life in the Twin Cities, and while this book draws on that literature, it does not seek to reproduce it. To be clear, this book is *not* an Indigenous history of postwar Minneapolis, nor is it a postwar history of Indigenous Minneapolis. Rather, it is an attempt to shed new light on the ways that settler constituencies produced and reinforced a racialized economy of power in the second half of the twentieth century. For this reason, the analyses that follow are mostly focused on the non-Indigenous side of the settler colonial relation. Of course, there can be no compelling history of the "institutions and ideologies" of settler societies "that is not simultaneously a history of . . . settler-native relations," so my analysis is necessarily informed by Indigenous sources and interpretations of events.[15] With that said, however, the focus of this book is to illuminate how settler prosperity, entitlement, and advantage have been realized and secured, rather than interpret Indigenous experiences that would be better interpreted by Indigenous people themselves.

At the same time, this book seeks to convey that while settler colonists and their descendants undeniably benefit from inequitable arrangements, they are also diminished by them. By this, I do not mean that settlers are "victims" of colonization, but rather that a society built on the predatory accumulation of land, the destruction of plurality, the reinforcement of racial hierarchies, and the group-differentiated distribution of advantage and opportunity is a society in which the possibilities for human flourishing are already contracted. "No one colonizes with impunity," observes Aimé Césaire, because a society grounded in the violence of colonization is a society that is animated by a collective sickness.[16] This book starts from the premise that non-Indigenous people (and especially people like me who descend from European ancestors who "settled" in the North American West in the nineteenth century) have a role to play in analyzing this sickness and an ethical obligation to be part of obstructing its reproduction. "The Dreamers will have to learn to struggle themselves," writes Ta-Nehisi Coates in a memorable passage in *Between the World and Me*, "to understand that the field for their dream, the stage where they have painted themselves white, is the deathbed of us all."[17]

Settler Colonialism and the Making of Minnesota

What is "settler colonialism" and how has it shaped the history of what it is now Minnesota? In recent years, a growing chorus of scholars has begun to insist that settler colonialism is a distinct form of imperialism.[18] The anthropologist Patrick Wolfe, who was the leading proponent of this position before his untimely death, argues that the forms of imperial conquest that were (and are) practiced in places such as Australia, Canada, and the United States ought to be distinguished from the metropolitan forms of European imperialism (sometimes called "franchise colonialism") that have long dominated mainstream understandings of what "colonialism" is. In Wolfe's terms, settler colonists differ from metropolitan colonists in that they "come to stay" and are foremost concerned with the establishment of a "new" society on an expropriated land base.[19] They are driven by a desire to settle and govern the land in perpetuity, while remaking themselves as its legitimate users and occupants. Such efforts are never undertaken in a social vacuum, and because the territories claimed by settler colonists are already occupied by Indigenous people, the imposition of settler colonial orders necessarily requires explicit forms of territorial alienation, as well as cultural forms of disavowal.[20] For this reason, settler colonialism is "inherently eliminatory."[21] "Supersession," or the "displacement of Indigenous peoples and their replacement with settlers," is its "central dynamic."[22]

Of course, settler "replacement" is never achieved in the materiality of actually existing situations and such impositions are contested at every stage. Indeed, Indigenous peoples are not the "tragic subjects of history" despite a long tradition of settler writing that has represented them in that way.[23] Rather, they continue to thrive amid the toxicity of settler colonial cultures in defiance of settler strategies of "elimination" that have ranged from explicit forms of frontier violence to coercive assimilation, strategic exclusion, selective securitization, and integrative pacification.[24] As Audra Simpson demonstrates, colonialism endures in its settler mode but continues to fall short of its own objectives; the North American colonial enterprise is a failure, she contends, because it has not accomplished what it has set out to do, namely, "eliminate Indigenous people; take all their land; absorb them into a white, property-owning body-politic."[25] Thus, while foundational inequities persist in settler colonial societies, the colonial project is "partial and incomplete." As the settler colonial relation "endures through time" it both "reconstitutes new dimensions of oppression and new possibilities for decolonization."[26] Settler colonial projects remain contingent and interruptible.[27]

Settler colonization is at the center of Minnesota's modern history. To elucidate this point, it is necessary to return to a moment when Indigenous peoples were the only inhabitants of the region that would come to be called the American Upper Midwest. For generations "beyond remembering," the lands that form the present state of Minnesota were part of the vast territorial homeland of Dakota people.[28] Indeed, "Minnesota is a Dakota place."[29] This is true both in the sense that "the Dakota people named it and left their marks in the landscape and in its history" and in the sense that it remains central to Dakota identity and culture, as well as a place where Dakota people continue to live.[30] In the period before the first European travelers made their way to this section of the North American interior, Dakota groups were spread over a vast geography.[31] Those who lived in the woodlands of the Upper Mississippi Valley (in addition to large swaths of what is now northern Minnesota) harvested an array of resources in long-established seasonal rhythms.[32]

Most histories of Minnesota identify an expedition that brought French Canadian travelers Pierre Radisson and Médard Chouart des Groseilliers to the heart of Dakota country in the 1650s as the harbinger of profound change, but European trappers were not the only outside group to make inroads into these lands in the seventeenth century. In this period, the northern stretches of what is now Minnesota were first contested between the region's longtime inhabitants and Anishinaabe (Ojibwe) migrants from the east. The latter have had a long history of relocation and "migration has always been a key component in Anishinaabe adaptation strategies."[33]

Throughout the eighteenth century, northern Dakota country was transformed into a contested zone of intertribal conflict.[34] In

Waziyatawin's terms, these conflicts were part of a broader "chain of events" that were set in motion by colonial processes that would "eventually be detrimental to all Indigenous people."[35]

The United States accelerated its process of assertive territorialization in the wake of its revolutionary founding in the late eighteenth century. But full inclusion of the northern plains and forests was still several generations away and the Upper Midwest remained marked by a degree of cultural and political mixing among Indigenous people and European transplants. This fluidity was not destined to last, and the frontier "borderland" was eventually overwhelmed as the region was integrated into the territorial ambit of the United States. This integration undermined generations of "syncretic and symbiotic Indian–European arrangements" as the nascent republic unleashed a "virulent model of homestead property" and assumed unilateral authority to "confer or deny rights to peoples within their borders."[36] Successive waves of settlers altered territorial relationships as they accelerated a process of enclosure and predatory redefinition. These transformations mark the true arrival of settler colonial dispossession in what would become the Upper Midwest. In this context an explicit politics of settler dominance began to overwhelm nearly every vestige of mutual reliance and respect.

By the 1850s, the mercantilist mode of production that had been synonymous with the fur trade was beginning to be replaced by the conventions of liberal capitalism. The extension of transportation networks and other infrastructures into the region brought new opportunities for settlers to extract surplus from the state's vast stretches of arable land and unlogged forests. Land and timber replaced furs as the region's most coveted assets and settler constituencies increasingly imagined Indigenous peoples as barriers to economic development.[37] Efforts to reduce Indigenous landholdings and remake Minnesota in the settler colonial mode ramped up as settler migrants began to dominate the region demographically and politically. In fact, this process had begun in earnest a few decades earlier when representatives of the United States brokered an agreement with the Dakota that allowed them to establish a foothold in the region. In 1805, U.S. Army Captain Zebulon Pike secured title of one hundred thousand acres of "prime real estate" in what is now the Twin Cities region for the "unconscionable price" of two thousand dollars.[38] By 1819, the United States had established Fort Snelling at the confluence of the Mnisota Wakpa (Minnesota River) and the Wakpa Tanka (Mississippi River), or the place the Dakota call Bdote.

The 1805 arrangements were the opening salvo of what would become a comprehensive effort to seize control of the eastern sections of the Dakota homeland. Treaties signed in 1851, most notably, reduced Dakota holdings to two narrow strips of land along the Minnesota River. These agreements transferred an estimated twenty-four million acres of land to the United States for promised annuity payments that would amount to little more than three cents per acre. In fact, the mutuality implied by the term "treaty" is deceptive in this case. The 1851 accords were so shot through with settler deception and manipulation that they have been described as a "monstrous conspiracy" that is "equal in infamy to anything else in the long history of injustice perpetrated upon the Indians by the authorized representatives of the United States government."[39]

The events of 1851 also set the stage for the U.S./Dakota War of 1862 and its devastating consequences. Ten years after the dubious treaties were brokered, an Indigenous revolt—provoked to a large degree by hunger and delayed annuities—was met with a settler counterinsurgency program so comprehensive that it ended in what remains the largest single mass execution in U.S. history (the subject of Durant's *Scaffold*) and the outright expulsion of Dakota people from their traditional territory. Waziyatawin uses definitions outlined in the 1948 *United Nations Convention on the Prevention and Punishment of the Crime of Genocide* to make the case that these events are consistent with contemporary definitions of ethnic cleansing.[40] She argues that the eviction of Dakota people from their traditional territories, finalized through the war of 1862 and its aftermaths, constitutes an "act of genocide" perpetrated by white Americans, "primarily so that they could continue to occupy Dakota lands unhindered."[41]

The treaties also facilitated settler migration into northern Minnesota in ways that were different from the fur trade era. "Previously, [the Anishnaabeg] had been acquainted with the few

Euro-Americans who lived among them in their country," writes one historian, but "now strangers were everywhere."[42] By the middle of the nineteenth century, Bureau of Indian Affairs (BIA)–administered Indian reservations had become the dominant spatial form of Indigenous life in Minnesota as settler governments sought to make room for the acquisitive advance of the settler frontier.

Regional settlement strategies were part of a broader project of invasion that aimed to remake vast swaths of the continent according to the ambitions of Euro-American settlers. Deploying strategies that ranged from outright removal to resettlement and reservationization, federal policy makers engaged in what Donald Meinig calls a project of "geographical social engineering."[43] Their efforts were comprehensive, and by the final decades of the nineteenth century much of the arable land in the American West had been transferred to state and private hands.[44] In the Upper Midwest, reservationization made it possible for railway companies, land speculators, and non-Indigenous settlers to seize territory on an unprecedented scale.

Yet by the end of the nineteenth century, reservationization efforts had begun to lose favor among American lawmakers. Starting in 1887, a range of initiatives were launched to break up collectively held Indigenous territories and convert them into alienable fee-simple property. Most famously, the passing of the federal Dawes Severalty Act by the U.S. Congress initiated a new round of territorial alienation so thorough that by the mid-1930s Indigenous landholdings had been reduced from 138 million acres to roughly fifty million acres.[45]

This process continued apace until Congress adopted the Indian Reorganization Act (IRA) in 1934, which put a temporary end to the federal efforts to transform reservations into fee-simple allotments and slowed the massive territorial attrition of Indigenous lands inaugurated by the Dawes Act.[46] By the late 1930s, the IRA was already being scorned by settler lawmakers and a variety of forces had begun to clamor for its abandonment. Such calls invoked a language of emancipation, insisting that the American state "liberate" Indigenous people from the paternalistic restrictions of federal control. The force of this argument even won over one of the IRA's principal legislative sponsors who by 1937 had begun to fear that the legislation's "community emphasis" bore the ideological impress of the "collectivist and totalitarian movements then sweeping the world."[47]

In this context, state interest in assimilation became explicit once again. After 1945, federal officials introduced efforts to terminate federal trust responsibility for tribal groups and integrate reservation dwellers into the "mainstream" wage economy through urban relocation.[48] Needless to say, the motivations for these shifts were not exclusively "humanitarian." The twin policies of "termination and relocation" offered officials an opportunity to unburden themselves of the significant cost of tribal administration, service delivery, and the protection of tribal territories from further encroachment.[49] Legislators were also motivated by the opportunity to free up resources to offset the growing cost of the Cold War.[50] At the same time, the opening up of Indigenous lands that these programs promised to deliver would facilitate non-Indigenous access to Indian Country's rich resource base. The list of the tribal territories that were deemed ready to be terminated revealed that more than administrative savings and ideological commitment was at play.[51]

Meanwhile, the upheaval of the Second World War amplified a process that would see thousands of reservation residents leave their home communities and settle in urban environments across the United States. More than twenty-five thousand Indigenous people enlisted in the war effort (a participation rate higher than any other group) and more than forty thousand others found work in wartime production.[52] After the war, the GI Bill and other federal initiatives encouraged reservation residents to pursue new lives in urban America. All told, public programs contributed to the urban "resettlement" of more than one hundred thousand Indigenous people in the period between 1952 and 1972.[53]

In Minnesota, wartime relocations merely added momentum to a trend that had been "ignited" by significant reservation land loss and the economic deprivations of the Great Depression, among other factors.[54] The Indigenous community in Minnesota's Twin

Cities of Minneapolis and St. Paul mushroomed from only a few hundred people at the start of the war to more than six thousand by the formal end of hostilities in Europe and the Pacific.[55] By the late 1960s, conservative estimates pegged the urban region's Indigenous community at about ten thousand.[56]

In the Twin Cities, Indigenous people built a diverse and resilient community in the postwar decades, but they also had to contend with a host of economic and social challenges. Racism was widespread and it manifested in multiple forms, some explicit, others more subtle. In nearly every facet of life, Indigenous residents of Minneapolis and St. Paul encountered structural impediments and individual hostilities. Economic insecurity was endemic and, broadly speaking, Indigenous people had far less access to the benefits of the postwar economic boom than did white Minnesotans. In her classic memoir *Night Flying Women,* Ignatia Broker recounts how her wartime move from the White Earth Reservation to the Twin Cities demanded that she cope with a complex range of hostilities and privations, including predatory landlords, institutional exclusions, and interpersonal discrimination.[57] Broker's experience was not unique, of course, and these challenges were persistent features of the lives of many who left reservation communities for the Twin Cities throughout the latter half of the twentieth century.

By the late 1950s, this pattern was having demonstrable spatial effects as the Indigenous community came to be increasingly concentrated in inner-city South Minneapolis, especially the Phillips neighborhood. In 1957, *Minneapolis Tribune* reporter Carl Rowan described sections of South Minneapolis as an "unofficial reservation."[58] Much of this concentration was produced by volition, of course, as Indigenous people sought to live among one another in a context of considerable adversity. At the same time, inner-city rental units were often the only living spaces that Indigenous people could secure in a profoundly discriminatory housing market. Indeed, the emergence of Phillips as an Indigenous neighborhood (chronicled in the next chapter) was also an explicit product of a racialized economy of power that ensured that certain groups would have access to resources and opportunities and others would not. Thus, when the *Minneapolis Tribune* lamented in a 1968 editorial that many Minneapolis "Indians" were living in the "poorest sections of the city," wracked by a sprawling crisis of unemployment, poverty, and trying to make a life "even without telephones," it was describing a pattern of group-differentiated inequity in broadly accurate terms.[59]

This schematic history offers a general sense of how a settler colonial political project is at the very core of Minnesota's modern history. As the paragraphs above demonstrate (and the chapters that follow will affirm), settler colonization is not a static political project. The methods employed in pursuit of its objectives are often altered. In Taiaiake Alfred and Jeff Corntassel's terms, colonial power frequently shifts shape; its instruments and techniques evolve to suit the needs of new situations.[60]

The core chapters of this book pick up where this historical sketch leaves off. They consider events that transpired in the latter half of the twentieth century in an effort to demonstrate that settler colonial inequity has cast a shadow that extends from the earliest efforts to remake Minnesota as a settler geography into the contemporary moment. And to point out that these dynamics have a contemporary existence is not abstract. Indeed, recent events are reminders that the project of tracing the endurance of the settler colonial relation is not a historical effort. While this book is focused on how these dynamics shaped events in the five decades that followed 1945, the recent crisis of Indigenous underhousing in the Twin Cities—dramatized most directly through the "Wall of Forgotten Natives"—makes it altogether clear that settler colonial inequity remains a potent force in the urban region today.[61]

Minneapolis as a Settler Colonial City

In geography and other disciplines, there is a well-established literature on how urban centers have been integral to projects of colonization.[62] From the fifteenth century through to the aggressive pursuit of overseas territories that animated the late nineteenth and early twentieth centuries, European imperial states relied on disparate urban sites to accomplish a variety of functions. In this literature, "colonial cities" are generally described as places that are designed to facilitate the smooth flow of human and resource surpluses from a colonized "periphery" to a metropolitan "core." Empirical studies show how these sites were linked to shifting interests in Europe, functioning as key sites of imperial administration, military coordination, wealth extraction, and missionary embarkment, as well as arenas for symbolic displays of the colonizer's strength.[63] They also demonstrate that such cities had a bipolar organization, with segregated zones of privilege existing in close proximity to zones of appalling insecurity.[64]

Such interpretations are of limited use in making sense of urban life in a place like Minneapolis. The colonization of the American West was not driven by the accumulative desires of far-flung sponsors, at least not in quite the same way. The "colonial cities" literature's characteristic emphasis on parasitical forms of metropolitan colonization (where surpluses are extracted from a "periphery" and returned to a "core") has a limited explanatory purchase in contexts where a demographically majoritarian group has settled permanently on existing Indigenous territories and asserted a sovereignty distinct from that which emanates from a far-flung metropolitan "center." Illuminating this distinction, a new generation of theorists has begun to think through the question of what makes settler colonial cities distinct from their "colonial city" counterparts.[65] In part, this book is an attempt to build on the momentum of these earlier interventions by considering how the theoretical innovations of settler colonial theory might help us renovate and extend existing geographic thinking about the urban implications of colonization.

What is a settler colonial city and how does it differ from other forms of imperial spatial organization? At the most basic level, three points of distinction stand out. It is worth dwelling on each of them to explain why I apply this label to Minneapolis.

In the first place, settler colonial cities are shaped by accumulation strategies that are primarily oriented around the enrichment of localized settler constituencies. Indeed, the political economy of settler colonial cities is more internally oriented than that of conventional colonial cities. Long-established geographic understandings of the latter have tended to emphasize their status as nodes in the networked geographies of European empires. The role of colonial cities, in these theorizations, is to function as instruments for the reproduction of European power and the facilitation of European accumulation. For this reason, colonial cities must be distinguished from settler colonial cities whose raison d'être, by contrast, is to ensure the economic well-being of local (or at least national) settler constituencies rather than far-off metropolitan sponsors.

In a certain light, all forms of imperialism are premised on what historian James Belich calls processes of "mass transfer," but what, precisely, is being transferred marks a key point of distinction between patterns of colonial and settler colonial accumulation.[66] In the case of the former, the "mass transfer" takes the form of human and material resources steadily flowing between sites in the colonized world and the metropolitan "core." Indeed, colonial cities were built and sustained to coordinate the transit of extracted raw materials and the fruits of colonial labor to Europe. In the case of the settler colonial city, the "mass transfer" manifests as a transplantation of settlers from Europe to the colonized territory, or the importation of what will become a majoritarian settler population that is concerned with the founding of a new political order grounded in comprehensive territorial appropriation. Indeed, settler colonial cities are built and sustained to serve the interests of this transferred population above all else. In settler colonial contexts, then, there is "no spatial separation between metropole and colony," as Eve Tuck and K. Wayne Yang put it.[67] The fundamental aim of settler colonial projects is "replacement" rather than exploitation, although the former need not preclude the latter.[68] Of course, nearly all North American cities are built on geographies that were already used and occupied by Indigenous peoples, and an important body of literature has shown that Indigenous presence in those cities has been continuous.[69] But only in rare circumstances have Indigenous people been organized as a geographically contained exploitable workforce.

None of this means that settler colonial cities were (or are) isolated from transnational circuits of institutional, cultural, political, or economic exchange.[70] In fact, the work of a number of theorists has traced such connections, marshaling evidence that shows how settler colonialism articulates with (or is organically linked to) the deployment of "outward"-looking forms of imperial violence (see also chapter 4 of this book).[71] Nevertheless, it is critical to draw a clear line of distinction between such forms of integration and the explicit mode of metropolitan command that defined "colonial cities" in the classic era of European imperialism.

The history of Minneapolis offers clear evidence of a settler colonial political economy at work. The most significant beneficiaries of the early stages of the settler colonial transformation of Minnesota invested considerable portions of their accumulated surpluses in Minneapolis and nearby St. Paul. For example, T. B. Walker, like other "empire builders" (a term that came to be synonymous with "ambitious men of Anglo-Saxon descent" who migrated to the American Midwest in the years that followed the Civil War), was able to secure massive personal benefit from the dispossession of Indigenous peoples, as we have already seen.[72] Importantly, though, the wealth that Walker and others extracted from these opportunities was not destined to be exported to a far-flung metropolitan core. Rather, it became the economic engine of a project of settler colonial "replacement" that would see Mni Sota reimagined as a settler society. Indeed, Walker was devoted to the development of Minneapolis as a powerful urban center. He showed a serious commitment to the city, as both a developer and a booster. Like other settler colonial elites, Walker's local engagement was motivated by a desire to secure his city's ascendancy in a context of robust interurban competition *and* to convert surpluses extracted from the regional hinterlands into productive urban investments. In part, this entailed significant reinvestments in the urban built environment. It was a process of literal city building.

But to understand the history of Minneapolis (and other settler colonial cities) as a creation of "big-minded" men is to obscure the material and social relations on which their actions rested. The degree to which life in Minnesota's Twin Cities was linked to surpluses accumulated through productive activities on recently seized

Indigenous lands cannot be overstated. To ignore these vital linkages is to divorce the city from its material embeddedness in the violence of dispossession. Against such mystifications, it is critical to point out that urbanization and settler colonization are linked. To do so is both to challenge the "mythic separation of the city from its surrounds" and to undermine the view that contemporary "Indigenous" and "urban" geographies have little to do with one another.[73] Indeed, one of the clearest ways to trace the endurance of settler colonial dynamics is to look at the ways that both the city and the reservation are products of long-standing processes of political, cultural, and spatial negotiation that are inextricably linked to one another.[74]

These linkages are observable in both human and nonhuman contexts. In his study of nineteenth-century Chicago, William Cronon observes that for many that city seemed to "break free from the soil and soar skyward as a wholly artificial creation."[75] Yet the interpretation of Chicago as a "triumph of human labor and will," Cronon shows, "concealed long-standing debts to the natural systems that made it possible."[76] The same can be said for nineteenth-century Minneapolis. The latter is a city that owes its status as an urban center of regional consequence to the commodification of its surrounding hinterlands, though these debts are rarely acknowledged in urban origin narratives. More often, Minneapolis is presented as a kind of miraculous settler achievement, a triumph of individual or collective ingenuity. Of course, such narratives obscure a basic economic truth: in order for urban interests to prosper from the development of the colonial interior, that interior had to be cleared for their benefit and remade according to their ambitions. As Cronon shows, the natural abundance of the nineteenth century American West contained immense wealth in and of itself. But the process by which vast stores of natural resources were accessed and converted into wealth in the form of capital required a process of transformation through which the existing "quilt" of Indigenous commons were enclosed and colonial-capitalist property relations were imposed.[77] The alienation of Indigenous people from their lands and the conversion of Indigenous resources into tradable commodities were (and are) the twin bases of Minneapolis's emergence as an urban region.

Second, settler colonial cities are places where the colonial relation endures as a significant element of everyday life. By contrast, conventional theorizations of colonial cities tend to interpret colonial urbanism as a "historical" process of city building, as the property of a now-concluded "age of empire." By the mid-1980s it was unremarkable for geographers to use the term "excolonial" to refer to cities where formal processes of decolonization had been achieved.[78] In short, the "colonial cities" literature tends to promote the idea that the time of colonialism has passed (even if many studies that use this framework observe that contemporary inequities have their roots in colonial occupation and administration).

Settler colonial theory, by contrast, maintains that colonization is not a historical artifact. It insists that the colonial relation endures in societies where colonizers have "come to stay" and no formal process of decolonization has been accomplished. Colonization, in other words, is a contemporary phenomenon in places like the United States because settler colonial political societies remain, by definition, animated by the "unreformed immanence of fundamentally unequal relations between Indigenous peoples and their nonindigenous counterparts."[79] To paraphrase Wolfe's oft-repeated phrasing, settler colonization is not so much an "event" as an enduring element of the broader field of power relations that structure outcomes in settler societies. Accordingly, one of the core objectives of settler colonial scholarship is to understand how these power relations have been recalibrated, recomposed, and transformed in ways that have allowed them to continue to shape relationships in the present. Thus, while dispossession, genocide, and other forms of colonial violence "are still with us," as Owen Toews observes, "the task is to figure out how they've survived in new times, what exactly they have become, and what they are doing now."[80] In Wolfe's terms, this work entails charting the "continuities, discontinuities, adjustments, and departures" through which the logic that animates historical practices of dispossession reemerges in different "modalities, discourses and institutional formations."[81]

Building on these insights, this book rejects the idea that a *singular* colonial logic has persevered across generations, impressing its dark prescriptions on the minds of successive generations of settler colonists. Rather, it starts from the premise that a complex politics of colonial group-differentiated inequity has continued across time precisely because it has adapted, mutated, and transformed in accordance with the demands of new social and political conjunctures.[82]

The enduring power of wealth amassed in the earliest chapters of the settler colonization of Minnesota offers evidence of one of the ways that settler colonial inequities persist. Capital accumulated through the initial project of dispossession is not locked in a hermetically sealed past but continues as a dynamic source of economic and cultural power. It is the explicit basis of new rounds of accumulative enclosure, privatization, and commodification. (The same is true of subsequent rounds of settler dispossession, including those that extend into the contemporary moment.) In many cases, the fortunes amassed by regional "empire builders" were reinvested in Twin Cities enterprises, infrastructures, built environments, and cultural amenities. The "influential" families that came to Minnesota in the mid-nineteenth century to establish industrial and financial enterprises and were rewarded with spectacular personal wealth are, in many cases, the same families that continue to be key players in the political, social, and cultural life of the state. It is no coincidence that major urban amenities continue to bear names like Walker, Weyerhaeuser, Dayton, and Hill. In everyday contexts, these names tend to take on a degree of banality, evidencing Lawrence Berg's observation that settler colonial naming practices often fetishize and efface "the social relations of dispossession that underlay modern property relations."[83]

These links are often obscured by the cultural pervasiveness of an imagined epochal break between a past moment of colonial contestation and an urban afterlife in which that contestation is presumed to be absent. Many accounts—from school textbooks to academic histories—interpret the emergence of the Twin Cities as a process of radical metamorphosis. In such interpretations, the rise of an urban region of significant consequence is understood as a sudden and transformative act of creation. Of course, most of these narratives acknowledge that the area on which the Twin Cities now sit was once used and occupied by Indigenous people—noting, for example, that it was an integral part of the lived geographies of Mdewakanton Dakota people at the time that the United States initiated the first treaties in what is now Minnesota, and later an important meeting point and trading hub for a range of Indigenous peoples and their Euro-American counterparts. In most such accounts, these early moments of intercultural negotiation are the last time Indigenous people are encountered as significant players in the life of the city. Indeed, the process by which Euro-American settlers secured title over the present site of the urban region is generally presented as a prelude to urbanization, a kind of prehistory to a period in which settler migrants would conceive, build, and develop a fundamentally new geography, independent of the area's first inhabitants. The city, in other words, is understood to be a settler creation that exists outside of ongoing negotiations with the region's Indigenous peoples. Such interpretations reinforce settler ownership of the Twin Cities, rendering it natural and quarantining it outside of the realm of contemporary politics.

Of course, the idea that urban geographies are "settler" creations is false. Almost without exception, North American cities are constructed on geographies that have been parts of Indigenous worlds for generations (and in some cases since time immemorial). Minneapolis is no exception. It is built at the geographic heart of the Dakota territorial, cultural, and cosmological universe.[84] While processes of settler urbanization have interrupted and transformed Indigenous connections to urban space, they have not extinguished them. Indigenous people have always remained in cities (even if they have sometimes been ignored or rendered invisible by settler constituencies) and urban areas endure as key sites of Indigenous place making and opposition to settler colonial forms of domination.[85] In Minneapolis, for example, there is a long and impressive history of Indigenous (and *Indigenist*) political work and institution building that has been oriented around contesting the violence of the settler colonial relation *and* creating space for Indigenous flourishing/resurgence. Studies by Brenda Child and Sasha Suarez, among others, are helpful in illuminating this tradition.[86] Importantly, too, these arguments can and should be extended to suburban areas and zones outside of the historic centers of North American cities.[87] Kasey Keeler's innovative study of Indigenous life in Twin Cities suburbs demonstrates that the spatial expanse that would eventually be integrated into the metropolitan region has never been anything like a tabula rasa. Indigenous people have long remained resident in these areas, in spite of settler efforts to physically and discursively remove them.[88]

Third, settler colonial cities are places where Indigenous people have more often been excluded from, rather than exploited in, core economic activities. While the abundant literature on "colonial cities" demonstrates how urban environments were organized with the explicit intention of facilitating the exploitation of colonized people, urban environments that developed through processes of settler colonization have not necessarily followed the same developmental trajectory. Although many of these cities were (and are) divided along ethnic and "racial" lines, Indigenous peoples themselves were more often removed from city life through a series of evictions, expulsions, and relocations than they were contained in urban enclaves.[89] Because settler colonists have generally been more interested in seizing the lands belonging to Indigenous peoples than they have been in accumulating surpluses generated by Indigenous labor, their preference was often to seek removal rather integration or local containment for the purposes of economic exploitation. Thus, while settler colonists did (and do) sometimes rely on Indigenous labor to achieve their objectives, their primary interest lies less in the systematic exploitation of a colonized workforce than it does in the eventual clearing of the expropriated territory for settler use and the incorporation of that territory into the regulatory ambit of settler institutions of governance.[90] In other words, Indigenous land, not Indigenous labor and its associated surpluses, is the sine qua non of settler colonial desire, as a range of North American empirical studies demonstrate.[91] For this reason, settler colonial cities occupy a "paradoxical kind of site in relationships between colonizer and colonized," according to Porter and Yiftachel. "They occupy Indigenous lands and form a central component of settler society, yet at the same time render Indigeneity profoundly out of place."[92]

To be clear, my point here is not that Indigenous people have never been exploited as laborers in settler colonial societies but rather that such exploitation has always been peripheral to the core objective of settler accumulation strategies, which hinge on the exploitation of expropriated lands. In Coulthard's terms, the fundamental organizing principle of settler colonial political orders is to "shore up" sustained access to territory "for the purposes of state formation, settlement and capitalist development."[93] For this reason, settler colonial "urban landscapes are emblematic of the logic of replacement," as Naama Blatman-Thomas and Libby Porter point out, both in the sense that they are sites of physical displacement and in the sense that they are sites of symbolic dispossessions that work to code urban spaces as non-Indigenous.[94]

The history of Minneapolis is consistent with this trend. Historical demographic data suggests that a relatively small number of Indigenous people lived in the Twin Cities urban region during the first half of the twentieth century.[95] This is significant because the urban region was (and is) at the very center of the Dakota homeland and proximate to a diverse range of Indigenous communities. While the methods through which this data was collected are decidedly problematic, the comparatively small number of Indigenous residents in the Twin Cities is a reflection of the degree to which Indigenous people had been pushed out from a region in which they once dominated demographically.

This does not mean, of course, that there was *no* meaningful Indigenous presence in the Twin Cities before the postwar growth of the urban Indigenous community. Quite to the contrary, Kasey Keeler's careful analysis demonstrates that Indigenous people have continued to live and build community in the urban region for as long as there has been an urban region to speak of, even if those communities were not always noticed by non-Indigenous observers.[96]

Nevertheless, zones of urban Indigenous residential life certainly did become more apparent in the period after the Second World War. The emergence of an Indigenous neighborhood in the South-side Phillips district (chronicled in chapter 1) offers evidence that Minneapolis began to see a form of racialized concentration that was similar to the divisions that theorists have suggested dominated conventional "colonial cities." Nevertheless, it is important to stress that the postwar emergence of an inner-city Indigenous neighbor-hood in Minneapolis (and other cities across the North American Prairie West) was driven by a different set of imperatives.[97] While most Indigenous people who built lives in the Southside Phillips neighborhood after 1945 worked in the wage economy, they did not, as a group, serve the same function as Indigenous people did in classic "colonial cities." If the labor of an Indigenous workforce was at the very center of "colonial city" organization, the same cannot be said in most settler colonial urban milieus. Far more often, In-digenous people in places like Minneapolis have had to overcome considerable barriers to find a place in the wage economy.

Limits of the Settler Colonial Framework

It is important to be clearheaded about what the settler colonial ap-proach does, and what it does not do. There are good reasons to be cautious about a wholehearted embrace of this framework.

Settler colonialism is a broad and malleable analytic, for better and worse. On the one hand, this generality allows settler colonial insights to be deployed in a diverse range of contexts. It is not sur-prising, given this fact, that the scholarly subfield of settler colonial studies has become consciously outward-looking and comparative in its orientation. At their best, multisited or comparative settler co-lonial analyses work to undermine nationalist narratives of unique-ness by demonstrating that settler colonialism is a "global process," rather than "a haphazard array of discrete historical phenomena."[98] On the other hand, this generality demands that analysts think care-fully about what can actually be learned about a particular situation through the use of a tool with such far-ranging applicability. Indeed, ideal-typical constructs (such as "colonial city" and "settler colonial city") will always fail to capture the dynamic fluidity of actually existing social environments.

Settler colonial analyses tell particular kinds of stories. In general, they are concerned with understanding the ways in which settler constituencies and their political representatives impose dominion over Indigenous lands, undermine the cultural and political forms of Indigenous people, and interrupt the autonomy and sovereignty of Indigenous collectivities. While these are important stories to tell in societies where a culture of "organized forgetting" buttresses a widely shared sense of entitlement among settler communities, their routinized repetition also risks overstating the stability and power of settler colonial projects. Alfred and Corntassel observe, for example, that settler colonial analyses risk allowing colonization to be "the only story" that is told about Indigenous lives. "It must be recognized," they observe, "that colonialism is a narrative in which the Settler's power is the fundamental reference and assumption, inherently limiting Indigenous freedom and imposing a view of the world that is but an outcome of perspective on that power."[99] Tim Rowse cautions that settler colonial analyses in Australia have often problematically asserted Indigenous "helplessness" in the face of "overbearing colonial pressure."[100] The effect of such presentations, he contends, is to reproduce a "sorrowing" form of outrage in which "defeat and marginality are highlighted at the expense of understanding the nature and limits of Indigenous agency."[101] In the North American context, meanwhile, Eve Tuck cautions against the effects of trading in "damage-centered research" that frames Indigenous and racialized communities as fundamentally wounded, defining them primarily as "sites of disinvestment and dispossession."[102] Connectedly, Alissa Macoun and Elizabeth Strakosch argue that scholarship in this emergent subfield has sometimes promoted a kind of "colonial fatalism" that presents settler colonial domination as structurally embedded, "highly stable," and relatively impervious to interruption.[103] They also suggest that analyses that rely too heavily on this structuralism can lead non-Indigenous scholars to interpret "settler action" as "always already colonizing" in ways that present anticolonial practice as futile and/or tacitly excuse those scholars from the ethical demand of engaging in it.

Just as troubling is the risk that the considerable attention being heaped on settler colonial scholarship may operate to "displace, overshadow, or even mask over" forms of knowledge production that have emerged from the political and intellectual work of Indigenous people themselves.[104] If settler colonial theorizing is to make a valuable contribution, it must put itself in conversation with the many promising and generative insights that have emerged from a recent surge of work in that vein, including, for example, analyses that have sought to move beyond the oppression/resistance binary in order to demonstrate how autonomous forms of Indigenous resurgence are flourishing across the North American continent, not least in urban areas.[105] Indeed, analysts of settler colonization have much to learn from the latter, particularly insofar as Indigenous movements for resurgence are calling for nothing short of "a comprehensive transformation of the settler colonial present" through the renewal of Indigenous political and legal orders, as Michelle Daigle and Margaret Marietta Ramírez demonstrate that they are.[106]

At the same time, it should be stressed that settler colonial analyses have sometimes obscured the ways that colonization intersects with other systems of oppression, offering only a partial picture of how racialized inequity shapes American life. It is worth pointing out that no study of urban racism in Minneapolis could be considered comprehensive if it did not take seriously the constitutive importance of anti-Black racism. New efforts to think through settler colonization's relationship to racial capitalism in general point to some of the ways that scholars are drawing these lines of connection.[107] Daigle and Ramírez encourage analysts to center these connections explicitly, arguing that the "decolonial" ought to be understood broadly to include the "affirmative refusal of white supremacy, anti-Blackness, the settler colonial state, and a racialized economy of containment, displacement and violence."[108]

Settler colonial theory is also menaced by big picture conceptual challenges. While it is analytically tempting to draw bright lines of distinction between settler colonial and other forms of imperialism, for example, it is critical to stress that multiple forms of imperialism "interpenetrate each other and overlap in a variety of ways," often in the same place at the same time.[109] It should also be said that settler colonial theory has been perhaps overly focused on places that were first colonized by the British and French (most research has focused on Canada, the United States, and Australia, for example), but these are not the only places where projects of demographically majoritarian settler invasion are ongoing.[110] Additionally, it is worth paying heed to Renisa Mawani's observation that settler colonial theorizing often trades in crude binaries, including "imposed divisions between settler and native, colony and settler colony, and land and sea" that are incapable of capturing the complexity of colonial power and the varied movement of "people, ideas, and legalities" across a diverse range of imperial spaces.[111] Of course, recent interventions have attempted to move settler colonial analyses beyond this tidy binarism. Iyko Day's effort to "triangulate" settler colonialism within a broader field of white supremacist racial capitalism is particularly promising in this regard.[112] In her terms, the "music" of settler colonialization must be understood in its dynamism, as a series of formations that are "transnational but distinctively national," "repetitive but without predictable rhythm," "structural but highly susceptible to change."[113]

Finally, there are good reasons to be cautious about the concept of the "settler colonial city," particularly if this framing works to reinforce the problematic idea that cities are settler spaces, that they are spatial productions brought to life exclusively by acts of settler inventiveness (however politically suspect those acts might be).[114] North American cities are constructed on geographies that have been parts of Indigenous worlds for many generations, almost without exception. To suggest that cities are "settler" spaces is to mask their contested nature and obscure the fact that Indigenous people have consistently "negotiated, resisted, unsettled, and transcended the limits of settler activity."[115] Moreover, it is critical to emphasize that this contestation continues in North American urban environments. Fine-grain critical work by Julie Tomiak and Natchee Blu Barnd, among others, offers robust evidence of the political, economic, and cultural stakes of these engagements.[116] At the same time, the "settler colonial city" frame risks reifying problematic ideas about the city itself, presenting it as a bounded object that is radically distinct from other geographies. Settler colonial ideologies have often traded on the maintenance of a dubious differentiation between urban and nonurban space, a distinction that imagines "the city and the reserve/reservation as completely disconnected spaces," for example, and "renders invisible the violence upon which settler city-building relies."[117]

In spite of these very real limits, the settler colonial framework can also be instructive and generative. This book uses settler colonial theory because it orients interpretive energies toward the persistence of the colonial relation in a context where that relation has been routinely obscured. It aims to offer a series of analyses that undermine exculpatory narrations of Minneapolis's urban history. Having said that, I am under no allusions that the framework it deploys offers anything like a *definitive* account of the social totality. Settler colonial theory is not a total system of explanation. Like all theoretical ways of seeing, it is partial and incomplete. Its insights must be supplemented by other forms of interpretation, especially those that chronicle Indigenous strategies to interrupt and transform settler colonial power.

Organization of the Book

Settler Colonial City develops its main arguments over the course of four chapters. In different ways, these chapters demonstrate how settler institutions, accumulation strategies, public-policy approaches, and forms of knowledge production operate to sustain or reproduce distinctly settler colonial forms of oppression. When considered together, these disparate "sites" of articulation offer evidence of a broad pattern of group-differentiated inequity. They demonstrate that the settler colonial relation remained an enduring feature of life in Minnesota's largest city in the five decades that followed the Second World War.

The first chapter, "Urban Change and the Settler Colonial Relation," considers how and why a spatially concentrated Indigenous community emerged in South Minneapolis in the years after 1945. It argues that the racialized production of this inner-city geography is inseparably bound up with sweeping transformations that remade the Twin Cities metropolitan region in the aftermath of the Second World War, as suburbanization, urban renewal, interstate construction, and other publicly subsidized projects transformed the urban landscape. It then turns to a consideration of how and why Indigenous people relocated to Phillips in the postwar period, while chronicling the persistence of a complex pattern of urban racism and the important work that sought to counter it. Next, the chapter demonstrates how a "white spatial imaginary" has shaped interpretations of the neighborhood in ways that are consistent with a longer history of settler colonial racism. It concludes by making the case that the South Minneapolis Indigenous neighborhood must be understood in its specificity and not flattened as a generic expression of postwar urban racism.

The second chapter, "Liberal Antiracism as Political Dead End," examines the work of two influential nongovernmental research organizations that were motivated to contest the exclusion of Indigenous people from the prosperity of postwar American life and published extensively on urban Indigenous issues in Minneapolis: the Minnesota League of Women Voters and the Training Center for Community Programs at the University of Minnesota. Paying close heed to the ideologies that informed their efforts, the chapter argues that both groups produced assessments of anti-Indigenous oppression that stopped well short of interrupting its reproduction. Specifically, it makes the case that while both groups were serious about their desire to support Indigenous people, they were never seriously committed to challenging the prevailing political order and its core assumptions about the world. To contextualize this point, the chapter shows that the research and advocacy work of both groups was constrained by a politics of liberal antiracism that allowed them to voice opposition to the oppression of Indigenous people without ever challenging the generative conditions that produced (and reproduced) that oppression. Ultimately, it contends that because these knowledge-producing organizations treated inequity as a manageable public-policy problem rather than a foundational social cleavage (inherent to a settler colonial society, for example), their work fell well short of its ambition to meaningfully combat racialized exclusion in the Twin Cities.

The third chapter, "Cops and Counterpatrols," considers the fraught relationship between the Minneapolis Police Department and Indigenous residents of South Minneapolis, with an emphasis on events that took place in the 1960s and early 1970s. It makes the case that the targeting of Indigenous people by urban law-enforcement agencies is inseparable from the persistence of broader ideologies of racialized privilege, arguing that the settler colonial relation manifests in a culture of "racialized policing" through which particular kinds of "knowledge" operate to depoliticize the disproportionate entanglement of urban Indigenous people with all branches of the criminal justice system. It also demonstrates that this "knowledge" has often been contested and considers how key moments of mobilization have operated to *repoliticize* the violence of racialized policing.

The fourth chapter, "Land Mines at Home and Abroad," demonstrates how the settler colonial relation intersects with other forms of imperial violence in the U.S. context. It challenges Minneapolis's "progressive" reputation by arguing that the city was and is produced by forces that are the source of immense suffering and displacement domestically and internationally. It argues, in other words, that the production of the Phillips neighborhood and other Twin Cities districts cannot be understood without tracing their relationship to economic and migratory flows that are explicitly connected to the violent pursuit of American "interests" at home and abroad. It troubles the idea that the effects of American state violence and militarism are exclusively experienced in faraway theaters of war by demonstrating some of the ways that American imperial practice has shaped life in South Minneapolis.

What these chapters have in common is that they are largely focused on the ways that settler attitudes, assumptions, commitments, and practices operated to produce, consolidate, and reinforce a racialized economy of power in Minneapolis during the second half of the twentieth century. Like the book as a whole, each is concerned with making sense of the settler or non-Indigenous side of the settler colonial relation. Before proceeding, it is important to reiterate two points. The first is that is that the settler colonial oppression described in this book has always been vigorously contested in Minneapolis. Where it has been possible to do so, I have included some accounting of how Indigenous people and their allies have confronted the various forms of inequity that the chapters consider. The second is that while this book is historical in its orientation, many of the issues that these chapters discuss continue as features of life in the Twin Cities today. Where it has been possible to do so, I have included some accounting of this continuation. With that said, I want to stress that the accounts provided in this book are necessarily incomplete. I urge readers to supplement the analysis that they encounter in this text by consulting some of the many excellent works that have been produced by analysts and historians from the Minneapolis Indigenous community.

1

Urban Change and the Settler Colonial Relation

The Making of an Indigenous Neighborhood

East Franklin Avenue emerged as one of South Minneapolis's principal commercial corridors at the end of the nineteenth century and remained a symbol of urban middle-class propriety for much of the next sixty years. In the mid-1950s, the avenue began to be sapped of its economic vitality, however, as businesses and upwardly mobile residents decamped to the booming suburbs at an ever-quickening pace. As the broader inner-city Southside started to slip in bourgeois esteem, the Phillips neighborhood, and the areas around East Franklin Avenue in particular, emerged as the residential center of the metropolitan region's growing Indigenous community. Already by 1957 the area was being described as an "unofficial reservation" in at least one of Minneapolis's major daily newspapers.[1]

What lies behind these changes? The most straightforward explanation is that the emergence of an Indigenous neighborhood in South Minneapolis is inextricably linked to suburbanization, urban renewal, interstate construction, and other publicly subsidized projects that transformed the urban landscape in the aftermath of the Second World War. As in other urban areas across the United States, the Twin Cities metropolitan region was remade after 1945 in ways that consolidated and produced distinct geographies of racialized inequity. At a moment when white Minnesotans were accessing unprecedented levels of material comfort, many Indigenous residents of the inner-city Southside—some new, some long-standing—were forced to contend with structural impediments and interpersonal hostilities in nearly every facet of life.

This explanation is supported by the evidentiary record, to be sure, and the first three sections of this chapter are committed to demonstrating how and why these changes unfolded. The analysis that follows begins by considering how a series of political-economic developments and urban strategies transformed the Twin Cities metropolitan region in the period after 1945, producing discrete zones of privilege and deprivation while cementing the "structured advantage" of white Minnesotans in urban space. With this established, it turns to a consideration of why Indigenous people relocated to Phillips in the postwar period. In doing so, it traces the persistence of a broad pattern of urban racism that operated to relegate Indigenous renters to the city's "worst" housing and most precarious tenancy situations.

At the same time, this chapter also demonstrates that the growth of an Indigenous neighborhood was not strictly a function of racist "involuntary relegation." Indigenous people had many good reasons to make their homes in Phillips. Indeed, the neighborhood was (and is) a place of significant political and cultural flourishing. It is a district where Indigenous people have lived and worked among each other, constructed robust community institutions, and confronted settler colonial inequities. For these and other reasons, Phillips remains a key node in the networked geographies of the Twin Cities' diverse Indigenous community.

But is the emergence of an Indigenous neighborhood in South Minneapolis merely another expression of a well-documented history of postwar urban racism or does it deviate from the standard script in some way? There is, of course, a robust scholarly literature on the ways that the postwar "metropolitan revolution" operated to consolidate racialized advantage in geographic space, especially through the vehicles of publicly subsidized infrastructure projects and loan schemes, and most notably at the expense of African Americans. Does the South Minneapolis case merely offer another local example of a pattern of group-differentiated inequity that prevailed in cities across the United States or does it demand to be theorized differently? Specifically, does the neighborhood's explicit relationship to a longer history of settler colonial inequity demand that analysts think about its postwar development differently? The final two sections of this chapter consider these questions and argue that the standard explanation is not sufficient to account for circumstances in South Minneapolis. The chapter concludes by arguing that the Indigenous neighborhood defies easy categorization, pointing to the complexity of the area's status as part of a broader geography of Indigenous life.

Remaking the Metropolis

In the years that followed the Second World War, the United States was remade by a sweeping "metropolitan revolution" that reoriented urban life and cast asunder a wide range of existing spatial and social certainties.[2] Explosive suburbanization ushered in an unprecedented deconcentration of the urban population. The expansion of automobile-based transportation networks facilitated sweeping urban growth. Processes of urban renewal razed and remade large sections of downtowns. Core neighborhoods entered periods of protracted decline. Once bustling inner-city districts came to be associated with destitution, abandonment, and the people excluded from the country's growing prosperity.

Public-policy strategies aimed at sustaining the strength of wartime accumulation and expanding economic growth were at the center of postwar processes of metropolitan decentralization. In the years after 1945, policy makers faced significant challenges in attempting to create conditions in which the enormous productive capacity of the war economy could be preserved. American contributions to the reconstruction of a shattered Europe offered a partial fix, but export markets could not fill the massive gap left by the cessation of wartime production.[3] To meet this and other postwar challenges, state planners and corporate elites promoted a sweeping expansion of domestic consumptive capacity.

This was an era of activist government. The Keynesian view that the public sector could play a leading role in promoting economic growth by encouraging consumption enjoyed broad bipartisan acceptance.[4] Building on strategies inaugurated in the New Deal era, policy actors worked to consolidate a grand "settlement" between capital and organized labor that would ensure economic expansion by growing middle- and working-class incomes. Under these new arrangements, federal policy encouraged and underwrote private consumption while union movements curbed their militancy. The results of this approach were immediate and dramatic. The organized American working class was transformed into the "backbone of a high-wage and high-consumption proletariat."[5] Personal consumption increased by $72 billion between 1945 and 1950, a jump that was more than enough to offset a $69 billion postwar decline in defense expenditures.[6]

These changes accelerated the peripheralization of American residential life. Nationally, suburban areas grew about ten times faster than core areas did in the 1950s.[7] Federal public policies encouraged this shift. Generous tax incentives motivated commercial developers to build on a scale that was hitherto unimaginable. The Interstate Highway Act of 1956 and other automobile-based postwar transportation policies transformed once-inaccessible peripheries into viable bedroom communities. New Deal–era loan programs were expanded and federal monies were freed up to secure personal mortgages, making home loans more accessible than ever before. These and other policies facilitated immense levels of suburban decampment as the availability of affordable housing on the urban fringe hastened a historic exodus of working and middle-class families. In this context, the American metropolis emerged as a key participant in the "fiesta of fossil fuel combustion" that would come to define the period after 1945 in the industrialized West.[8]

The Twin Cities metropolitan area was no exception to these trends and the urban region expanded outward at a breakneck pace in the decades that followed the war. Regional suburban growth outpaced central city growth by a margin of five to one in the 1950s.[9] By the end of that decade, the Twin Cities would rank among the twenty least dense metropolitan areas in the country.[10] During the war and the turmoil that preceded it, new housing construction had all but stopped in Minneapolis and St. Paul.[11] At war's end, acute housing shortages in both cities were exacerbated by the return of an estimated eighty thousand veterans to the region.[12] Private developers (benefiting handsomely from public subsidy) embarked on a broad range of new projects on the urban fringe and drove suburban migration at a furious pace.[13] The municipalities of Minneapolis and St. Paul lost a cumulative total of about four hundred thousand people in the generation that followed the war.[14]

The suburban dream was not available to everybody, however. Across the United States, postwar housing policies were mobilized to sustain and secure white advantage. State-subsidized home loan programs, in particular, disproportionately funneled public support to white Americans in ways that reinforced and extended already existing forms of racialized exclusion.[15] Scholars have documented how the discriminatory distribution of government-supported mortgages and other techniques of racial separation operated in this era. (In the Twin Cities, the Mapping Prejudice project has done important work in this regard.)[16] Nevertheless, white Americans have often failed to recognize the degree to which their prosperity has been subsidized by state support, in spite of the wide availability of documentary evidence. "[I]nstead of recognizing themselves accurately as recipients of collective public largesse, whites came to see themselves as individuals whose wealth grew out of their personal and individual success in acquiring property on the 'free market,'" George Lipsitz observes.[17]

The metropolitan revolution required the production of a new urban infrastructure. In particular, new transportation networks were needed to make it possible for people to commute across a vast metropolitan expanse. To achieve this end on a national scale, the federal government and its local partners constructed the Interstate Highway System between 1956 and the mid-1970s in what was once described as the world's largest public infrastructure project. Interstates were the condition of possibility for urban decentralization in the postwar period and "few public policy initiatives have had as dramatic and lasting an impact on modern America," notes the urban historian Raymond Mohl.[18] In Minneapolis, the completion of Interstates 35 and 94 in the late 1960s facilitated rapid development on the urban fringe as developers began to "devour newly urbanized land at a brisk pace."[19]

Downtown boosters praised the new corridors for their capacity to "whisk" central-city workers to and from suburban communities in mere minutes.[20] But those same boosters were mum about what, precisely, was being "whisked" over. New interstates ripped through the existing urban fabric and disrupted the lives of residents in affected areas, many of whom had already been excluded from the security and prosperity of the postwar boom. The cartographer Geoffrey Maas argues that interstate construction in the Twin Cities disproportionately disrupted Black and working-class communities, following a racialized "path of least resistance" through areas that had long been stigmatized in the dominant urban imaginary.[21]

One Southside resident described the sense of isolated *in-betweenness* that these changes provoked: "From a low-income perspective there was no more community . . . we were caught up in the middle, we weren't involved downtown or out in the suburbs. We became transient. You don't feel like you have any roots, you're stuck in purgatory. It was like a whole area blown away."[22] Observations like this one are not surprising given that interstate corridors impose immense physical barriers that have the unavoidable effect of destroying the "connectivity of the city."[23] At points, they extend between ten and twenty lanes of traffic, not including access roads, medians, paved shoulders, and massive wooden sound barriers. Automotive commuters remain neatly contained in these concrete canyons. They move "quickly in and out" and are often oblivious to what is around them, observes the Twin Cities urbanist Judith Martin.[24]

In Phillips, the isolation produced by interstates was not merely symbolic. The new urban expressways offered no direct access point to East Franklin Avenue and their construction exacerbated the negative effects of decentralization and hastened the avenue's transformation from a viable "working-class neighborhood" to one where poverty was concentrated.[25] In this way, the Indigenous neighborhood was physically and psychologically cut off from its surroundings.

State-initiated processes of urban renewal and slum clearance played a decisive role in concentrating economically marginal and racialized people in the inner city. In the 1960s, downtown cores contained most of the last remaining densely populated mixed-used districts. This was true in Minneapolis, where the urban core of the prewar city had grown up around the milling and timber industries that were located near St. Anthony Falls on the Mississippi River. By the late 1940s, city leaders were faced with an increasingly obsolete city center that seemed destined to continue losing residents and business to the booming periphery.

These challenges were widespread in urban America and the federal state responded by creating opportunities for local governments to "rejuvenate" declining downtowns through processes of urban renewal. The American Housing Act of 1949 authorized municipalities to seize properties through eminent domain and assemble them as large tracts that could then be sold to private developers. Its ambitious goal was to "revive downtown business districts by razing the

The construction of Interstates 35W (pictured here in 1967) and 94 tore through the urban fabric of the Twin Cities and disrupted the lives of residents in affected areas. Courtesy of Hennepin County Library.

slums, bringing new businesses into the core, and attracting middle-class residents back to the city."[26] Minneapolis policy actors were quick to act on this legislative opening and proposed a sweeping renewal project that would raze large swaths of the historic city center. The newly formed Housing and Redevelopment Authority (HRA) set to work developing plans for key sections of the downtown core

IMPLOSION
IN MINNEAPOLIS

AN INVITATION TO SHARE IN THIS DYNAMIC MARKET

In the early 1960s, urban boosters sang the praises of the wrecking ball and argued that comprehensive demolitions were making space for an unprecedented revitalization in the center of Minneapolis. Courtesy of Hennepin County Library.

Minoru Yamasaki's "temple of insurance," Northwestern National Life Building, opened in 1965 and is emblematic of the corporate sterility that dominated renewal efforts in downtown Minneapolis. Courtesy of Hennepin County Library.

and won federal funding to achieve their ambition by the late 1950s. Between 1959 and 1963, about 40 percent of the built environment of central Minneapolis was razed, as the wrecking ball took aim at more than two hundred buildings.[27] New builds began to transform the downtown core. Sterile structures like Minoru Yamasaki's Northwestern National Life building (once described as a "temple to the gods of underwriting") proliferated.

The elimination of Minneapolis's Skid Row was an explicit objective of these efforts. In the first half of the twentieth century, downtown sections of Washington and Nicollet Avenues, in the city's Gateway District, had become increasingly synonymous with a rough homosocial drinking culture connected to the area's transient population of seasonal male workers. Railroad construction, timber extraction, and labor-intensive forms of agriculture were central components of the industrial economy of the Upper Midwest, and they all demanded a flexible seasonal workforce, particularly from the 1870s to the 1920s. Minneapolis became a key node in the migratory circuits of this pool of laborers and much of the Gateway's storefront activity was oriented around serving its needs, not least on the city's "Skid Row." Cheap restaurants, bars, residential flophouses, "cage hotels" (featuring stacked sleeping quarters divided by chicken wire), pawnshops, thrift stores, and Christian missions came to dominate the area.[28] Life on Skid Row was precarious, and occasionally violent, to be sure, but as bar owner Johnny Rex (sometimes called the "Mayor of Skid Row") reveals in documentary footage that he shot in the area in the late 1950s, it was also a place of mutual aid and comradely coexistence.

Ultimately, transformations of the industrial economy of the Upper Midwest spelled Skid Row's doom and the entire district was razed by renewal efforts. The industries that had employed Skid Row's mobile workforce were "all but dead" by the 1950s and urban leadership was far less inclined to tolerate a "vice" district if it did not serve the function of providing a "ready supply of cheap labor."[29] This coupled with an elite desire to remake Downtown Minneapolis as a modern urban center that was free of "blight" and capable of attracting new enterprise. At the same time, the elimination of Skid Row was seen as a vital step in stemming the migratory tide of commercial and residential life to the suburbs.

The dismantling of Skid Row as a geographic fact required the removal of its residents. The area's permanent population of about twenty-five hundred people was primarily composed of single men over thirty, many of whom "didn't really have any other place to go."[30] In Minneapolis, most of the displaced Skid Row residents ended up in a series of nearby inner-city neighborhoods, including the Southside area around East Franklin Avenue.[31] The elimination of Skid Row was thus not simply a process of dismantlement but also a process of displacement. Skid Row poverty wasn't eliminated but was relocated. None of this was lost on Johnny Rex. "They called it Skid Row then, now they call it the inner city," he told a documentarian in the late 1990s.[32]

In short, urban renewal programs remade American downtowns at a significant social cost. Far more low-income housing was destroyed than was built, and little of substance was done to counter the effects of suburbanization or improve conditions in the inner city. The initial Minneapolis HRA plan had promised a housing component that would provide shelter for displaced residents but political hurdles prevented that from being realized.[33] The situation in Minneapolis mirrored outcomes in other cities across the United States. The 1949 federal law that authorized urban renewal had provided for the construction of more than eight hundred thousand units of public housing across the country, but by 1960 only 320,000 of those units had been built, falling well short of actual need.[34] These investments only helped a small number of the four million people estimated to have been displaced by urban renewal and freeway construction between 1956 and 1972.[35]

The decline of the inner city was not strictly a process shaped by state planners, however, and the internal political economy of core neighborhood "slums" cannot be ignored. Phillips, for example, was dramatically transformed in the postwar decades by an exodus of owner-occupiers. These departures hastened the conversion of much of the neighborhood's stock into rental units as new housing became available with the postwar suburban boom. In the late 1970s, the Phillips Neighborhood Improvement Association (PNIA) conducted a comprehensive inventory of buildings and found that most former single-family homes had been subdivided into rental units. By 1980 this transformation was so advanced that renters outnumbered owners by a margin of more than four to one.[36] The PNIA study also found that nearly one-third of surveyed residents cited "poorly maintained housing" as a major problem, while one-fifth cited "absentee landlords."[37] It is important to recognize, however, that this deterioration was not simply about neglect. Indeed, slum landlordism could be a profitable enterprise in a context where racialized people had few other places to turn and city officials paid little heed to housing code and other violations. Indigenous renters were overrepresented among those who lived in the area's low-quality housing, as chronicled below.

Collectively, then, state subsidized processes of suburbanization, interstate construction, urban renewal, and slum removal, coupled with profitable forms of slum landlordism and a range of other factors, contributed to the production of an urban geography in which privilege and deprivation were isolated from one another. These processes were both creative and destructive. The policy prescriptions that subsidized the well-being of some Twin Cities residents are the same ones that coordinated the "organized abandonment" of others.[38]

The Making of an Indigenous Neighborhood

The sweeping reorganization of metropolitan space that I have just described coincided with the dramatic acceleration of Indigenous relocation to American cities. Many of those who left remote and reservation communities to make new lives in places like Minneapolis arrived at a time when new geographies of privilege and deprivation were emerging. These changes ushered in undreamed-of levels of prosperity for many, to be sure, but they did so with considerable collateral damage. In spatial terms, inner-city neighborhoods were the principal casualty of these shifts. In human terms, African Americans and other racialized communities, including Indigenous people, suffered most. They were overwhelmingly relegated to the declining urban core, while suburbs bloomed and boomed all around them. Minneapolis's Indigenous neighborhood did not emerge as part of an organic process of development but through an explicit set of decisions that worked to distribute advantage, privilege, and security in uneven ways. The urban strategies that delivered unprecedented comfort and abundance to a new generation of suburban Minneapolitans are the same strategies that hastened the decline of Phillips and other inner-city districts, remaking them as geographies of racialized exclusion and economic insecurity.

Urban poverty was not new to the United States in the postwar period, of course, but the "forms and distributions" of its postwar variants had no substantial precedent: "In previous periods of American history, poverty and unemployment were endemic," observes the historian Thomas Sugrue, "but poor people did not experience the same degree of segregation and isolation."[39] Indeed, the "urban crisis" that emerged in the quarter century that followed the Second

World War was qualitatively new. It was animated by a complicated alchemy of social and economic forces that worked to concentrate and isolate groups of economically marginal and racialized people in distressed inner-city districts in ways that had not been seen. The color and spatial location of American poverty was consolidated, especially after 1960, though the absolute number of people living below federal poverty line did not increase all that much.[40]

Minnesota's Twin Cities were not immune to this trend. By the 1960s, new pockets of impoverishment had begun to emerge in the inner cores of both Minneapolis and St. Paul. The 1970 census revealed that the two cities had a combined total of seven Census Tracts (CTs) with "extreme" poverty rates of 40 percent or more, nearly all of which were clustered around their respective central business districts.[41] By 1990, that number had grown to more than thirty, with inner-city CTs still comprising a significant majority of these "extreme" poverty zones.[42]

Growing core area insecurity corresponded to a crisis of joblessness. In 1960, only a few pockets of the inner-city Southside had unemployment rates higher than 3.5 percent.[43] By 1990, that rate had risen to roughly 15 percent of the area as a whole, more than twice the city average.[44]

The intensification of inner-city poverty in the Twin Cities intersected with the growth of racialized communities in core neighborhoods.[45] By the end of the 1980s, racialized people in Minneapolis and St. Paul were more likely to live in low-income neighborhoods than their counterparts in any other metropolitan region in the United States.[46] In Phillips, African Americans and Indigenous people began to emerge as significant demographic minorities in the early 1960s.[47] The number of racialized neighborhood dwellers grew in the years that followed and by 1990 "nonwhite" residents constituted a majority for the first time.

The dramatic growth of the Twin Cities inner-city Indigenous community in the postwar decades was an aggregate effect of a number of intersecting factors. In the most general sense, Indigenous urbanization was driven by the desire of reservation residents to pursue opportunities that were not available in their home communities. In this way, Indigenous people who left reservations shared ambitions with thousands of other Americans who departed from rural and agricultural districts seeking opportunities that could only be found in cities. At the same time, the economic challenges associated with reservation life were not generalizable to the nonurban population as a whole. Reservation insecurity was inseparable from the inequities of settler colonization. Indeed, successive rounds of territorial alienation and the disastrous effects of BIA policy produced severe economic consequences. Throughout the first half of the twentieth century, reservations in every part of the country were wracked by poverty, not least in Minnesota. At the midcentury mark, about half of all adult reservation dwellers were earning less than five hundred dollars annually.[48] It is no wonder, given this context, that such a large number of Indigenous people seized opportunities to contribute to the American war effort, either as soldiers or as workers in the urban defense industry.

The migratory pressures produced by these privations were amplified after 1945 by a federal policy climate that was increasingly oriented around the connected goals of breaking up the reservation system and assimilating Indigenous people into the urban wage economy. In the wake of the Second World War, these twin objectives were made explicit as state actors laid the political groundwork for what would become the federal policies of termination and relocation. The former was intended to divest the federal government from trust responsibility for tribal groups and territories, whereas the latter was intended to provide the means for reservation dwellers to integrate into the economic and social "mainstream" of American life through urban relocation. By 1951, BIA commissioner Dillon Myer—who had distinguished himself during the war years as the head of the War Relocation Authority and its program of Japanese internment—had established a Branch of Placement and Relocation and opened a number of urban field offices with the intent of facilitating and supervising Indigenous urbanization.[49] The relocation program brought about two thousand migrants to select urban areas in its first year, offering them a modest transportation allowance (usually in the form of a one-way ticket *away* from the reservation), and start-up funds for housing and living costs. Deploying a strategy that echoed the objectives of the assimilationist boarding school program, most relocatees were settled far from home to discourage easy return to the reservation.[50] Donald Fixico, the eminent analyst of Indigenous urbanization in the United States, demonstrates that state efforts to facilitate urban relocation in this era should be historicized as part of a longer pattern of geographic engineering through which policy makers have encouraged (and at points enforced) Indigenous mobility.[51]

The Twin Cities metropolitan area was not an official federal relocation site, but postwar in-migration to Minneapolis and St. Paul was encouraged through less explicit means. In 1948, the local BIA area office opened an employment placement center and other agencies launched "smaller-scale relocation programs" of their own.[52] Minneapolis and St. Paul were obvious choices for many people who engaged in such negotiations, whether they had BIA assistance or not. While the broader phenomenon of Indigenous urbanization in this era was characterized by wide dispersal to cities across the United States, Indigenous people who left Minnesota reservations tended to stay in their home state at a much higher rate. Between 1955 and 1960, an estimated 59 percent of the state's Indigenous "outmigrants" relocated within Minnesota. Only California had a higher rate of intrastate relocation.[53]

Indigenous people who moved to Minneapolis and St. Paul in the postwar decades tended to arrive from fewer and more proximate places than their counterparts in other cities. The metropolitan area's status as a regional economic center and its relative proximity to several large reservations also made it a logical destination. Anishinaabe people have consistently been in the majority in Minneapolis. Many of the Indigenous people who moved to the city's core neighborhoods in the period after 1945, for example, came from, or were affiliated with, Ojibwe reservations in the Upper Midwest, especially White Earth and Red Lake.[54] Smaller numbers of Dakota and Lakota people have also long formed a substantial minority of the city's Indigenous community. Members of other tribal groups, including Ho-Chunk people, are also numerically significant.

The vast majority of Indigenous people who moved to the Twin Cities in the postwar period took up residence in the inner city. In Minneapolis, clusters of Indigenous people initially congregated in the inner-city Northside, Elliot Park, and Phillips neighborhoods, where an abundance of rental housing had been opened up by the suburbanization of earlier inhabitants.[55] Throughout the 1960s, Phillips, above all others, came to be synonymous with the urban Indigenous community. By 1970, about two-thirds of the region's Indigenous residents were living in this Southside neighborhood, many in the environs around East Franklin Avenue.[56] In this context the area came to be understood as the cultural, residential, and po-litical center of Indigenous life in the Twin Cities, a so-called urban reservation.[57]

In part, this clustering reflected a shared desire on the part of Indigenous people to build community in a context of considerable adversity. Since the early 1960s, a diverse range of Indigenous insti-tutions has been established in the neighborhood. The construction of Indigenous housing complexes, health centers, service organiza-tions, administrative offices, political projects, businesses, and com-

Kids pose for photographer Randy Croce outside a powwow on East Franklin Avenue in 1978. Courtesy of Randy Croce.

munity centers has solidified a multicultural Indigenous sense of place in the built environment of the Phillips neighborhood and East Franklin Avenue. The Little Earth of United Tribes housing complex— which was founded a few blocks south of the Franklin Avenue strip in 1973 with the explicit intention of providing a focal point for the urban Indigenous community—is significant in this regard. So too is the Minneapolis American Indian Center, which opened its doors at 1530 East Franklin Avenue in 1975. The latter became an important hub for a diverse range of activities and cemented (quite literally) an Indigenous claim to the avenue and the city.

In recent years, this claim has been extended and reaffirmed by the establishment of an American Indian Cultural Corridor along a five-block stretch of East Franklin. These institutions have served as an important counterweight to the stigmatization of the area, functioning as brick-and-mortar symbols of Indigenous achievement, resilience, and resurgence.[58]

The Southside Indigenous neighborhood was produced by more than just an active desire for congregation, however. In 1969, Alfreida

Young men converse in front of the Minneapolis American Indian Center at 1530 East Franklin Avenue in 1986. Photograph by Russell Crea. Courtesy of Hennepin County Library.

An aerial view of Little Earth of United Tribes at Cedar Avenue South and East Twenty-fifth Street in South Minneapolis, 1973. Courtesy of the Minnesota Historical Society.

Beaver, a planner with the Model Neighborhood Project in Minneapolis, told an investigative committee that Indigenous urbanites faced de facto forms of involuntary relegation. "There is a higher concentration area [of Indigenous people] in the south . . . [because] that is the only place they are allowed to move to," she testified.[59] Dennis Wynne, an official with the Minneapolis Housing and Redevelopment Authority, told the same committee that Indigenous people often had to contend with extraordinary constraints in securing decent shelter:

> We have a rental market in Minneapolis wherein an Indian family who may have been here for some time, comes in and has few options where to live. For the most part, they are limited to substandard housing, apartments which are, in many cases, barely livable. Often these are owned by absentee owners. I think they can best be described more accurately as an exploitation market because that is what it really amounts to—exploitation of families, or individuals—many times by absentee owners and sometimes by governmental structures themselves.[60]

Meanwhile, a 1968 report prepared by the League of Women Voters of Minnesota made the same case in even starker terms. "Finding decent inexpensive housing, a major problem for all poor people in the cities, is especially hard for American Indians," the group observed:

> The poorest segment of the population, Indians have the least to spend on rent. They therefore must take the worst available housing—often buildings slated for demolition. These and other old apartment buildings embroiled in frequent code violation complaints under frequently changing ownership make up the neighborhoods where the majority of urban Indians live. The reality of nowhere else to go leaves Indians at the mercy of indifferent landlords. Housing is in such short supply that there are no alternatives.[61]

In other words, the emergence of an Indigenous community in and around Franklin Avenue is inseparable from a particular political economy of exclusion, as these interventions attest.

Indeed, Indigenous urbanites routinely found themselves residing in Phillips and other inner-city districts because the dilapidated and subpar rental units that dominated these neighborhoods were the only housing options available to them. Already by the mid-1950s, the paucity of decent shelter available to Indigenous people was being described as the "gravest threat" to that group's health and well-being.[62] The situation had not changed much a decade later, and one City Planning Department official would describe the shelter occupied by Indigenous people as the "worst housing in the worst neighborhoods in the city."[63] At that time, a survey of Indigenous housing found that 72 percent of dwellings were in substandard condition, 75 percent had broken doors, plaster, and stairs, or lights that did not work.[64] Although Minneapolis had a robust housing code, the report observed, it lacked serious enforcement: "The Housing inspection crew is so short staffed that it can only keep up with complaints," and "legal loopholes" make it possible for landlords to ignore rules.[65] In this context, housing long slated for demolition wasn't brought up to code and functioned instead as a "considerable resource for poor Indian renters." This unenviable condition persisted in the decade that followed. Through the 1970s, more than 90 percent of Indigenous Southsiders lived in rental units, many of which were in a state of advanced deterioration.[66]

Indigenous renters faced problems that extended far beyond the indifference and neglect of Southside landlords, however. A rich material record reveals that many encountered explicit forms of racist discrimination in their efforts to find and secure housing. Alongside various studies that allude to the pervasiveness of this problem, case files from the Minneapolis Department of Civil Rights (MDCR) offer a glimpse at some of the ways that this abuse manifested.[67] Common themes persist across these official complaints.

For example, Indigenous renters often described contacting a landlord by phone to confirm the vacancy of a unit and being assured that no tenant had been found. After meeting in person, however, the would-be renter often found that the landlord had had a change of heart or insisted that the unit was no longer available.[68] The files reveal that MDCR investigators sometimes followed up with landlords, appointing "testers" to present themselves as white or non-Indigenous prospective renters. Often such testers learned that the apartment was, in fact, still available.

In most cases, landlords were cunning enough *not* to reveal their racialized preferences to MDCR officials. One file, for example, recounts the experience of a complainant who contacted a landlord by phone to inquire about a vacancy and was asked if she was "white." "When she replied that she was Indian," the report notes, "he said that he was sorry, no hard feeling [sic], but he couldn't rent to her because she was Indian."[69] When MDCR investigators followed up, the landlord was shrewd enough to change his rationale. This time he complained that the would-be renter's credit rating was poor, while admitting that he had not actually looked it up. When investigators learned that the complainant was receiving a significant bank loan to open a restaurant on nearby Franklin Avenue (hardly an indication of poor credit), they again followed up with the landlord. The MDCR investigator's report of that conversation is revealing:

I contacted [the landlord] again on May 1. He was, again, very hostile. He immediately went into a tirade about the [complainant], the key sentence being, "Her credit stinks." I told him, quite calmly, that I had checked with [the complainant], and that I believed she wouldn't be a particularly poor credit risk, but that if he was worried about it, the logical procedure would be a more thorough reference and credit check. He said something about not wasting his time on people like that . . . he could tell they were poor credit risks. (From a brief phone conversation.) He also said he had a good deal of experience in real estate and saw what different kinds of people did to property, and that he would rather have the property vacant than have problems. He didn't want a whole lot of people living there, property damage; etc. He did not ever say "Indians" but there is no doubt in my mind that this is what he was talking about.[70]

In this and other cases, the landlord's actual motivations were only revealed after considerable prodding.

At the same time, complaint files reveal a range of incidents where landlords were less circumspect, openly revealing their racism and announcing their unwillingness to rent to Indigenous people. In one such case, a BIA Housing Guidance Assistance worker reported that a landlord told her, "I just won't take any more of your people."[71] The landlord noted that his complex already housed a number of Indigenous people. "They give me trouble," he said. "Don't bother to fill out the application. I wouldn't rent to you anyway and besides, it cost me 2 cents so give it back to me."

MDCR complaints also offer evidence that even renters who had the financial backing of social-service agencies encountered explicit prejudice. In one telling incident, a young woman was referred to a South Minneapolis apartment by a social worker who had spoken to a caretaker about the prospective renter. The social worker had explained that the renter was young, reliable and that her rent would be covered by an institutional source. The MDCR report indicates that the caretaker seemed pleased, but when the renter arrived to see the apartment, her attitude shifted. Again, the complaint is revealing:

I proceeded to 2507 Nicollet on September 19, 1972 for the pur-
pose of renting an apartment. I met a female inside who indi-
cated to me that she was . . . the Caretaker of the apartment.
[She] looked at me a long time and said, "Where did you come
from?" She also asked if I had a home and family in Minneapolis. I handed [her] the "landlord statement" which indicates
public relief will pay my rent from the public relief department.
[She] said, "I can't take that." On the way to show the apartment,
[she] asked if I were married or single and if I were employed.
I informed her I was single and had just returned from an employment interview. She then said, "We don't want parties." [She]
opened the apartment but did not show me around. I asked [her]
if the apartment came furnished and she said, "No." The apartment was in fact furnished at the time. When we returned up-
stairs, [she] kept telling me the apartment was for older persons,
but she never said how old. [She] never offered me an application. I learned later that same day from the Social Service Aid
that she had called [the caretaker] after I had come to the apartment. The Social Service Aid informed me that [the caretaker]
had said pertaining to me, "well I didn't know she was Indian."[72]

These complaints offer a tiny glimpse at the diverse forms of abuse
that renters encountered.

The production of an Indigenous neighborhood in South Minneapolis was thus not the net effect of an organic process of development. Rather, it was the outcome of two intersecting, if contradictory,
patterns. On the one hand, the neighborhood was produced by the
efforts of Indigenous people to find ways to be together in Minneapolis by building institutions and networks for community flourishing that were concentrated in geographic space. On the other hand,
the neighborhood was produced by racism, and especially forms
of racism that shaped housing-market dynamics and public-policy
approaches in ways that secured advantages for white Minnesotans
and denied them to others.

The White Spatial Imaginary and the Settler Colonial Relation

How are we to make sense of the radical inequity that animates these distributions of power, privilege, and material comfort? In Lipsitz's terms, the "structured advantages" enjoyed by the dominant segments of the American public, who are almost always white, are not haphazard. Rather, they are the product of a long line of political practice that has funneled opportunity and enrichment to white people at the expense of others. He argues that a "wide range of public and private actions" have operated to safeguard the advantages that white people "have inherited from their ancestors," including "wealth originally accumulated during eras when direct and overt discrimination in government policies, home sales, mortgage lending, education, and employment systematically channeled assets to whites."[73] This list surely includes other postwar public policies that amplified the American city's economic and "racial" divisions by directing public resources toward the ends of expanding a largely white middle class, reorienting urban infrastructure around the needs of a growing suburban population, and "renewing" central cities as places of orderly commercial activity, while neglecting the needs and aspirations of increasingly racialized inner-city communities.

Of course, this pattern extends far beyond the postwar period, as Lipsitz demonstrates. Indeed, he argues that the politics of white advantage have roots in much longer histories of exclusion, including processes of settler colonial dispossession that alienated Indigenous people of their lands. More than forty-five million white Americans can trace their inherited family wealth to the Homestead Act of 1862, just as more than thirty-five million white families benefited from discriminatory federally insured home mortgages between 1934 and 1970 (2). Importantly, Lipsitz insists that these were not one-off moments of subsidy. "Because money is passed down across generations through inheritance," he observes, "the patterns of the past still shape opportunities of the present" (ibid.).

Although Lipsitz is concerned with the way that racialized public policies disadvantage African Americans, his observations are applicable to studies of American settler colonization as well. By stressing the ways that racialized advantages have afterlives that continue beyond the policies that produce them, he offers an interpretive language that allows analysts to trace clear lines of continuity. For the purposes of this book, for example, Lipsitz's work offers a way to make connections between the earliest forms of Indigenous dispossession in the region, the postwar policies that contributed to the production of an Indigenous neighborhood in South Minneapolis, and the persistence of contemporary forms of racialized group-differentiated inequity. Indeed, Lipsitz's observations offer a way to interpret the production of an "urban reservation" as a continuation of a longer settler colonial history of distributional unfairness through which Indigenous people (and peoples) have been confined to spaces of economic and infrastructural marginality, even as considerable prosperity and abundance has been enjoyed all around them. If nineteenth-century processes of expulsion and reservationization constituted forms of "organized abandonment," then so too do modern forms of inner-city deprivation. These geographic strategies are not identical, of course, but they are animated by a common set of commitments.

Durable meritocratic myths have often absolved white Americans of the burden of examining the politics that undergirds the "structured advantages" of whiteness. Exculpatory thinking has often taken a spatial form. What Lipsitz calls the "white spatial imaginary" is linked to an interpretation of American urban space that allows "whites" to see themselves as "individuals whose wealth grew out of their personal and individual success in acquiring property on the 'free market'" rather than as a privileged subset of the population that includes many who benefited from their capacity to access an "expressly discriminatory" pool of government-backed mortgages and other advantages (27). This same "spatial imaginary" has allowed "whites" to view racialized inner-city populations not as "fellow citizens" denied certain structural advantages but as "people whose alleged failure to save, invest, and take care of their homes forced the government to intervene on their behalf" by building public-housing projects and other amenities, all of which were then "ruined" by the willful neglect of their inhabitants (ibid.). The degree to which public monies and efforts were invested in the production of white suburban prosperity is almost always excluded from such interpretations.

There is much in his thinking that can help illuminate discussions about Minneapolis's Indigenous neighborhood. There is considerable evidence that the "white spatial imaginary" has animated interpretations of Indigenous marginality in the inner city. Indeed, prevailing explanations of why Indigenous social and economic insecurity persists have often relied on cultural/behavioral interpretations that assign blame to Indigenous people themselves. The pervasiveness of Indigenous occupancy in cramped, dilapidated, and underrepaired housing units has, for example, sometimes been explained as a function of the moral and proprietary failings of the tenants.

Illustrative here is the reaction that Gerald Vizenor received after he reported in the *Minneapolis Tribune* that hundreds of Indigenous families were paying extortionary rents to live in roach- and rat-infested units in the Southside "poverty area."[74] Although Vizenor laid the blame for these conditions on the public policies that had produced them, the prevailing reaction does not seem to have been widespread calls for a municipal crackdown on predatory landlords or new rounds of investment in affordable inner-city housing. In fact, at least a few readers doubled down on precisely the racist assumptions that Vizenor's reportage ought to have disabused them of. One, for example, wrote to Vizenor to register his concern about what he interpreted as a lack of basic cleanliness on the part the people depicted in the article:

> What caught my eye was filth and garbage all over the place. It seems to me the first step for anybody to live with pride is to be clean. I wonder if these people really care where they live. If they were given a $20,000 home rent free would it be neat and clean or littered with garbage and filth? Perhaps, these people need to be educated in how to maintain their dwellings. Perhaps some church organizations could secure volunteers to teach these people the basics of clean living and home maintenance.[75]

The reader acknowledges that repairs may well be needed but notes that he can't understand why a landlord would bother to "fix up a dwelling if it will just be wrecked again."[76] In another letter received by Vizenor, a "disgusted taxpayer" offers a similar set of reflections:

> The article you had in the Sunday paper was very disgusting. I don't feel one bit sympathetic for these people. I don't donate 5¢ to the welfare. I have heard too much about these people on welfare. If these people want to live like pigs why spend money on them. They can at least be clean, and . . . [indecipherable] be responsible for the damage they do. I am sure there are thousands of people that agree with me.[77]

The preposterous view expressed in these letters, that a *culture* of uncleanliness is the reason why Indigenous residents of the inner city were living in such conditions, was not limited to irritable *Tribune* readers. In 1978, for example, a Minneapolis building inspector named Martin Thompson allowed a local reporter to tail him as he made stops in the Phillips neighborhood, or what he called "the hell hole of the city."[78] Thompson held forth, voicing outright contempt for racialized people living in poverty, observing that social-assistance recipients rarely bothered to maintain their rented homes, and waxing philosophical on the apparently transhistorical nature of Indigenous filthiness: "They used to be able to crap all over everything and move the teepee but they can't do that anymore," he is purported to have said.[79]

The deployment of such cultural explanations to account for Indigenous insecurity was not limited to explicit racists. It seeped into sympathetic interpretations as well. For example, a report prepared by the League of Women Voters of Minnesota acknowledged the role of persistent structural problems in limiting the housing options of Indigenous people, but also mobilized cultural explanations to help explain why this was the case. Consider, for example, this partial interpretation:

> One reason for poor Indian housing is overcrowding, some of which seems to be due to an Indian philosophy that even dis-

tant relatives are part of the family and should be taken into the household. This practice makes household budgeting difficult for the Indian, even when he is motivated to budget his expenses; it may also cause unpleasantness with the landlord. On the other hand, Indians seldom request repairs, and put up with really deplorable conditions without complaining.[80]

It is, of course, a matter of demonstrable fact that Indigenous residents of the Southside often shared large households. It may also be true that this was sometimes motivated by a (laudable) "philosophy" of accommodation that was out of step with the unwritten rules of certain bourgeois households. But to cast this philosophy as a major *cause* of "poor Indian housing" is to explain the dramatic paucity of spaces where Indigenous families could secure accommodation as the result of a cultural preference for togetherness that is "unpleasant" for landlords. To explain group-differentiated housing insecurity through narratives of cultural deficiency or incompatibility is to risk obscuring the constitutive importance of what Lipsitz calls the "structured advantage" of the dominant group.[81]

These and other expressions of the "white spatial imaginary" are not articulated in a historical vacuum. They are formed within the complex and shifting articulations of the settler colonial relation. It is through this dynamic that racist forms of "knowledge" about Indigenous people have been reified and naturalized. With varying degrees of emphasis in different periods, settler colonists and their descendants have interpreted Indigenous people and practices as uncivilized, primitive, debauched, and backward.[82] In more recent decades, they have been depicted as out of step with the presumed orderliness of settler society and contemporary urban life. The persistence of these discourses shapes and reshapes the epistemological contours of how the lives of Indigenous people are understood by non-Indigenous Minnesotans. In shifting and incomplete ways, they produce "knowledge" about who Indigenous people are and where they are properly "in place."[83]

Critically, though, to interpret Indigenous people as belonging to an inner-city geography of destitution and filth is not merely an expression of racist contempt. The emergence of Minneapolis's

Indigenous neighborhood is inseparable from a longer history of social and political negotiation through which settler colonists and their descendants have consolidated material advantages for themselves. "White supremacy does not exist or persist because whites foolishly fear people with a different skin color," notes Lipsitz. "It survives and thrives because whiteness delivers unfair gains and unjust enrichments to people who participate in and profit from the existence of a racial cartel that skews opportunities and life chances for their own benefit."[84] Processes of settler colonization enshrine spatial and political orders in which "unfair gains and unjust enrichments" are channeled to settler constituencies. This process does not end once Indigenous communities have been thoroughly (though not entirely) divested of their lands. The "structured advantages" of settler colonization, key expressions of the inequity that animates the settler colonial relation, persist in contemporary life in myriad forms. And yet, because these advantages are so naturalized as common sense, so dissolved within the self-absolving contours of the "white spatial imaginary," they no longer appear to be advantages at all. The "machinery of enforcement," to invoke Sarah Schulman's phrase, is obscured.[85]

Distinguishing the Indigenous Neighborhood

The association of the term "inner city" with racialized poverty is well established in the United States, even if that association seems to have less of a grip on reality with every passing year.[86] Indeed, most Americans are acquainted with some version of a broadly circulated cultural script that establishes white suburbs and nonwhite cores as the twin geographic poles of the divided American metropolis. The most simplistic (and exculpatory) versions of this script have long been offset by critical retellings that emphasize the definitive role that white supremacy has played in the production of these divided geographies. It is important to stress, however, that the history of the South Minneapolis Indigenous neighborhood does not always fit within the confines of these familiar interpretive frames. While it is true that the changes that occurred in Phillips in the second half of the twentieth century are bound up with state-subsidized suburbanization, interstate construction, urban renewal, slum clearance, and a predatory rental economy, among other things, these developments offer only a partial glimpse of how the Phillips neighborhood (and especially its East Franklin Avenue corridor) came to be understood as an Indigenous place, albeit a multicultural one. The emergence of an Indigenous neighborhood in South Minneapolis is not a generic expression of the racialized effects of the "metropolitan revolution," in other words. It is not an Indigenous analogue for African American ghettoization but a distinct urban phenomenon that ought to be understood in its particularity. Accordingly, it is necessary to qualify the analysis above with a few observations.

Indigenous people often have distinct relationships to urban spaces and the territories on which they are built. Minnesota's Twin Cities are constructed in the heart of the Dakota homeland, at the center of the Dakota cultural, spiritual, and political universe. They also sit in relative proximity to territories that were home to Anishinaabe communities before widespread Euro-American settler colonialism began to transform the region. Given this context, it is misleading, to put it in the mildest terms possible, to use the language of "migration" to describe the process that saw thousands of Dakota and Ojibwe people move to the Twin Cities in the postwar period. Sarah Hunt argues that "migration" narratives have the problematic effect of naturalizing reserves (reservations, in the U.S. context) as "Indian space" while naturalizing cities as "white space."[87] This crude division obscures the degree to which settler ideas about what urban space is (and who belongs in it) are often contradicted by Indigenous ideas about territoriality and space. Evelyn Peters observes that Indigenous people often move to cities with a different sense of place than others, particularly when they are traveling within their traditional territories.[88] Of course, this is not necessarily a generalizable claim in the United States. The vast majority of Indigenous people who participated in the official Indian Relocation program, for example, moved to urban centers that were many hundreds (if not thousands) of miles away from their traditional territories, and many participants would not have felt that they were journeying in a familiar place. In Minnesota, however, Indigenous people tended to relocate to cities from nearby places at a much higher rate than they did elsewhere. Given this fact, it is worth stressing that questions of sovereignty, entitlement, and belonging are vital in this urban context. If the language of migration is nonsensical in the context of the Twin Cities, it might make more sense to conceptualize postwar Indigenous urbanization as a process of what Sasha Suarez calls "re-indigenization."[89] In the case of Dakota people in the Twin Cities, she contends, the process of making claims on urban space can be understood as a project of reclaiming a homeland, whereas in the context of other Indigenous people, it is perhaps better understood as a process of "claiming space" for community continuation. Suarez's observations are consistent with the idea that the reinterpretation of urban space is one of the key ways that Indigenous people have undermined colonial interpretations of geographic meaning.

At the same time, the Indigenous neighborhood cannot be understood as an isolated geography. This is true in at least two ways. First, it is critical to dispense with the problematic tendency to understand cities as disconnected from their broader surroundings. Cities are not islands. They are products of complex and enduring entanglements with other places. In the North American West, the most salient of these entanglements is the embeddedness of cities in Indigenous forms of territoriality. While places like Minneapolis are often imagined as stand-alone products of settler ingenuity—as settler spaces par excellence—such interpretations are always already menaced by alternative interpretations of territoriality, jurisdiction, sovereignty, and entitlement. Indeed, long-standing and resurgent Indigenous interpretations of North American geography make plain that cities are not "island[s] of settler becoming" but places that are "embedded in broader Indigenous networks and territorial relations."[90] Accordingly, one of the most important ways that Indigenous people have "advanced an anti-colonial understanding of cities and the lands upon which they have been built" is by "remapping urban areas as part of traditional and treaty territories" in ways that challenge conventional interpretations.[91] Such claims defy settler fantasies of creation, ownership, and exclusivity. Second, it is critical to avoid the suggestion that the Indigenous neighborhood is itself isolated or contained (an interpretation sometimes implied, wittingly or not, by analyses that emphasize Indigenous concentration in the inner city). This is true not only in the sense that urban spaces are always shaped by relationships with their putative "outside," but also in the sense that the Phillips neighborhood is better understood as a node in a networked Indigenous geography than it is as a terminal point for Indigenous relocations. Indeed, the neighborhood is not a collection point for people leaving reservations but a place that exists in dynamic relation with Indigenous communities across the region. Thick circuits of mobility and exchange have persisted between South Minneapolis and these places since at least the early 1960s. Indeed, Indigenous politics and modes of being together routinely escape "the divide between city and non-city that is inscribed in layered histories of settler urbanization," to borrow a phrase from Stefan Kipfer.[92]

These observations are reminders that to take note of the Indigenous character of the Phillips neighborhood is to do more than make an ethnographic qualification to an otherwise generic case of urban racism (if such a thing could even exist). While familiar interpretations of the inner city as a site of racialized concentration should be complicated in all cases, this task is urgent in the context of the Indigenous neighborhood of South Minneapolis, where the complexity of Indigenous relationships to place defies tidy categorization.

2

Liberal Antiracism
as Political Dead End
The Limits of Non-Indigenous Advocacy

In 1968, the *Minneapolis Tribune* published an editorial lamenting the social and economic exclusion of Indigenous people in the Twin Cities. "Indians began migrating to the cities after World War II to escape reservation poverty and seek a better life," it summarized. "Instead, they found a mirage."[1] The *Tribune*'s interpretation reflected a growing popular discomfort with the persistence of Indigenous insecurity in Minnesota's urban areas. It also echoed the concerns of a new generation of non-Indigenous advocates that had begun to emerge as key players on the urban region's political scene, buoyed by an increasingly mainstream climate of liberal reform.

This chapter considers the work of two Minneapolis-based non-governmental research and advocacy organizations that were motivated by the ambition to contest the exclusion of Indigenous people from the prosperity of postwar American life. The first is the League of Women Voters of Minnesota (LWV), which began to take a keen interest in "Indian affairs" in 1961 and committed significant resources to research, advocacy, and legislative lobbying over the course of the next two decades. The second is the Training Center for Community Programs (TCCP), an academic and community outreach institute at the Twin Cities campus of the University of Minnesota, which, from 1967 through the mid-1970s, engaged in a range of federally funded projects concerned with understanding and brokering solutions to the exclusion of Indigenous people from the social and political life of "mainstream" America.

These organizations (and the knowledge they produced) merit attention for at least four reasons. First, they were responsible for the production of a huge volume of information about Indigenous people in the Upper Midwest in general and the Twin Cities in particular. Their research was well funded, well circulated, and consequential. Second, their work had tangible public-policy implications. Both organizations had close ties to Minnesota's liberal political establishment and drew on those connections to advocate for a range of proposals. Third, they occupied positions of considerable public profile and their interventions commanded popular attention. Fourth, their work offers present-day observers an informative glimpse into the political limits of liberal antiracism.

This fourth point is at the center of this chapter's intervention. The analysis that follows demonstrates that the LWV and the TCCP understood themselves as advocates for Indigenous people, but their commitments stopped well short of a desire to fundamentally challenge the core inequities of settler colonial society. Both groups were serious about their desire to support Indigenous people, but they were never interested in confronting the prevailing political order, its distribution of resources, and its core assumptions about the world. This is significant because it is this political order, its distributions, and its assumptions that structure settler colonial inequities and sustain their endurance. To illustrate this point, this chapter demonstrates that the research and advocacy work of these two organizations was animated (and constrained) by a politics of liberal antiracism that allowed them to express their opposition to the marginalization of Indigenous people without confronting the generative conditions that gave rise to that marginalization and facilitated its reproduction. Specifically, it makes the case that by framing Indigenous marginalization in the Twin Cities as a manageable public-policy challenge rather than a substantial social cleavage rooted in the persistence of the settler colonial relation itself, the work of the LWV and TCCP impeded the serious political work of seeking to understand (and ultimately transform) racialized inequity.

This chapter begins by looking at the context in which these organizations emerged as influential participants in debates about Indigenous issues in Minnesota. It then turns to a discussion of the key assumptions that undergirded the knowledge that they produced. In doing so, it argues that both organizations were committed to a politics of liberal antiracism and demonstrates how this shaped the way that they interpreted the "problem" of Indigenous urban insecurity and conceived of solutions to it. It concludes with a critical assessment of the implications of this framing.

The Emergence of the LWV and TCCP as "Indian Affairs" Advocates

In his celebrated 1962 investigation of American poverty, *The Other America,* the political theorist Michael Harrington observed that while the postwar boom had ushered in the "highest mass standard of living the world has ever known," there remained millions of Americans yet "maimed in body and spirit, existing at levels beneath those necessary for human decency."[2] Harrington's work is often credited with having inspired a new generation of advocacy groups, social scientists, and policy elites that were committed to smoothing over this contradiction and extending the unprecedented prosperity of the period to all parts of American society.

In the American Midwest, Indigenous communities were routinely identified as sites where the new abundance had yet to penetrate, although not initially by Harrington.[3] In the 1960s, two non-Indigenous Minnesotan advocacy organizations launched comprehensive efforts to understand and overcome these racialized inequities. Convinced of the righteousness of their endeavor, they set out to understand the sources of Indigenous exclusion and broker solutions that could help overcome them.

One of these groups was the Minnesota affiliate of the League of Women Voters. The statewide organization's first foray into Indigenous issues was driven by the advocacy efforts of key activists from White Bear Lake, an affluent Twin Cities suburb. The central figure behind this push was Elizabeth Adams Ebbott, who, by the early 1960s, had made it known that she wanted the LWV to contribute to the amelioration of the situation of what she called the state's "ignored minority."[4]

It is not clear what sparked Ebbott's interest in the marginalization of Indigenous Minnesotans but the presence in her personal files of an annotated copy of a series of articles by journalist Carl Rowan (published under the title "Plight of the Upper Midwest Indian" in the *Minneapolis Tribune* in 1957) offer some hint. Her marginal notations on these texts cohere enough around a series of specific themes that it is possible to make some assumptions about what she found noteworthy in the fifteen pages of broadsheet text.[5] Nearly every passage underlined, starred, or otherwise flagged relates to either the depth of Indigenous hardship or the failure of the political establishment to address it. Ebbott's markings suggest that she was not merely concerned with the widespread exclusion of Indigenous people from the prosperity of American life, but also that she understood that exclusion to be political, and therefore solvable.

In this, she shared the national LWV's long-standing position that the formal political institutions had a fundamental responsibility to promote "general welfare by positive action."[6] This conviction dates to the organization's founding in 1919. The national LWV was born as an auxiliary of the National American Woman Suffrage Association in the wake of that group's victorious campaign to secure the Nineteenth Amendment to the Constitution of the United States, which prohibited individual states from denying the right to vote on the basis of gender. The civic education of newly enfranchised women was the national LWV's original raison d'être, but from its inception it also pursued "nonpartisan" legislative advocacy on a range of issues. The organization's earliest publications make it clear that LWV members believed they could be a "new force for the humanizing of government."[7] They also make clear that the LWV was committed to the idea that government itself could be a "humanizing" force within American society. The first iteration of the organization's "legislative program" is illustrative of this point. It envisions a robust regulatory role for government on a broad range of issues, including labor conditions, public welfare, public education, "social hygiene," and the consumption of alcohol.[8]

In other words, state-led intervention, in the organization's official view, was critical to ensuring the general well-being of American people. LWV historian Louise Young summarizes this long-standing orientation:

> Laissez-faire doctrines, from a feminist perspective, have served too well the bastions of male privilege, offering discouragement to the feminists' desire to aid the disadvantaged, including themselves. The League [repudiated] the concept of a passive, noninterventionist government, standing aside while competition guaranteed the survival of the strongest.[9]

Perceiving itself an advocate for the oppressed, the LWV supported legislative attempts to curb the exclusion of particular groups from the full benefits of American citizenship.

The efforts of the White Bear Lake chapter to encourage the Minnesota LWV to take up "Indian affairs" as one of its central research and advocacy foci resonated with organization activists who felt that one of the League's indispensable functions was to challenge the injustice of group exclusion. It was to this sense of moral calling that Ebbott and her White Bear Lake colleagues appealed when they sent a letter to all other Minnesota chapters in the lead-up to the organization's 1961 statewide convention. Their missive, which urged the Minnesota LWV to combat Indigenous disadvantage, began as follows:

> Life expectancy—37 years.
> One third of the children die before the age of five.
> Estimated per capita income of the most affluent group—150 per year.
> If the total wealth of the land were divided equally among the residents, it would come to about $500 per person.
> These statistics are not from some report about the Congo,

the natives of India or the people of Korea. These foreign people with similar statistics have our sympathy, have our support, have the League working for their betterment.

No, these facts state briefly and dramatically the condition and plight of about 20,000 Minnesota citizens—our ignored minority, the Chippewas of Minnesota.[10]

The letter goes on to invoke the moral authority of the popular Christian journalist Harold Fey in order to remind readers that "as a whole the Indians live in deeper poverty than any other racial group in the nation," a destitution, it notes, not even shared by "our latest newcomers," Puerto Ricans. Indigenous people, or, more specifically, "the Chippewas of Minnesota," were suffering. (It is curious that the LWV had little to say to about other Indigenous peoples.) And it was the responsibility of their fellow citizens to ameliorate that situation.

Invoking this imperative, the White Bear Lake activists convinced the statewide organization to adopt "Indian affairs" as one of its primary advocacy issues. In the decades that followed, the League engaged in an ambitious (and sometimes successful) lobby program aimed at influencing public policy at both the state and national levels. The organization helped push legislators to defend traditional hunting and ricing rights, provide basic services to Indigenous people who were not living in reservation communities, fairly distribute Johnson–O'Malley funds, and restore the territorial rights of the Menominee people of Wisconsin (which had been forfeited as part of the federal government's dubious termination program in the 1950s), among other things. It also developed working relationships with a range of Indigenous and Indigenous-serving organizations and agencies.

The League's most significant contribution in the realm of "Indian affairs," however, was its effort to produce informational resources about the "needs" of Indigenous people in Minnesota and their relationship to government, including the publication of five editions of the influential survey text *Indians in Minnesota*, a book that is still used in many Minnesota classrooms (albeit in an updated form). The

Minnesota LWV invested significant energy in getting its research into the hands of influential people and was often quite successful at doing so. Ebbott was the primary force behind these efforts and her personal files contain a broad range of correspondence to this effect, including letters of thanks from powerful judges, elected officials, and top bureaucrats.[11]

Yet, while LWV members were able to establish ties to leaders in the upper echelons of local and national political power, they were not entirely disengaged from grassroots organizations. There is evidence, for example, that the group had a complicated and occasionally productive relationship with the American Indian Movement and others. Indeed, AIM organizers sometimes relied on the LWV for particular kinds of support, just as the LWV relied on AIM to confer a certain kind of legitimacy on its activities. When AIM activists picked up on the efforts of earlier Twin Cities organizers by reinaugurating a picketing campaign in front of the Minneapolis Area Office of the BIA to protest the lack of services available to Indigenous urbanites in 1970, for example, the League marshaled its institutional clout to support the demonstrators. In the days that followed the demonstrations, Minnesota LWV President Irene Janski published a letter in the *Minneapolis Tribune* expressing unequivocal support for the demands that had been articulated. "Indian Citizens have made their statement eloquently," she noted, and expressed the League's hope that it would be heard at all levels of government.[12] This was no empty demand coming from a group that was as well connected to institutional power as the LWV. In the weeks that followed, Minnesota Senator Walter Mondale built on the organization's lead by making a statement of his own and entering Janski's letter into the Congressional Record. AIM Chairman Dennis Banks wrote to Janski to thank her for her support.[13]

Members of AIM also called on the League for support in more dire circumstances. The LWV's 1971 statewide convention coincided with an AIM occupation of an abandoned Twin Cities naval base. Occupiers were evicted while the convention was in full swing. Internal LWV documents reveal that AIM activists turned to League leadership and requested an opportunity to address the convention in order build support for those who had been arrested. After certain complications were smoothed over, AIM leaders were allowed to speak and a box was placed at the door so League members could contribute to efforts to raise bail money. It is a testament to both the persuasiveness of those who spoke and the formal political clout of the LWV that following the convention more than thirty attendees "went unofficially to the Governor's office and presented him with a signed statement declaring their concern over the incident."[14]

At the same time, the LWV leadership understood that the legitimacy of their "Indian Affairs" work required that they cultivate positive relationships with leading Indigenous organizations and agencies. In the early 1970s, AIM was still counted among these ranks by members of the establishment. When Ebbott wrote to the powerful Hill Family Foundation requesting funds for the publication of the 1971 edition of *Indians in Minnesota,* she was told that securing endorsements from some of the "Indian leadership in Minnesota" would help improve prospects. Foundation representatives suggested that she seek recommendations from the State Office of Indian Affairs, the State Department of Education and, notably, the American Indian Movement.[15] It is hard to imagine that just two years later—after AIM activists had engaged in an armed confrontation with the FBI at Wounded Knee—the movement would still be included in such a lofty list of institutional authority.

For the purposes of this chapter, the key fact in all of this is that LWV research emerged as a significant mainstream source of information about Indigenous people living in the Twin Cities. The first edition of *Indians in Minnesota,* self-published as a pamphlet in 1961, did not contain a separate section on urban Indigenous issues, either in the Twin Cities or elsewhere. It made peripheral mention of problems that were specific to Indigenous urbanites but stopped well short of interrogating the city as a site of injustice or community strength.[16] In future editions, the LWV began to address this oversight and in 1968 it even published a pamphlet titled *Indians in Minneapolis.*[17] As the authors explained: "League members decided . . . that they wanted to take a closer look at what has been called 'Minnesota's largest reservation,' Minneapolis." From 1971 on, new editions of *Indians in Minnesota* featured at least one chapter on issues that were unique to urban environments. This development is not surprising given that by the mid-1960s a number of urban Indigenous groups had emerged as key voices in the region's urban politics. It's hard to imagine that the LWV could have continued to give urban issues such short shrift in this context.

The second non-Indigenous organization that sought to understand the sources of Indigenous exclusion was the Training Center for Community Programs (TCCP) at the University of Minnesota. In the years that followed the Minnesota LWV's arrival as a major institutional voice in Indigenous advocacy, the TCCP emerged as the most prolific producer of social-science research on "Indian affairs" in the Upper Midwest.

The TCCP's path to this position was circuitous. The Center was formed in 1963 as one of a series of research sites tasked with tackling issues of "youth delinquency," a Kennedy administration project that both anticipated, and would eventually be subsumed by, the Johnson administration's Great Society and War on Poverty efforts.[18] TCCP researchers approached "delinquency" as a social product (rather than an individual failing) and their work focused on the functioning of society's "major institutions" (public schools, government agencies, the criminal punishment system, etc.) rather than the "intrinsic nature of the disadvantaged or deviant."[19] Accordingly, their work focused on the everyday protocols of these institutions and sought to make recommendations about how existing approaches might be adapted to "meet the needs of those who are outside of the mainstream of American life."[20] In this sense, they shared the basic ideological orientation of the Great Society initiative. They believed, in other words, that the "basic structures of American society were satisfactory," as Ira Katznelson summarizes, but that they needed "adjustment, fine-tuning, [and] enhanced access," goals that could be achieved through training programs, expanded participation, and effective neighborhood-level programming.[21]

The TCCP's work was not merely ideologically linked to the federal approach to fighting poverty, however. Its decade of research activities, from the humble beginnings already described through a considerable expansion in the late 1960s, was financed almost entirely by the core funding bodies of the War on Poverty program and its predecessor initiatives, especially the federal Department of Health, Education, and Welfare (HEW). For the purposes of this chapter, the most significant federal investment in the Center came in 1967 when HEW funded the TCCP's "laboratory for social change," which targeted four areas where research efforts and experimental programming were deemed most needed. The project sought to expand community awareness about organized labor, promote and experiment with educational and training opportunities for low-income people, build training programs for board members of social agencies, and establish a center for "Indian affairs" that would bring together community and university resources to address key needs of the Indigenous peoples of the region.[22]

The importance of the latter initiative was exemplified by the TCCP's decision to hire sociologist Arthur Harkins as its new director. Harkins identified himself as a "student of American Indian life" and, at the time of his appointment, was in the process of editing a book titled *Modern Minnesota Ojibwa*.[23] His War on Poverty credentials were well established. Harkins had spent two years working as a consultant on "Indian Community Action programs" for a private research firm.[24] Building on these experiences, he sought to mobilize TCCP resources to study the status of "the urban Indian," among other things.[25]

Under Harkins's leadership, the TCCP emerged as a prolific publisher of a broad range of research about Indigenous people. Much of this work focused on questions of "Indian education" but the more than seventy reports that the research center released between 1968 and 1973 span a diversity of topics.[26] Importantly, they are a significant source of information about the experience of urban Indigenous residents of the Twin Cities, including those who lived in the Phillips neighborhood. These reports, written by Harkins, his TCCP collaborator Richard Woods, and a range of others, provide some of the earliest academic research on the Indigenous experience of labor market exclusion, housing discrimination, quotidian racism, and public education, among other things. Center researchers believed that the university had a vital role to play in addressing social divisions and deprivation. They argued that "informing the citizens of our communities of the nature and problems of poverty" was essential to building public support for efforts to ameliorate the lives of the disadvantaged.

This, then, is the context in which the LWV and the TCCP emerged as two of the most influential and prolific producers of institutional knowledge about urban Indigenous life in Minnesota. In spite of their pretension of scientific objectivity, however, the research that these groups produced was profoundly political. To elucidate this point, it is critical to assess the ideological commitments that undergirded their work.

The Politics of Liberal Antiracism

In general terms, the efforts of the Minnesota LWV and the TCCP were oriented around finding policy fixes that would diminish the social and economic insecurity of Indigenous Minnesotans, particularly in the Twin Cities. Their approaches to these problems were not identical but both organizations were oriented around a common set of interpretive and political commitments. Specifically, they were both adherents to a politics of liberal antiracism.

The political orientation of the LWV and the TCCP was "liberal" in two senses. The first is that both shared and articulated a series of assumptions about the nature of individuals and society that are consistent with the core tenets of the modern liberal philosophical tradition.[27] While there is considerable differentiation between and among the kind of thinking that might be reasonably collapsed under this banner, there is also a "core set of ideas" that marks its distinction from other traditions.[28] Liberals are committed to the primacy of the individual as the basic unit of moral and political life. Liberals believe in equality in the sense that they recognize a "common moral standing" between individuals.[29] Liberals are universalist in that they believe that human beings are united by a common foundation that transcends "particular historical, social, and cultural differences."[30] Or, at the very least, liberals believe that such differences are "secondary."[31] And liberals are meliorist in their thinking. They believe that social arrangements can be reformed and improved through rational intervention, that "moral, political, economic and cultural *progress* is to be brought about by and reflected in carefully planned institutional improvement."[32]

The second is that the TCCP and the LWV were ideologically aligned with a form of statecraft that has long been branded "liberal" in the United States. They shared, in other words, the core convictions of what has sometimes been called the "New Deal Order," a midcentury political coalition and approach to governance grounded in Keynesian economics, expanded social provision, tempered labor militancy, and modest forms of wealth redistribution. Acolytes of this approach put their "faith in the wisdom and legitimacy of a strong federal government" and believed in its capacity "to secure the greatest possible good for the greatest possible number of Americans," as Maurice Isserman and Michael Kazin summarize.[33] At the center of this politics is the conviction that the work of an enlightened and interventionist state can and should be mobilized to resolve the core contradictions of American capitalism.[34] What distinguished the New Deal Order from other political currents interested in harnessing the power of the state as a vehicle of redistributive justice was its commitment to the preservation of capitalist democracy as the fundamental basis of American life. Accordingly, the term "liberal" in no way implies an oppositional politics grounded in collective deliverance from the injustices and inequities of capitalist social organization. Indeed, the liberal coalition that emerged through the politics of the New Deal was born out of the crushing *defeat* of the organized anticapitalist left. Its ascendance required the transformation of radical constituencies from opponents of the capitalist state into what political journalist Chris Hedges calls "domesticated negotiators *with* the capitalist class."[35] Parenthetically, it is this intimacy with the capitalist mode of production that has made liberals the political opponents of socialists, in spite of the slippage between these two categories that now often occurs in mainstream American political discourses. In fact, liberalism is in conflict with socialist visions of liberation precisely because it is grounded in a politics of possessive individualism.[36]

There are obvious tensions between these two interpretations of the term "liberal," but they are not necessarily antithetical to one another. Postwar liberals in the United States believed in interventionist government but remained committed to the idea that the values held sacrosanct in classical liberalism, such as the moral primacy of the individual, were best protected in a capitalist social formation. In this sense, the politics of New Deal liberalism should not be historicized as a deviation from classical liberalism, with its characteristic hostility to collectivism, but as a movement that sought solutions within the "framework of the liberal faith" at a challenging moment, as the political theorist Louis Hartz observed in 1955.[37] In Hartz's estimation, postwar American liberalism ought to be understood as a movement of resilient reform that sought to "extend the sphere of the state" while retaining the "basic principles of Locke and Bentham." This brand of interventionist liberalism was the dominant political current in postwar Minnesota and the LWV and the TCCP were ideologically and politically connected to some of its staunchest champions.

At the same time, the politics of these groups was "antiracist" (if in a restricted sense) because it was driven by genuine discomfort with what they perceived to be a generalized exclusion of Indigenous people and other racialized groups from the prosperity of postwar American life. They found it unacceptable, even odious, that Indigenous residents of their state were disproportionately disadvantaged and they sought affirmative strategies to correct this group-differentiated imbalance. Their antiracism, like their politics more generally, was animated by a prevailing faith in the liberatory potential of modest institutional reform. They believed, that is, that racialized inequities in general, and those shouldered by Indigenous people in particular, could be addressed without challenging the basic structures of American social and political life. Oriented in this way, they did not approach racism or colonialism as constitutive elements of contemporary experience in the United States. Rather, their work was in line with the antiracism of contemporary social-science knowledge production, which, as critical theorist David Theo Goldberg argues, sought to manage "race relations" and "identify the individual and intentional causes of racial conflict and the means for its alleviation."[38]

To contextualize these ideas, it is useful to consider some of the ways that researchers from the LWV and the TCCP characterized the "problem" of urban Indigenous exclusion and, by extension, how they conceived of solutions to it. In particular, I want to dwell on two of the core convictions that animate the liberal forms of antiracism at the center of both organizations' approach to urban Indigenous insecurity. The first is a steadfast belief in the liberatory potential of social-scientific research. The second is a steadfast belief in the fundamental reformability of existing institutions. Taken together, these commitments form the broad contours of the liberal antiracist "theory of change" that motivated both organizations.

Leading figures at the LWV and the TCCP were convinced that social-scientific research was an important tool for tackling the problem of Indigenous insecurity in the Twin Cities and beyond. In part, this commitment stemmed from the conviction that the ignorance of legislators, academics, and the general public was at the very center of the *problem* itself. Indigenous insecurity persisted, they believed, because it was understudied, misunderstood, and/ or ignored. Minnesota LWV activists identified a prevailing "public attitude" of "apathy and ignorance," for example, as one of the key sources of enduring Indigenous disadvantage.[39] Both organizations assumed that the development of an extensive body of knowledge about the nature of these difficulties, and the dissemination of that knowledge, was a necessary precondition to negotiating solutions. They also assumed that formal institutions were the key vehicles through which that knowledge could be acted upon and lasting change could be brokered. For both organizations, knowledge production was thus a critical task.

In asserting their faith in the transformative capacity of knowledge *and* institutional reform, the LWV and the TCCP revealed their ideological proximity to one of the dominant currents of postwar political thinking in the United States. The idea that a strong and "integrationist" state can (and ought to) be a "harmonizing force" in a plural society was sacrosanct to a generation of liberal thinkers who had come of political age in the shadow of the New Deal.[40] Proponents of this view were politically dominant in Minnesota. It was from that state, after all, that a number of titanic figures in the postwar Democratic Party first ascended to prominence, including Hubert Humphrey, Eugene McCarthy, and Walter Mondale. These men and their allies had a decisive impact on state and national politics for about four decades, from at least the mid-1940s to Mondale's crushing defeat in the 1984 presidential contest.

It is critical to point out that while these figures enjoyed a national reputation as progressive reformers, their politics was far from radical. The postwar Minnesota Democratic-Farmer-Labor Party (DFL), which this generation of liberal welfarists came to dominate, was not the "natural heir" of its socialist Farmer-Labor predecessor; it was the progeny of that party's evisceration.[41] The dominant figures of the postwar DFL did not learn their politics in the mines of northern Minnesota's Iron Range or on the shop floors of the Twin Cities, as some of their predecessors had, but mostly in law schools and university classrooms. It was in these academic spaces that a number of these future leaders came to see themselves as "postideological" proponents of competent and compassionate statecraft.[42] This conceit, however earnestly felt, brings to mind Terry Eagleton's cheeky suggestion that "ideology," like "bad breath," is always something that somebody else has.[43]

The political science department at the University of Minnesota, where Humphrey and others were trained, was dominated by thinkers who sought to "convince the American public of the beneficence of a strong central state, fairly administered by trained scientists, who alone understood the complexity of modern social and economic problems."[44] Humphrey and his fellow travelers were not driven by visions of class struggle and proletarian deliverance. They were driven by faith in the capacity of disciplined governments to solve complex social problems through scientifically informed policy prescriptions that balanced diverse interests. The leading figures in the Minnesota LWV and the TCCP shared this faith, and their efforts to produce research about the causes of Indigenous disadvantage were reflective of it.

Consistently, the LWV and the TCCP were optimistic that prevailing divisions could be conquered. Their forays into "Indian affairs" were motivated by the idea that American society was polarized between two distinct camps: those that were sharing in the prosperity of the postwar economic boom *and* those that continued to toil on what Lyndon Johnson called the "outskirts of hope."[45] When activists from the White Bear Lake LWV invoked the specter of an "ignored minority" to encourage colleagues to get behind their push for the inclusion of "Indian affairs" in the organization's statewide agenda, they were articulating a moral position that prefigured a broader liberal anxiety about the persistence of poverty amid unprecedented material abundance. In this, their appeal anticipated the central thesis of Harrington's *The Other America,* published a year later, which popularized the idea that economic insecurity was so pervasive in the United States that the impoverished had come to constitute a separate society. Harrington's contribution enjoyed wide circulation and favorable reviews that helped extend its influence, even to the highest echelons of American power. John F. Kennedy reportedly read the book at a time when he was considering comprehensive antipoverty legislation and it is cited as one of the influences on Johnson's decision to declare his "unconditional" War on Poverty in 1964.[46] It is not surprising, given this success, that the TCCP would endorse Harrington's findings and invoke his authority in a 1966 request for federal grant money. "The United States in the sixties contains an affluent society within its borders," the proposal quoted from *The Other America.*[47] Yet, "at the same time, the United States contains an underdeveloped nation, a culture of poverty. Its inhabitants do not suffer the extreme privation of the peasants of Asia or the tribesmen of Africa, yet the mechanism of misery is similar." Meanwhile, just as *The Other America* invited readers to be "angry and ashamed to live in a rich society in which so many remained poor," LWV activists started from the premise that Indigenous insecurity was an outrage that could only be conquered through compassionate and enlightened reform.[48] Meanwhile, the

TCCP articulated its work as an explicit effort to bridge the gulf between these two Americas. "In the broadest possible terms, the goal of our Training Center is to help bring these two nations together" and "open doors of opportunity for the 'Other America,'" wrote an organization researcher in 1966.[49]

In sum, then, both organizations were oriented around negotiating access points into a mainstream from which many Indigenous people were presumed to be alienated. By the mid-1960s, the LWV had reached "consensus" that the "ultimate goal of all programs for Minnesota Indians should be self-sufficiency of the Indian population and acceptance into American life."[50] "But this acceptance or integration," they cautioned, "does not imply altering their reservation status or cultural patterns except as Indians may desire it . . . It is to be accomplished on their own terms." Comparably, the TCCP's work in "Indian affairs" started from the premise that public-policy efforts could intervene and interrupt the "plight of Minnesota's Indian" in order to create a situation in which "the Indian, like all other Americans, has a range of opportunities open to him."[51] Rhetorically at least, it remained agnostic on the question of which of the "variety of alternatives" ("reservations or city, assimilate or emphasize the ethnic," for example) Indigenous people ought to pursue. In fine liberal form, it emphasized personal choice as the principle that needed to be defended above all others: "In time, clearer answers for the group will emerge when freedom of choice exercised by the individual has illustrated which alternatives most effectively serve the interests of the Indian."[52]

Of course, both organizations were cognizant of the foundational role of settler colonial violence at the center of these questions, even if they did not put it in those terms. Both were unequivocal about their belief that the Indigenous people of the region had to contend with a long line of injustices. The assertion that Indigenous people were living in an "other America" was often accompanied by an acknowledgment that a history of colonial violence was at least partly to blame. In fact, recurring illusions to the effects of that violence animates the writing of both groups, though not always explicitly. In what is perhaps the most direct such acknowledgment, the White

Bear Lake activists encouraged their colleagues to remember that "our whole country" and the "basis of our standard of living" is rooted in the "conquest" of Indigenous lands, noting that this implied that a "very real debt" was owed to "the Indian."[53] In this and other statements, LWV members showed a willingness to concede that contemporary American prosperity was not merely the product of an ever-extending democratic freedom but a kind of plundered treasure won at the cost of regrettable activities. In response to this history of violence, both organizations felt an obligation to distinguish themselves from those that denigrated Indigenous traditions and cultures. Accordingly, their writings rhetorically challenged assimilationism, rejecting the chauvinistic conviction that the best way to ensure Indigenous deliverance from disadvantage and insecurity was to absorb Indigenous difference into the cultural and economic "mainstream" of American life.

In contesting the politics of assimilationism, the LWV and the TCCP were not just shadowboxing. Throughout the 1950s, a range of Twin Cities groups had explicitly promoted the benefits of "integration" to Indigenous people. Organizations like the United Church Committee on Indian Work (later renamed the Division of Indian Work) were exemplary in this regard.[54] Daisuke Kitagawa, one of the organization's first leaders, spoke from personal experience as he extolled the virtues of cultural integration with the American "mainstream." Kitagawa had been interned alongside other Japanese Americans during the war years and had come to the conclusion that integrative urbanization was the best way to extend the full benefits of American citizenship to Indigenous people. "As one who has gone through the whole experience . . . of mass-evacuation, life in an assembly center and a relocation center, and finally the resettlement in an utterly unknown city, I firmly believe that the current policy of 'off-reservation resettlement' is ultimately the only way to assure American Indians of their future as American citizens," he wrote in an article for the Missionary Research Library.[55] Similar sentiments prevailed among the leadership of a nondenominational evangelical "Indian church" that had been formed in the 1950s. One *Minneapolis Tribune* profile noted that the congregation had been formed with the support of an organization called the Global Gospel Fellowship that had taken an interest in "Indians who need help" and sought to provide them with preparatory tutelage for joining the dominant society.[56]

This approach began to be significantly challenged in the years that followed. By the early 1960s, Indigenous urbanites in Minneapolis were declaring pride in their identity and seeking "new ways of controlling their destinies, both through the system and in defiance of the system," according to one community historian.[57] This emergent spirit manifested in a number of ways, including demands for greater representation on the organizations that claimed to serve the interests of Indigenous people. It was in this era that Indigenous urbanites began to insist on a role in determining how the "assistance" that was intended for them would be administered and delivered. Local observers, including the reporter Sam Newlund, took note of what seemed to be an unprecedented Indigenous investment in urban politics. "With a new gusto, the activists among them are getting involved in anti-poverty work, serving on committees, writing their Congressmen, visiting the mayor and demanding a voice in programs designed to help," he noted in a 1966 report for the *Minneapolis Tribune*.[58] Gerald Vizenor, then a community organizer in Minneapolis, saw "the new Indian participation" as a watershed. "I believe . . . this is the first time that the Indian community as a subculture has been approached positively, without restrictions, or justifications or value limitations," he said at the time.[59]

In this context, then, the LWV and the TCCP began to make their interventions. Indeed, their work was developed in a moment when the politics of explicit assimilationism had become politically toxic and the writings of both groups reflect this emergent reality. At the same time, the "theory of change" that they promoted was animated by the belief that American institutions were not only transformable but also that they could be primed to play a remedial role in addressing racialized injustice. While their work was not without its merits, it was also constrained by a number of very significant limitations, as all forms of liberal antiracism are. It is worth considering a few of them in detail.

The Limits of Liberal Antiracism

The prevailing optimism with which organizations such as the LWV and the TCCP embraced the agenda of postwar welfarism betrayed an excessive faith in the fundamental decency of the institutions of American political rule, as well as their fundamental reformability. Both organizations assumed that those who had been excluded from the full benefits of American citizenship, including Indigenous people, could be integrated into the American mainstream if only the levers of state power could be properly manipulated.

This approach is based on a naive interpretation of what the American state is and how it responds to political demands. By promoting the idea that Indigenous insecurity could be overcome through modest bureaucratic reforms of existing state practices, both organizations made plain their conviction that state power is broadly benevolent, harnessable, and responsive to reasonable demands. This view is misinformed, I think. The state is a "strategic field formed through intersecting power networks" that constitute particular kinds of political possibilities; it is a material expression of a "relationship of forces."[60] In the United States and elsewhere, this relationship was and is shaped by a long history of racialized power through which the interests of certain blocs have been consistently privileged over and above those of others. This includes the ways that the interests of Euro-American settlers and their descendants have been routinely promoted and defended. In short, states are not neutral arbiters of competing claims but complex and shifting "condensations" of these histories of contestation.[61]

If we understand the organization of state power in this way, then the assumption that genuine social change springs from enlightened governance is untenable. The LWV and the TCCP would have us believe that the inequities shouldered by Indigenous people are largely the product of ignorance on the part of "mainstream" Americans, but they rarely ask how those "mainstream" Americans also benefit from these arrangements. As George Lipsitz points out, the endurance of white supremacy is not merely a product of troublesome attitudes. Rather, white supremacy "survives and thrives because whiteness delivers unfair gains and unjust enrichments to people who participate in and profit from the existence of a racial cartel that skews opportunities and life chances for their own benefit."[62] Social gains have always been won through processes of vigorous collective contestation and not the benevolence of informed rulers. By promoting modest adjustments of existing institutional practices, liberal reformers, and their allies in the liberal state, do not meaningfully challenge the "generative structures" that are constitutive of the settler colonial relation.[63]

The liberal approach promoted by the LWV and the TCCP is also limited by the kind of "inclusion" that it prescribes for Indigenous people. Both groups wanted to facilitate reforms that opened points of entry into the prosperity of the dominant society but emphasized that any such integration must happen on the terms of the people who were being integrated. In rhetoric, at least, both groups expressed respect for Indigenous desires to pursue different sorts of futures and assume sovereignty over the conditions of their collective existence.[64] But while there is much to be lauded in such declarations of support, how exactly the sorts of strategies that these organizations promoted were oriented around supporting Indigenous forms of alterity and self-determination is a murky question. It is worth asking, for example, what liberal reformers from these two groups had in mind when they promoted the desirability of "self-sufficiency" and "personal choice" in their writing. The answer to this question is never clear in their published work. What is clear is that both groups retained a fundamental faith in the essential desirability of dominant forms of social organization. By acknowledging that the "ultimate goal" of their efforts was to broker Indigenous points of entry into the mainstream of "American life," the LWV offered a qualified endorsement of that mainstream.[65] In so doing, it presented American life as a broadly neutral field in which individuals are free to pursue their own interests. By making this case, it betrayed its ideological proximity to the universalist conceit at the center of its liberal antiracism. By assuming that American citizens were united by a common foundation that transcends "particular historical, social, and cultural differences," it minimized the degree to which American life is organized around an economy of power relations that has been hostile to the needs, aspirations, and desires of Indigenous people.[66] Instructive here is Kevin Bruyneel's observation that the "core political constraint" of the American liberal imagination is its incapacity to recognize that its commitment "to such institutions and beliefs as private property and liberal individualism is created out of and built upon, in no small part, settler-colonial logic, practices, and structures."[67] By setting the horizon of its ambition as the inclusion of Indigenous people into the ranks of the comfortable, relatively prosperous, and wage-earning dominant society, it failed to engage with more comprehensive demands for a rethinking of the settler colonial order of things.

At the same time, the approaches promoted by the LWV and the TCCP do not grapple with the idea that the settler colonial relation endures as a "structural" dimension of contemporary life. Their work is shaped by a temporal politics that operates, unwittingly or not, to confine colonial violence to the past. While "past treatment by government" may well be the "basis of current problems," the unforgiveable transgression itself is relegated to a distant horizon.[68] The "crime" of dispossessive and assimilative settler invasion into Minnesota, in such interpretations, is denounced for the horrors it unleashed, but that violence is also presumed to have occurred in an epoch of American history that is now closed. In this, the violence of settler colonization is compartmentalized as a series of past events, while contemporary manifestations of that violence are categorized as residual symptoms of that "past treatment." Insofar as violence is understood as continuing, moreover, it is presumed to do so as a trace of the original sin of historical colonization. The LWV's sense that contemporary American prosperity ("our standard of living") was won at the cost an earlier period of violence implies a debt, to be sure, but it is also rooted in a denial that the persistence of a settler colonial forms of inequity continue as constitutive dimensions of contemporary American life.[69] The moral imperative for those who seek to overcome this original violence is understood as one of settling accounts. But debts, like apologies, create a sense of "pastness" in which the transgression for which the debt is owed is no longer present.[70] Decolonization, in this limited view, is understood as a matter of acknowledging historical wrongs rather than a process of actively dismantling settler colonial structures in the politics of the present. Inherent in this approach is a refusal to see Indigenous political claims as contemporary. Indeed, the solution is not to negotiate new forms of being together but to bring Indigenous people "up" to the "standard of living" so cherished by LWV analysts. The desirability of that "standard of living" itself—its basic foundations as well its contemporary promise—is taken for granted.[71]

This thinking is exemplary of what Audra Simpson calls "settler time," or, more specifically, the "unequal power to define what matters, who matters, what pasts are alive and when they die."[72] To acknowledge troubling origins while advocating integration into a contemporary order that is very much the product of those troubling origins is, at the most basic level, a refusal to accept that the "troubling" dimension of those origins persists. Indeed, "the more liberal versions of hegemonic settler narratives may admit that along the otherwise glorious path to creating a nation bad things were done to indigenous people," writes Gabriel Piterberg.[73] But these same interpretations, sympathetic or regretful as they usually are, nearly always "deny that the removal and dispossession of indigenous peoples is an *intrinsic* part of what setter nations are—indeed the most pivotal constituent of what they are—rather than an *extrinsic* aberration or corruption of something essentially good." For Piterberg, the "exclusionary fundamental that inheres in these white hegemonic narratives lies not in the sovereign settler's denial of the wrong they have done to those whom they have disinherited or enslaved (though such denials are protested all too often), but in their denial that the interaction with the dispossessed is the history of who the settlers collectively are."[74] In my view, this kind of selective thinking is at work in the analyses of the LWV and the TCCP and animates their certainty about the fundamental decency of the contemporary order. Indigenous people were wronged in the past and are worthy of sympathy, they contend, but those wrongs are part of a historical trajectory that is now completed. These past events are regrettable, to be sure, but in no way do they demand a substantive rethinking of the contemporary order.

At the same time, the LWV and the TCCP promote a spatial imaginary that exempts the contemporary city from the regrettable aspects of Minnesota's past. Specifically, their analyses make a surgical distinction between frontier or reservation geographies that function as the spatial instantiations of a violent past and an urban geography where that past is experienced only as a residue. If we follow the logic of the LWV, and to a lesser degree the TCCP, the "crime" of colonization (land theft, containment, assimilationism) is something that is presumed to have happened *out there*. The reservation, in this view, is understood as the supreme expression of this violence. In such interpretations, the confinement of Indigenous people to a series of "shrinking islands" constitutes the central transgression of settler colonial invasion. Meanwhile, the economic devastation of present-day reservations is a residual expression of the original transgression. Absented in this presentation, however, is the degree to which urban environments (for the purposes of this book, Minneapolis) are also products of settler colonial violence. In fine liberal form, the city, in such presentations, is imagined as a neutral time-space, a geography of the present in which diverse peoples come together and negotiate their lives on even terms. Insofar as problems associated with the colonial crime persist, they do so either as remnants of the violence of that *other* place, as burdens that have been imported to the city from elsewhere, or as manageable interpersonal problems that can be overcome through education and the effective management of "race relations." This thinking exempts the contemporary city from the long history of settler colonial spatial negotiation; it renders it as an exceptional place, cut off from the messy negotiation of settler colonial contestation, and bounded by a kind of temporal cordon sanitaire. But urban and reservation geographies have never existed in isolation from one another; they are relationally entwined outcomes of a unitary process of geographic production grounded in the settler colonial relation. In the same way that Harrington's "other America" has always been intractably

connected to the America of postwar affluence, so too has Indigenous economic insecurity always been intractably linked to settler
prosperity, and not least its urban manifestations. To spare the contemporary city from association with the foundational violence of
the settlement of Minnesota is to conceal the degree to which that
violence has shaped the distribution of advantage and disadvantage
in the urban contemporary.

3

Cops and Counterpatrols

Racialized Policing on East Franklin Avenue

The Minneapolis Police Department's (MPD) official motto is "to protect with courage, to serve with compassion." But neither of these commitments was paid much heed when officers Michael Lardy and Marvin Schumer responded to a complaint that two men were sleeping in front of a downtown Minneapolis apartment block one spring evening in 1993. One of the sleeping men remembers being thumped awake with a nightstick, handcuffed to his companion, and "dumped" in the trunk of a squad car. The officers then transported their captives to the nearby Hennepin County Medical Center. But they were not in a hurry to get there.[1] The short journey took an "unreasonably long time" and involved a good deal of erratic driving.[2]

Word that two Indigenous men had been picked up and transferred in such an unorthodox fashion soon reached the media and the MPD found itself at the center of a growing public relations scandal. "There's a certain segment with the Police Department that has a John Wayne frontier mentality about Indian people," said Clyde Bellecourt of the American Indian Movement.[3] "I don't care whether you are transporting people 2 feet, 2 blocks, or 2 miles, you must treat them with dignity," Pat Amo, the City of Minneapolis's Indian Community Liaison told the *Star-Tribune,* as she accused the officers of treating the men like animals.[4]

These expressions of outrage were articulated with a well-established historical context in mind. Reactions to Lardy and Schumer's actions were animated by an enduring sense of grievance. If the police murder of George Floyd became a symbol of a broader pattern of anti-Black police targeting in the spring of 2020, the "trunk incident" became a symbol of a broader pattern of anti-Indigenous police targeting in the spring of 1993. Indeed, many in the Minneapolis Indigenous community noted that the actions of Lardy and Schumer were only the most recent in a long line of episodes in which MPD officers had been exceptionally violent in their dealings with Indigenous people.

This chapter takes this history of targeted aggression as the starting point for a broader discussion about how knowledge practices and cultural expressions that are rooted in the settler colonial relation have shaped local policing strategies and interpretations of them. Its objective is not to establish that the MPD has been especially brutal to Indigenous people. Numerous studies and a robust evidentiary record that spans from the 1960s to the 1990s (and into the present) already make this plain.[5] Rather, this chapter attempts to assess the broader cultural field in which MPD actions have been articulated. In doing so, it builds on Elizabeth Comack's observation that to understand "racialized policing," we need to "broaden our gaze" in ways that allow us to locate the roots of targeted violence in a larger context.[6] Through a series of empirical studies in other cities, Comack has shown that Indigenous peoples' encounters with police are often shaped by particular ideologies of "racialized privilege" through which the inequity inherent in the settler colonial relation is depoliticized and rendered natural.[7] In her terms, racialization is a process by which racial "categories, identities, and meanings" are constructed and assigned to particular groups, whereas privilege is precisely the capacity to define situations in the cultural terms of one's own experience and to "have those judgments stick."[8] Drawing on these insights, this chapter considers how the reproduction of particular kinds of "knowledge" about Indigenous people has rendered their disproportionate entanglement with the criminal justice apparatus understandable, tolerable, and even natural to certain publics. At the same time, it is also keen to show that this cultural "knowledge" is always contested and that key moments of Indigenous political organizing have interrupted the potency of its ideological impress.

The analysis that follows begins by demonstrating some of the ways that the MPD and the coercive arm of the state have targeted Indigenous people in South Minneapolis. Building on Comack's insights, it demonstrates that a series of broadly circulated racist assumptions about Indigenous people have operated to motivate, legitimize, and depoliticize aggressive targeting by police. It then turns to a discussion of how certain forms of organizing and intervention worked to counter these assumptions by dramatizing the culpability of police and the broader society of which they are a part.

Racialized Policing in South Minneapolis

The "trunk incident" provoked outrage in part because it confirmed the continuation of a long tradition of hostile and humiliating policing in Minneapolis's inner core. Those who expressed anger over this event tended to interpret it as only the most recent in a long string of incidents in which Indigenous urbanites had been singled out for aggressive treatment by police. The evidentiary record makes clear that many Indigenous residents of the inner-city Southside have experienced some form of police brutality, whether we define that term broadly to include a "range of abusive police practices, such as the use of profanity, racial slurs and unnecessary searches" or more narrowly as the use of physical violence, or "excessive force," in the course of police work.[9] It is beyond the scope of this chapter to consider the full range of forms that this violence has taken, but suffice it to say that a rich evidentiary record—openly available to anyone who is interested in seeking it out—reveals that Indigenous Southsiders have regularly been brutalized by police.[10]

That evidence also speaks to the pervasiveness of far more mundane and routinized forms of police harassment. For example, the MPD directed an enormous amount of energy toward the policing of a series of East Franklin Avenue bars, primarily frequented by, and associated with, an Indigenous clientele. Beginning in the 1960s, these establishments were consistently targeted by MPD raids, which often led to dozens of arrests.[11] "There was a time on Franklin Avenue when you could set your watch when the patty [sic] wagon would come down . . . the officers would come in the bars, go in the front door and out the back, arrest people, put them in the wagon and take them downtown," recalled one Southsider.[12] "They rounded us up like cattle and booked us on 'drunk and disorderly' charges, even if we were neither," remembered another.[13]

For many, it was clear that this sort of targeting was not practiced in other parts of town. Fay Cohen's 1971 PhD research on the Southside's "Indian Patrol" (discussed at length below) notes that it was common among participants to believe that "non-Indians, drinking in fashionable bars in wealthy neighborhoods, rarely were arrested and taken to jail [while] Indians drinking in bars in poorer districts . . . were likely to be arrested and put in the drunk tank downtown."[14] One MPD official effectively confirmed this assumption in an interview with the Minneapolis League of Women Voters, noting that Indigenous people were more frequently brought in on drunk charges because they were more "visible" to police because "they were drunk on 'skid row' rather than at home or in front of a fashionable restaurant."[15]

Notably, too, the targeting of Indigenous people in and around Franklin Avenue bars was so acute that this group consistently made up a significant portion of the MPD's arrests for drunkenness. In 1969, for example, Indigenous urbanites accounted for nearly one-third of a weekly average of 156 such bookings.[16] Drawing on this and other evidence, sociologist Michael Indergaard concludes that police targeting of Indigenous people for minor "public disorder type offenses" was so intense that it constituted an institutionalized strategy to exercise "constant" "social control."[17]

In a certain light, the situation in Minneapolis offers a local illustration of sociologist Barbara Perry's observation that North American Indigenous communities, rural and urban, have tended to be both over- and underpoliced.[18] Indeed, the MPD routinely failed In-

Eric Almond's "Neanderthals in Our Midst" was published in *The Alley,* a Phillips community newspaper, in 1991. Cartoon by Eric Almond. Courtesy of *The Alley.*

digenous residents in two ways. It both acted as a source of predation *and* shirked its basic protective function. In the early 1970s, an "Indian community" survey revealed that many felt the police were either hostile to, or indifferent about, the needs of urban Indigenous people. "Call the police about anything and they'll just take one look at you and say—'another drunken Indian,'" observed one respondent.[19]

In the postwar decades, disproportionate targeting of Indigenous urbanites by the criminal justice system was not simply a matter of policing, however. "No matter what aspect of the justice system is examined in relationship to Native American people—law enforcement, courts, or corrections—Native Americans are disproportionately represented compared with their numbers in the Minnesota population," observed the U.S. Commission on Civil Rights in 1975.[20] Indeed, this problem was particularly acute in the realm of incarceration. Various studies reveal that Indigenous people were (and are) dramatically overrepresented among the ranks of those serving time in Minnesota's prisons.[21] In the early 1970s, one study revealed that while Indigenous people made up only half of 1 percent of the state's total population, they constituted roughly 10 percent of its male prison population, with a considerable majority of those inmates coming from urban areas.[22] Head counts only tell part of the story, however, and the form and duration of punishments meted out to Indigenous arrestees were often much stiffer than they were for others. Research conducted in 1979 found that Indigenous residents of Minnesota were considerably more likely than their white counterparts to be arrested and spend time in jail, and considerably *less* likely to secure bail, be acquitted, or receive probation.[23] Meanwhile, other evidence suggests that the consequences of being arrested were amplified for those who were economically insecure, particularly those who had difficulty proving they had stable work and housing.[24] Low-income people often faced tougher penalties and served fuller sentences. These and other discrepancies persisted through the 1980s, prompting one Minnesota League of Women Voters report to conclude: "comparatively Indians enter the correctional system younger, have more frequent contacts with the courts, and spend more time in correctional facilities."[25] (Notably, these trends have continued to this day. In early 2020, the Minnesota Department of Corrections identified nearly 10 percent of its inmates as "Native American." Indigenous people account for less than 2 percent of Minnesota's total population.)[26]

Depoliticizing Racialized Policing

To make sense of this group-differentiated targeting, it is helpful to return to Comack's insights about "racialized policing" and consider how the sustained reproduction of certain kinds of "knowledge" *about* Indigenous people has operated to problematically depoliticize police targeting on the Southside of Minneapolis. Following Comack, it is worth asking how certain recurring "categories, identities, and meanings" have shaped non-Indigenous interpretations of the urban Indigenous community and how these *ways of seeing* have rendered the group-differentiated aggressiveness of the criminal justice system understandable, natural, and tolerable to some observers. What is important for the purposes of this chapter is the way that the deployment of certain kinds of "knowledge" have rendered inequitable distributions *natural,* masking the degree to which a distinct "machinery of enforcement" has ensured the reproduction of those inequities.[27]

The analysis that follows highlights the troublesome potency of three interconnected interpretive frames, all of which reflect the cultural politics at the center of the settler colonial relation. The first is the idea that urban Indigenous entanglement with the law is a consequence of the traumatic alienations of urban migration. The second is the idea that this entanglement is a consequence of the fundamental "disorganization" of urban Indigenous communities. The third is the idea that this entanglement is a consequence of a group-specific predisposition to alcoholism. In practice, these dubious interpretive frames are inseparable from one another. They overlap and intersect in myriad ways. In the interest of elucidation, I consider them independently here.

The assumption that urban migration is traumatic for Indigenous people has helped naturalize Indigenous entanglement with the coercive institutions of the state and has been mobilized to explain the aggressiveness of police. "The American Indian living in Minneapolis is beset by problems inherent in his move from the reservation . . . he is faced with adjustment in a competitive, urban society which is alien to his culture," summarized one typical report in 1968.[28] In this and countless other assessments, the "problems" of Indigenous urbanites are explained and interpreted as an *inherent* effect of the trauma of migration. In the Twin Cities and other North American urban regions, this idea circulated widely in the postwar period and came to function as a core element of a coherent (and exculpatory) explanatory framework.[29]

In Minnesota, this commonsense view was often promoted by institutional research. For example, the Community Welfare Council of Hennepin County's "Indian Committee," a group established in the 1950s to respond to the rapid growth of the Minneapolis Indigenous community, noted, in one final report, that the large number of Indigenous urbanites who had begun to appear in Hennepin County courts, generally arraigned on minor charges, was a result of their unfamiliarity with city life and a series of connected difficulties, including the various discouragements of joblessness, the strain of substandard living conditions, and, most condescendingly, an "improper use of leisure time."[30] Less than a decade later, the (Minnesota) Governor's Human Rights Commission reiterated this sentiment, noting that while some Indigenous migrants have "succeeded" by finding work, shelter, and "identify[ing] themselves with their new community," others have found "nothing but trouble in the city."[31] The Governor's Commission identified this subgroup as the *source* of an "Indian jail rate" that was "far out of proportion with the number of Indians in the cities" and proposed that their failure to adapt to urban norms was making "successful" integration difficult for others. One report published by the University of Minnesota's Training Center for Community Programs (TCCP), meanwhile, suggested that difficulties of adaptation were key to the preponderance of Indigenous "trouble with the law."[32] The report's author proposed a number of possible explanations for these discrepancies, including "intercultural conflict," "alienation from a legal system that has frequently betrayed Indian interests," "deep conflicts between an older, traditional Indian way of life and the demands of a modern technological society," and a "self-defeating way of expressing rebellion against the dominant society which is *perceived* as having abused, exploited and discriminated against Indian Americans" (emphasis added). What each of these explanations has in common is that it identified the activities and behaviors of Indigenous people themselves as the decisive factor.

Similarly, non-Indigenous researchers have often insisted that the overrepresentation of Indigenous people in the criminal justice system reflected the inherent disorganization of urban Indigenous family units, as well as the community more generally. For example, the TCCP report just cited identified family "disorganization" as a key factor. The Minneapolis League of Women Voters, for its part, noted that "a disorganization of family life brought on by poverty and heightened by the need to balance new ways with old in a complex, urban society" was at the very center of the "disproportionately large" percentage of the local Indigenous community that found themselves "in trouble with the law."[33] These and other reports often stressed a profound distance between Indigenous "lifestyles" and established standards of propriety, though the latter are rarely (if ever) defined. The Community Welfare Council's Indian Committee, for example, worried that "slum" housing was part of a "total environment" that was not only "bad" but also represented "a serious hazard to Indian children and young people, morally, physically, and in relation to their educational opportunities," whether "Indian families realize it or not."[34] The broader urban community could not afford to "let such conditions persist," it concluded, because "they breed delinquency and backwardness." Indeed, non-Indigenous observers routinely assumed that a diverse range of "cultural" differences posed barriers to "successful" integration. These included, for example, the patronizing presumptions that Indigenous children lacked adequate supervision or guidance, that Indigenous women lacked skills in household management, and that Indigenous men had little sense of how to spend their time responsibly, among other things.

At the same time, the overrepresentation of Indigenous urbanites on arrest sheets, in court dockets, and in the carceral system was often explained as a consequence of an epidemic of Indigenous alcoholism. The conservative state representative Frank DeGroat, one of only a very few Indigenous people to serve in the Minnesota House of Representatives in the twentieth century, exemplified this position when, at a late 1960s prelegislative conference in St. Paul, he told the gathered audience that the "law enforcement problems with Indians" could be explained, in part, by "easy access to liquor" and the "leniency of law enforcement."[35] In fact, the view that Indigenous alcohol use and "trouble" with the law were intertwined was so well established in a certain public imaginary that one TCCP researcher simply used the high number of Indigenous people appearing in municipal courts on "drunkenness" charges as unambiguous evidence that a crisis of Indigenous alcoholism existed.[36] That this researcher did not feel compelled to complicate or justify such an assertion is evidence of the degree to which a commonsense image was already established.

As others have shown, this racist association has become a routine feature of news reporting about North American Indigenous people and communities.[37] For Joseph Westermeyer, a psychiatric epidemiologist, the "Indian drunk" is routinely imagined as a "powerless figure" in popular representations, one who has "no alternative to drunkenness with which to cope with poverty, the destruction of his culture and the undermining of his family."[38] Contemporary versions of this thinking link to a long history of stereotypes about Indigenous alcoholism, particularly the "firewater myth," which holds that Indigenous people suffer a genetic weakness to alcohol.[39] "Indians are the wild alcoholics in the literature of dominance," Gerald Vizenor observes, and the long colonial shadow cast by the "firewater myth" has proved remarkably resilient, particularly given its scientific groundlessness.[40] Indeed, the image of a community that is genetically predisposed to alcoholism has experienced an enduring cultural afterlife. As late as 1976, one South Minneapolis community newspaper still felt it was necessary to disabuse its audience of this illusion. "Stated simply, if Indians drink more than Whites, it's not because they were born drinkers," it informed readers.[41]

These distortions derive their cultural potency from the reproduction of a form of common sense. Following the cultural theorist Stuart Hall and his colleagues, I understand the Gramscian notion of "common sense" as a form of quotidian thinking that provides "frameworks of meaning" that allow people to make sense of the world around them. In Hall's terms, common sense is "a form of popular, easily-available knowledge which contains no complicated ideas, requires no sophisticated argument and does not depend on deep thought or wide reading."[42] Instead, "it works intuitively, without forethought or reflection." As Nick Estes observes in an instructive consideration of the reproduction of "anti-Indian common sense" in Mni Luzahan/Rapid City, common sense is largely inconsequential at an individual level. It only emerges as a force of "historic significance" when it begins to circulate in a collectivity.[43]

In settler colonial societies, commonsense interpretations often affirm and normalize "settler presence, privilege, and power" at the expense of Indigenous people.[44] In theorist Mark Rifkin's terms, "settler common sense" is at the root of non-Indigenous entitlement; it animates the cultural, social, and political processes through which the settler colonial project of dispossession is reframed as inevitable, given, and even legitimate.[45]

Commonsense assumptions about Indigenous vulnerability foreclose on reflection. They offer an explanatory frame that seeks answers in a series of problematic assumptions about the behavioral, cultural, and lifestyle characteristics of Indigenous people but leave the actions of the settler state (and settler individuals) unexamined. Through commonsense interpretations, Indigenous Southsiders have often been forced to bear the burden of being "woven" "out of a thousand details, anecdotes, stories" that are not their own, to borrow a phrase from Frantz Fanon, while the racialized functioning of the criminal justice system has received far less scrutiny.[46]

The work of frontline police officers themselves is also shaped by commonsense frames. "They carry into their interactions with Native Americans the same stockpile of stereotypes and images that shape broader patterns of cultural imperiality," assumptions that are "located in both the occupational and popular culture," observes Robynne Neugebauer.[47] In early 1976, reporters from *The Alley* spoke to MPD officers about their experiences patrolling the 6th precinct (which included parts of South Minneapolis, including East Franklin Avenue). The interviews reveal, among other things, that some officers understood themselves to be policing a profoundly troubled community, with one describing their work as maintaining a "fine line" between "what we have now" and "total chaos."[48] The officers described their function in stark Manichaean terms. When challenged on questions of brutality, one noted that "we don't have any contact with the good people . . . all we come in contact with are the bad people and it starts to seem like there's nothing but rats in the area."[49] The interviews also suggest that the police felt that one of the key sources of the "chaos" was, in fact, the product of a lack of concern on the part of conventional authorities. "Until the parents and the courts start showing concern things aren't going to get any better," suggested one officer. "You are not going to see businesses going down there. All you see is them leaving."[50]

Collectively, then, these and other cultural explanations coalesce into an explanatory frame that renders Indigenous people's disproportionate encounters with the law *understandable*. Taken together, the interpretations cited earlier, and others like them, worked to consolidate the idea that the urban Indigenous community was fundamentally at odds with an abstract standard of mainstream propriety. In making these claims, commentators joined a long tradition of U.S. urban research that has represented inner-city communities of color in terms of "disorder and lack," understanding them as repositories of "concentrated unruliness, deviance, anomie and atomization, replete with behaviors said to offend common precepts of morality and propriety, whether by excess (as with crime, sexuality and fertility) or by default (in the case of work, thrift and family)," as Loïc Wacquant has observed.[51] Although Wacquant's observations concern representations of the African American ghetto (and, importantly, he insists that the "ghetto" be understood as a "historically-determinate, spatially-based concatenation of mechanisms of ethnoracial closure and control" that is unique to the African American urban experience), they are clearly relevant in this context. These narratives not only traded in racist caricature and exculpatory distortion, they also worked to depoliticize police targeting by reframing it as a consequence of the actions and lifestyles of Indigenous people themselves. In effect, these interpretations decontextualized the practices of "racialized policing" and naturalized them as reasonable responses to a "troubled" community.

Repoliticizing Racialized Policing

Of course, racialized policing and the commonsense ideological commitments that underpin it were routinely contested and repoliticized by neighborhood organizers and activists. Most famously, the early activities of American Indian Movement (AIM), which formed in Minneapolis in 1968, were explicitly directed at challenging the violence of the criminal justice system. It is important to point out, however, that AIM was neither the first nor the only group to raise these issues. Indeed, the interpretive focus on AIM in writing about Minneapolis's Indigenous political traditions has sometimes overshadowed earlier efforts to organize around a range of urban grievances, including MPD brutality. Partial assessments of these histories have obscured the constitutive importance of work that predates AIM's activities, particularly organizing efforts undertaken by a generation of Indigenous activists that began to insert themselves into inner-city politics starting in the mid-1960s. Although a genealogy of Indigenous-led antibrutality organizing is beyond the scope of this book, such a study would make an important contribution to popular knowledge about the political life of South Minneapolis.

Indigenous organizations existed in the Twin Cities even before the Second World War. Political organizing changed considerably in the decades after 1945, however, particularly as the Twin Cities Indigenous community became concentrated in Phillips and other core districts.[52] In the inner city, the broadly shared experience of economic insecurity, police violence, and racist discrimination created a "shared sense of embattlement" and hastened the emergence of an activist community.[53] Thus AIM did not emerge in a political vacuum and its varied successes are in many ways indebted to a culture of contestation that began well before the organization came on the scene.[54]

The earliest evidence of antibrutality organizing that I have encountered comes from the mid-1960s. There had been some discussion about police targeting of Indigenous people in Minneapolis throughout the early 1960s (including some modest efforts by the Minnesota Civil Liberties Union to document it), but the intensity of these claims began to be amplified in the charged atmosphere of urban revolt that would sweep across the United States in the years that followed.

In 1967, future AIM leader George Mitchell ran as a candidate for alderman in the Southside's Ward 6 and made targeted policing an explicit part of his campaign. "I'll admit that I'm a bitter man," he noted in one campaign speech, "bitter because while driving here tonight I see the same things [that] I saw ten years ago."[55] His pitch to Southside voters voiced concern about the deterioration of the inner city and offered a full-throated condemnation of the routinized violence of the MPD. Mitchell invited Southsiders to join him "in the belief that real law enforcement does not involve police brutality" and insisted that "a better informed community is our best protection."[56]

Concern about brutality was also voiced by less prominent members of the community. Southsider Marvin Needham, for example, penned an article titled "Police Brutality, an American Indian Problem" and sent a draft copy to Gerald Vizenor in January 1967.[57] Needham's piece pulses with indignation. It begins by citing a number of recent beatings "administered to the Indians being arrested in the East Franklin Ave. area" as evidence that "discrimination and bigotry" were part of the MPD's quotidian culture. "If there is any doubt in anyone's mind about the dissimilarity in treatment of Indians and Whites, regarding arrests and their subsequent treatment in the Courts, all one has to do is sit in Court on a Saturday or Monday morning; or take a trip to the Workhouse and see the ratio of Caucasian inmates to the Minority inmates," he noted.

Later in 1967, Needham appeared prominently in coverage of an "Urban Indian Conference" convened by a mayoral task force.[58] Reports of the proceedings reveal that Needham vocalized concerns about the MPD and called for the establishment of a new Indigenous group that would monitor their activities in the inner city. The article notes that Needham had drawn inspiration from an incident in the city's Near North district, in which a group of residents (presumably African American) had actively "interceded" to thwart the arrest of a friend. He had found their commitment laudable. "I may not agree with all their methods," Needham said, "but I admire their desire to change their way of life."[59] This intervention is interesting both because it gives voice to a broader distrust of police among Indigenous Southsiders and because it anticipates a broader politics of contestation that was yet to materialize. In calling for the establishment of an Indigenous-led police-monitoring group, Needham portended tactical innovations that would garner a great deal of attention with the emergence of AIM and the early iterations of its Indian Patrol in the years that followed.

AIM's urban roots have often been overshadowed by the organization's participation in a series of rural rebellions, most notably the 1973 occupation of Wounded Knee. The hypermediation of a series of images connected to these events—iconic photographs of small groups of rifle-wielding men standing on the windswept South Dakotan plains, for example—have sometimes obscured the fact that the organization spent the first two years of its existence organizing around a series of local issues, especially police violence. According to most accounts, concerns about the MPD were at the center of the group's initial activities.

In fact, these issues were debated at the movement's hastily organized inaugural meeting in 1968. In the days leading up to the gathering, Dennis Banks, still a relative neophyte to Southside politics, and his friend George Mitchell, a well-seasoned Twin Cities activist, had gone door to door with leaflets that read: "we need to have a meeting."[60] The expectations of the organizers were modest. They were surprised when dozens of local people responded to their call. Finding himself at the front of a much bigger than anticipated crowd, Banks recalls opening the meeting with a broad question:

> People are fighting in the streets of Chicago. They're fighting to stop the Vietnam War and bring about changes in the political party system. They're fighting in the streets of Alabama to change the whole structure of universities. What the hell are we going to do? Are we going to sit here in Minnesota and not do a goddamn thing? Are we going to go on for another two hundred years, or even five, the way we are without doing something for our Indian people?[61]

According to Banks, this lofty invitation was brought to ground by the intervention of a young Clyde Bellecourt, who, speaking with an enthusiasm that "swept over us like a storm," put the question of police violence at the center of the group's discussion. In Banks's version, Bellecourt asked: "When do you propose to go down there to Franklin Avenue, to all those Indian bars where the cops inflict abuse on our people every night? . . . Let's go down there right now, tonight!"[62] Bellecourt's call for immediate mobilization did not materialize that evening. But it did anticipate the sort of interventions that AIM would soon be making, particularly on and around East Franklin Avenue.

Indeed, one of AIM's first interventions was to organize a volunteer monitoring force that would patrol the Southside streets in order observe police activity and offer help to people who needed it. These were volunteers "seeking safety for Indian people in a white world," observes Laura Waterman Wittstock.[63] On foot and in cars painted red, a shifting cast of activists spent weekend evenings monitoring activities on the avenue and reporting incidents back to a central command post, initially located in the basement of the American Indian Youth Center at 1304 East Franklin Avenue.[64] Armed with rudimentary equipment and matching red jackets, the Indian Patrol ran countersurveillance on the police and sought to help people avoid arrest.[65]

AIM's plan to monitor the police was an immediate headline grabber and journalists were dispatched to observe the new organization's activities. "The patrollers, about 20 strong and consisting of several blacks and whites, but primarily Indians, kept a watchful eye on E. Franklin near 14th Avenue S., the scene of alleged police harassment of drunks," reported the *Minneapolis Tribune* on the Indian Patrol's inaugural night in August 1968.[66]

The results were immediate. The patrol's first night was described as the "quietest night in 15 years," as few police cars trawled the area and the all-too-familiar paddy wagon made only one appearance, the *Tribune* noted. Building on the strength of this initial success, AIM voted to continue the patrol and agreed that non-Indigenous people could continue to participate.

Throughout the remaining weeks of the summer and into the fall, volunteers met every weekend and hit the streets by 11:30 p.m. The patrol's critical work happened during the hour that followed last call at bars on the East Franklin strip, a short stretch in which they felt their services were most needed.[67] On a typical evening, the patrol's work oscillated between escorting people home and gathering information about the police. As a matter of course, it recorded the details of any incident, collecting police badge and license plate

The American Indian Movement's offices at 1337 East Franklin Avenue in the late 1960s. Photograph by Robert Shistak. Courtesy of Fay Cohen.

numbers, alongside any other information it could glean. Members felt that doing so would allow them to measure the scale of police presence in the neighborhood.[68]

This monitoring work had an important impact. As Bellecourt put it:

> After we started our own surveillance of the police, officials here in South Mpls. and their conduct by photographing them, being there to witness the assaults, harassments, and taking down license numbers, badge numbers, etc. we started showing up in court the next day and telling people they didn't have to plead guilty anymore to something they didn't even know they were guilty about, a lot of these things began to stop.[69]

AIM activists argued that their approach had won important gains as the number of Indigenous arrests on the avenue dropped dramatically. By year's end, patrol organizers could claim that they had managed to go twenty-two straight weeks without any alcohol-related charges on the avenue, though the leaders themselves had to contend with a number of serious confrontations with police.[70]

The tactics employed by the AIM patrol were not conceived in a vacuum, however, and the organization drew consciously from the lessons of other contemporary "citizen patrols." According to Fay Cohen, who observed the first iteration of the Indian Patrol closely as part of her PhD research at the University of Minnesota, AIM's monitoring activities were inspired, in part, by similar groups—organizations, that is, that shared the conviction that local residents could do more to protect their community than the police, who were often viewed as a hostile presence.[71]

It has often been reported, for example, that the Black Panther Party (BPP) was one of AIM's key inspirations for its police monitoring activities.[72] The BPP was established in Oakland, California, two years before AIM came on the scene. The organization's initial objective was to provide community "self-defense," which primarily entailed protecting African Americans from police violence. "We believe we can end police brutality in our black community by organizing black self-defense groups that are dedicated to defending our black community from racist police oppression and brutality," reads the seventh point of the BPP's ten-point program, *What We Believe*.[73] For the Panthers, self-defense generally meant being heavily armed. Huey Newton, for one, took pains to be up-to-date on local and state gun laws and would routinely conduct patrol activities with a shotgun in hand.[74] The Panthers recruited comrades in Oakland's African American ghettos and organized armed cadres to counterpatrol the police.

Conspicuous displays of weaponry were not part of AIM's aesthetic in the early years, especially while the organization remained primarily grounded in the urban politics of the Twin Cities. "I rejected violence and some of the methods involving force adopted by the Panthers," wrote Banks in his memoir, "but I knew AIM would do what we had to do to achieve our ends."[75] Indeed, Banks and others invoked the specter of militancy from the very beginning. He was quoted at length to this effect in a *St. Paul Pioneer Press* article published in the fall of 1968: "I don't believe in violence, but I do believe in a form of militancy . . . to be effective as an organized group . . . we will probably have to come to the brink of rioting."[76]

Links between AIM and the BPP, however indirect, affirm historian Manning Marable's observation that the "inchoate black rebellion"—that spread across the United States in the decade between 1965 and 1975—both "inspired and, to a profound degree, initiated similar revolts" among other racialized Americans, including Indigenous groups.[77] Various organizations were forged in the crucible of that decade-long rebellion, Marable notes, but the Oakland BPP quickly emerged as the "most influential revolutionary nationalist organization in the US."[78] Notably, the Panthers had also drawn inspiration from elsewhere. Founders Huey Newton and Bobby Seale modeled their efforts on the work of activists in the Southern California city of Watts who had organized a project called the Community Alert Patrol to curb police violence against fellow African Americans in the wake of the historic rebellion there.[79]

Interestingly, there are also a number of historical and biographical similarities between the Minneapolis AIM and the Oakland BPP. Both were urban movements that emerged out of communities that were, for the most part, composed of relatively recent arrivals to the urban environments in which they organized. Nearly all of the Panthers' early leaders were "recent transplants" from the American South, observes historian Curtis Austin.[80] While their parents had left Dixie for California in search of "a better life," they had encountered "more of the same" in the ghettos of Oakland. In this context of renewed frustration and hardship, the young radicals "concluded their forebears had fought the good fight but had used the wrong tools," and turned to militancy as a tactic to challenge the persistence of African American oppression. Similarly, many of the people who would form AIM and other political organizations in the Twin Cities had arrived in Minneapolis from economically strained reservations or boarding schools throughout the Upper Midwest. Those who formed AIM interpreted the pervasiveness of the difficulties that they encountered as a function of enduring racist oppression and sought to forge a political movement capable of challenging its persistence. In both cases, too, organizational founders had become acquainted with the coercive arm of the state. The Panthers had been motivated by the omnipresent violence of the Oakland Police Department and the experience of coming of age in an environment where a predominantly white police force patrolled the African American ghettos with an aggressive zeal. AIM leaders, moreover, had for the most part encountered state coercion through their experiences of the criminal justice system, boarding schools, and MPD practices on the streets of Minneapolis.

Yet, while the influence of the Oakland Panthers is often cited as *the* central outside inspiration for AIM's police-monitoring activities, far less attention has been paid to the influence of local African American activism.[81] Indeed, the history of African American revolt in the Twin Cities has often been downplayed, though it has received some renewed attention in the wake the nationwide revolts that followed the murder of George Floyd in 2020. In spite of this inattention, however, Twin Cities African American activism has been very significant, both in its robustness and in its influence on other movements.

The organization of community "patrols" is an important part of this history. By the mid-1960s, mistrust of the police was widespread among African American communities in the inner-city Northside.[82] Knowing that they could not count on the MPD to serve and protect, members of the African American community assumed the burden of maintaining peace themselves at tense moments.[83] Reports from the aftermath of the assassination of Martin Luther King in April 1968, for example, demonstrate that community members took to the streets calling themselves "Black Patrols" and "Citizens' Patrol Groups" and were successful both at de-escalating tensions *and* encouraging police to reduce their presence in the neighborhood.[84]

The impact of the Black Patrol was not lost on those that would ultimately assemble the Indian Patrol, and some members of the latter felt that the "roughest officers" had begun to avoid the Northside because of this new form of community oversight.[85] Those same officers, they felt, were now "trooping into the Indian neighborhood" instead. Banks was explicit that the Black Patrol had been an inspiration: "[Northside activists] got rid of [police harassment] on Plymouth Av. with their patrol, and we're going to have to do the same thing," he told the *Minneapolis Tribune* as the Indian Patrol was first preparing to hit the streets.[86] "The only way to get any action is by a show of force."

For all its militancy, however, AIM maintained relationships with a number of liberal organizations and officials, secured funds from a range of antipoverty bureaucracies, and was adept at navigating connections with a number of corporate benefactors, particularly in its first two years. Groups such as the Minnesota League of Women Voters maintained a posture of cautious support for AIM and offered modest assistance at various junctures (see chapter 2). Meanwhile, Minneapolis AIM also managed to secure some financial support for its various activities from both private and public sources, including a series of Twin Cities churches and foundations, as well as federal antipoverty funds that flowed through the Office of Economic Opportunity.[87] Additionally, a number of AIM leaders managed to secure leave from their employers in order to pursue their community activism. In the relatively progressive atmosphere of ascendant civil-rights activism, Clyde Bellecourt was granted secondment from Northern States Power Company to pursue AIM activities, for example.[88]

In spite of these links to the establishment, AIM's approach to the MPD was often openly oppositional. For good reasons, the AIM leadership tended to view police as a hostile force or an "arm of the White establishment," according to Cohen.[89] The earliest issues of AIM's community newsletter reflected this position and one of the publication's core functions was to recount incidents of police brutality, often while naming names. Consider the following account of the arrest of one the AIM comrades in the early 1970s:

> Richard C. Johnson, the arresting "COP" is evidently a high-strung and sick young COP. He must feel that with a badge and the law behind him that he can do no wrong. He took it upon his own to incur punishment while doing his so called duty. [AIM activist] Mr. Obrien was hit with a closed fist twice in the

stomach and had his head banged on the squad car door simply because he asked a question and because he is an INDIAN. Mr. [Clyde] Bellecourt was also a victim of his brutality. He merely told Johnson that there was no reason to treat O'Brien in the manner he was doing. . . . Bellecourt was handcuffed and taken to a squad car. He was put in the backseat and Johnson got in with him. All the way to the Courthouse or Jailhouse, he was harassed by Johnson. Also, the Cop continually twisted and jerked the handcuff's [sic] on Bellecourt's wrists until they were raw, cut, and bleeding. Bellecourt was not informed of what he was being arrested for until he was completely booked downtown.[90]

After recounting this incident, the writer makes explicit that it was Bellecourt's Indigenous status that had prompted the officer to treat him with such contempt. "Other citizens are told what they are being arrested for and do not receive this treatment . . . why do we always have to remind the great white society that we are human beings?"

In these early years, AIM showed remarkable skill at channeling moments of crisis to contest police aggressiveness. By politicizing a range of confrontational incidents that occurred between AIM activists and the police in 1969, for example, the organization forced the MPD to respond to their accusations. That spring, Police Chief Donald Dwyer attended an AIM organized public meeting in which more than two hundred people turned up to voice their grievances with law enforcement. Cohen observed the meeting and described the scene:

[Bellecourt] led the meeting. He asked people to sign a list if they had been treated unfairly, so that they could be called upon to give "open testimony." Then he described his recent encounters with police and showed slides of his bruised and abraded wrists. He accused police of an "escalation of war against Indian people", [Bellecourt's] testimony was followed by other accusations: that police beat Indians; that police ridiculed Indians; that police invaded Indian homes. Police were said to ignore Indian requests for help. Nothing was done to meet Indian needs, said one woman, "because we've got Brown faces . . . you've got to be an affluent White or a Black militant to get anything done." The crowd cheered in agreement with her.[91]

Dwyer rejected Bellecourt's view that police actions were an "escalation of war against Indian people," but he did dutifully "write down specifics" and seem "conciliatory and concerned."[92] Through this and more subtle moments, the MPD was increasingly forced to acknowledge that routinized aggressiveness on the Southside was the source of considerable community anxiety.

The first iteration of the "Indian Patrol" was relatively short-lived and probably had only a limited impact on reducing police aggressiveness in the decades that followed 1968. What it did do, however, was provide an organizational vehicle to express outrage at MPD treatment of Indigenous people. While the sense that Indigenous urbanites were both "underpoliced" and "overpoliced" certainly predates the patrol, what these monitoring efforts did was channel that long-standing "sense of grievance" into an organizational form capable of capturing both Indigenous and non-Indigenous attention. In this sense, AIM patrollers and other activists contributed to a larger process of contestation. In doing so, they politicized the routinized brutality of racialized policing. By communicating the pervasiveness of aggressive policing in a mediagenic form, AIM activists were instrumental in denaturalizing its occurrence for non-Indigenous audiences.

Whereas dominant interpretations often relied on dubious narratives of migratory trauma, community disorganization, and the purported pervasiveness of alcoholism to explain why Indigenous Minnesotans were disproportionately entangled with the coercive arm of the state, the patrol sought to tell a different story. At the very least, this had the effect of consolidating the idea that institutions of the state were aggressively targeting Indigenous people. In so doing, it worked to erode the potency of these cultural explanations.

Of course, it is critical to note that this view is not universally shared. Vizenor argues that AIM's media profile effectively "created the heroes of confrontation for an imaginative white audience" while those dedicated to less mediagenic forms of institutional negotiation were largely ignored.[93]

*

The history of police violence in South Minneapolis is inseparable from reproduction of particular forms of racialized "knowledge" about Indigenous people which have operated to render Indigenous people's asymmetrical entanglement with the criminal justice apparatus understandable, tolerable, and even *natural* to certain publics. But this cultural "knowledge" is always contested, and key moments of Indigenous political organizing have operated to interrupt its potency. The Indian Patrol went some way in countering this knowledge by dramatizing the targeting of Indigenous people rather than seeking answers in the individual "shortcomings" of those caught up in the legal process. Its presence in the media and on the streets politicized that targeting by denaturalizing police targeting.

Of course, the Indian Patrol's moment was not the only time that questions about racialized police targeting have managed to reach a broader public. Headline-grabbing incidences of racialized police misconduct, including the 1993 "trunk incident," have periodically made media waves over the course of the last six decades. Although the incidents discussed in this chapter pertain primarily to the policing of Indigenous people—and, especially, the way that settler colonial assumptions about Indigenous trauma, disorganization, and weakness have served as a screen for the persistence of racialized coercion—the experience of "racialized policing" in Minneapolis is not exclusive to the Indigenous community.

As I write, Minneapolis is at the forefront of a nationwide revolt against racialized police violence that is demanding nothing short of a radical transformation of policing in the United States. In a climate that is reminiscent of the late 1960s, previously impossible demands are being taken seriously. The question remains, however, whether the present appetite for transformation will translate into concrete change, or if, as in the 1960s, demands for a radical revaluation of the relationship between law enforcement and racialized communities will mostly come to naught.

4

Land Mines at Home and Abroad

American Empire in South Minneapolis

Minneapolis is often touted as one of the most "progressive" cities in the United States. Consider, for example, its performance in a series of informal national studies through which it has been deemed the "gayest city in America," the "most literate city in America," and "America's best bike city."[1] Given these bona fides, it is not surprising that Minneapolis is routinely included alongside places such as Portland, Seattle, and Denver in efforts to identify American oases of livability, inclusiveness, and liberal enlightenment. Local promotional material often taps this reputation, citing, for example, the city's "vibrant" LGBTQ scene and ethnic diversity as sources of local pride and as amenities to be enjoyed by visitors.[2] At the same time, Minneapolis's purported openness is identified as a key asset in the intraurban competition to attract mobile capital and grow local prosperity. Urban guru Richard Florida included the Twin Cities on an updated list of twenty U.S. metropolitan areas best positioned to capture and retain the "creative class."[3] Florida's study cites "innovation, high technology, and tolerance for racial, ethnic and social diversity" as the key ingredients in the urban region's strong performance.

There are several problems with these rosy assessments. The first is that to present Minneapolis as a harmonious place where a climate of tolerance for "racial, ethnic, and social diversity"

115

prevails is to obscure an enduring history of urban racism and group-differentiated inequity. Of course, it feels a little strange to point this out in a moment when Minneapolis is at the center of a national revolt against racialized police violence and attention is being focused on the city's inequities as never before. Suffice it to say, however, that before most people had heard the name George Floyd, local analysts were working hard to make the point that distinct patterns of exclusion and marginalization were impacting the city's racialized communities. Researchers have long shown, for example, that nonwhite people are disproportionately excluded from sharing in the city's economic buoyancy.[4] Indigenous residents of the Twin Cities continue to cope with many of the problems considered earlier in this book, not least a crisis of economic hardship that affects about half of the local community.[5] At the same time, a recent study demonstrates that "foreign-born"–headed families in Minnesota are three times more likely to live in poverty than the nonimmigrant population, nearly half of all female-headed "foreign-born" households subsist beneath the official poverty line, and about 20 percent of "foreign-born" adults over sixty-five do, too.[6] Other research shows that the urban region's African American community is disproportionately exposed to endemic poverty, social exclusion, and the coercive violence of the criminal justice system. The gap between Black and white employment rates is larger in the Twin Cities than in any other metropolitan area in the country.[7] Twin Cities African Americans were particularly hard hit by the subprime mortgage crisis; even "high-income blacks" were about four times more likely to receive subprime financing than "low-income whites."[8] At times, Minnesota has arrested and incarcerated African American males at a rate higher than any other state in the nation.[9] Black men in the Twin Cities are routinely menaced by police violence, as the high-profile killings of Philando Castille, Thurman Blevins, and George Floyd make all too plain.

The second problem is that to present Minneapolis as a place of cosmopolitan prosperity obscures the degree to which that prosperity has been won at the expense of other places. Urban theorists Stefan Kipfer and Kanishka Goonewardena observe that by framing Western cities as endogenous producers of wealth, commentators camouflage the degree to which "economic and ecological parasitism," as well as a "dependence of commercial exchange on militarism, imperial expansion, and other forms of primitive accumulation," are all "formative" dimensions of those cities' past and present.[10] Geographers such as Doreen Massey have long demonstrated that local environments are relationally produced, that places "are what they are" as a result of their "relations with elsewhere."[11] To take these observations seriously in the context of Minneapolis is to observe that the city's status as a competitive urban economy and a lauded destination city is organically linked to a series of transnational relationships that complicate its "progressive" characterization. More bluntly, Minneapolis's prosperity and diversity are inextricably connected to a distinctly American political economy of violence.

To weigh these problems against the celebratory accounts that I started with is to confront a thorny contradiction. On the one hand, Minneapolis is a place that is rich in diversity and prosperity, a place of economic buoyancy animated by a much-talked-about spirit of cooperation, tolerance, and interpersonal decency. On the other hand, Minneapolis is a city acutely divided along ethnic and "racial" lines, a place in which opportunity, security, and prosperity are far from universally shared.

In describing this as a contradiction, my aim is not to suggest that these two interpretations are "so totally at odds that both cannot possibly be true," as the most common use of that term would suggest.[12] Rather, I have in mind something closer to a Marxian use of the term to describe a situation in which two "seemingly opposed forces are simultaneously present."[13] In the latter formulation, oppositional forces need not cancel each other out. Rather, they exist in dialectical tension with one another. This form of contradiction better captures the context that concerns me here because Minneapolis is a place where two realities persist alongside and within each other. It is a city that is shaped by tendencies that are progressive *and* regressive, open *and* exclusionary, cohesive *and* divisive.[14] Yet these oppositional tendencies do not merely coexist; they are also organically linked. The forces that *produce* prosperity, abundance, and inclusiveness are connected to the forces that produce insecurity, marginality, and death, at home and abroad.

In Minneapolis, the settler colonial relation articulates alongside, and intersects with, other expressions of imperial aggression. This chapter argues that the production of the Phillips neighborhood and other Twin Cities districts cannot be understood without tracing their relationship to a broader deployment of violence in defense of American "interests." Troubling accounts that celebrate Minneapolis as a desirable mix of economic opportunity, political enlightenment, and cultural diversity, it demonstrates that the forces that ensure that these sources of local pride persist are relationally linked to forces that are the source of immense suffering and displacement. In doing so, it also challenges the idea that the effects of American state violence are only experienced in faraway theaters of war or domestic sites of military coordination—in Baghdad or Fort Hood, for example—and demonstrates that they also articulate in what have been called "banal geographies of neo-imperialism," including Minneapolis.[15] Indeed, the benefits and the injuries of American empire coexist in the contradictory confines of this "progressive" urban environment.

This chapter is motivated by the idea that settler colonial analysis must look beyond the borders of the modern nation-state.[16] Specifically, it is inspired by Rinaldo Walcott's observation that a kind of methodological nationalism has often impeded settler colonial analysis, obscuring the ways that domestic settler colonial agendas have always been entangled with a broader series of outward-looking commitments. What Walcott calls a "critical engagement with coloniality" demands that analysts draw lines of continuity between domestic projects of colonization and broader forms of racialized devaluing. To do so, he contends, is to challenge the carefully constructed conceit that the enduring effects of settler colonial dispossession, the transatlantic slave trade, the racialized segregation of North American cities, and contemporary forms of imperialism (such as the ones chronicled below) are disconnected from one another.

"Building Better Lives with Land Mines"

Although nationalist dogmas have long cited universal liberty as the great source of American prosperity, such claims almost always obscure the "machinery of enforcement" that sustains the economic prowess of the United States. The disproportionate consolidation of wealth and privilege in the industrialized "core" in general, and the United States in particular, has a long imperial history, of course, but the ways in which that domination has been articulated in the wake of the Second World War have a different character. After 1945, the United States emerged as the world's most powerful economic force and preeminent military power. Unlike its predecessors, however, the American state sought to consolidate and sustain its position by promoting and managing a "fully global capitalism," rather than by ruling foreign polities directly.[17] This strategy has allowed it to play a "vital role" in "superintending capitalism on a worldwide plane," without the burden of administering a formal colonial network.[18]

This does not mean that the postwar defense of American hegemony has been achieved without coercion and violence. Since 1945, American military spending has grown to epic proportions. In 2019, American taxpayers invested nearly $700 billion in their military, a sum greater than the next seven countries combined.[19] Meanwhile, new spending commitments are pushing annual military spending ever closer to the $1 trillion mark.[20] Public investments continue to ensure that "martial accumulation" will remain one of the core dimensions of the American economy (hence Deborah Cowen's caution about drawing too stark a division between "markets" and "militaries").[21]

These have not been idle expenditures. Since the close of the Second World War, the American state has deployed military force in an enormous range of formal and informal conflicts. Such engagements have often been justified through an official rhetoric of democratization and humanitarian intervention, but critic William Blum argues that they have almost always been motivated by a series of self-interested guiding imperatives, including "making the world open and hospitable for [economic] globalization," bolstering the success of American defense contractors, "preventing the rise of any society that might serve as a successful example of an alternative to the capitalist model," "extending political, economic and military hegemony over as much of the globe as possible, to prevent the rise of any regional power that might challenge American supremacy," and creating "a world in America's image, as befits the world's only superpower."[22]

The strength of postwar American capitalism is inseparable from the violence that has been deployed to achieve these ends. In Minneapolis and elsewhere, this not an abstract point. Local corporations that form the core of the Twin Cities economy, from retail giants like Target and Best Buy to technology manufacturers like Honeywell and 3M, owe their spectacular strength to the benefits born of American-led economic globalization. In fact, the life of the Phillips neighborhood is intimately linked to a broader economy of American state violence.

To begin demonstrating how, it is helpful consider a series of events connected to the Honeywell Corporation, the neighborhood's most notable corporate resident. Honeywell International's present status as a global technology giant and stalwart in the top quintile of the Fortune 500 belies its humble beginnings. The corporation was born in the early twentieth century out of a merger between two modest Midwestern temperature control firms, the Electric Heat Regulator Corporation of Minneapolis and the Honeywell Corporation of Wabash, Indiana. On the eve of the Great Depression, the two firms consolidated their interests and chose Minnesota as a permanent home.[23] In 1927, the new enterprise set to work on the construction of a substantial inner-city headquarters on a vacant lot that would come to "anchor" the western portion of the present-day Phillips neighborhood.[24] From these modest beginnings, Honeywell set out on a meteoric ascent from regional to global dominance, becoming the world leader in residential and industrial temperature-control technologies by the mid-twentieth century.

The outbreak of the Second World War allowed Honeywell to diversify its activities. Wartime mobilization emboldened the corporation to pursue lucrative interests in aerospace and weapons manufacturing. In short order, it emerged as a significant supplier to various branches of the American defense establishment. In the decades that followed 1945, Honeywell began to develop and supply a range of destructive instruments, including large- and small-caliber tank ammunitions, torpedoes, artillery shells, and land mines, such as the Area Denial Artillery Munition (ADAM) and the Remote Anti-Armor Mine (RAAM), among others. It also began to develop guidance technologies for weapons with immense destructive capacity, including intercontinental nuclear ballistic missiles such as Boeing's Minuteman and Northrop's MX.

In Minneapolis, Honeywell's weapons work became a source of local controversy. Indeed, the corporation emerged as the primary target of the Twin Cities' significant peace, disarmament, and antiwar movements from the Vietnam era through the 1990s. As war raged in Southeast Asia in the 1960s, "dinner parties in certain Minneapolis neighborhoods were always at risk of being ground to a halt by guests who would produce a mock-up of [Honeywell's] fragmentation device and patiently explain the damage it inflicts on humans," write Paul Chaat Smith and Robert Warrior.[25]

For Twin Cities organizers, Honeywell was a local symbol of the perverse proximity between the interests of corporate America and what they perceived to be the morally suspect deployment of state violence in the Cold War era. In 1968, local New Left leader Marv Davidov and a number of allies formed the Honeywell Project (HP) in an ultimately unsuccessful effort to encourage the corporation to convert to peaceful production while protecting local jobs. Over the course of several decades, Davidov and others engaged in a diverse range of tactics aimed at impugning the reputations of Honeywell and other local firms. While the corporation's involvement with nuclear weapons remained the primary grievance, activists often also pointed to the devastation reaped by its land-mine cluster munitions. By the 1980s, HP was in coalition with a wide range of antimilitarist and disarmament groups and had begun organizing nonviolent civil-disobedience demonstrations that targeted the corporation's headquarters in the Phillips neighborhood.[26] These events ranged in size and influence over the course of the decades, but at points they were very effective at capturing significant local attention. The latter was particularly true when days of action led to mass arrests. In 1986, for example, about 140 demonstrators were detained outside of Honeywell's annual shareholders meeting, including the spouse of MPD Chief Tony Bouza.[27]

Honeywell took these public relations challenges seriously and sought to defend its reputation as a positive force in the Twin Cities. In response to the protests visited upon its corporate headquarters throughout the 1980s, executives and their spokespeople echoed President Ronald Reagan's view that military strength was the best means of ensuring peace. In one case, they responded to a mass demonstration by releasing a statement reminding the public that Honeywell's employees also "deplore war," insisting that they too were "working to assure peace by meeting the U.S. public preference for a strong defense."[28] The corporation's PR strategies were not merely reactive, however, and Honeywell made substantial investments in a diverse range of community education programs to demonstrate its apparent commitment to a world without war. In one

Honeywell Inc. headquarters at 2753 Fourth Avenue South in South Minneapolis, with I-35W in the foreground, 1972. Courtesy of Hennepin County Library.

case, for example, it provided most of the $240,000 operating budget of an initiative called "Prospects for Peacemaking" in which a coalition of groups that included the Minnesota League of Women Voters and the Humphrey Institute at the University of Minnesota hosted a series of public discussions about nuclear weapons.[29]

Marv Davidov, founder of the Honeywell Project, speaks at a protest against the weapons production work of Honeywell Inc. in 1982. Photograph by Mark Peterson. Courtesy of Hennepin County Library.

Honeywell's charitable and community investments extended well beyond efforts to mitigate its association with nuclear weaponry, however. Indeed, the corporation has sometimes been described as the driving force behind Minnesota's national reputation as "a place where business demonstrates social concern."[30] Honeywell did not seal itself off from the increasingly impoverished neighborhood that surrounded its headquarters and made commitments to invest in the social and economic well-being of Phillips. In 1957, the charitable Honeywell Foundation was established with the explicit intention of improving life in the neighborhood. Throughout the latter half of the twentieth century, it endowed a diverse range of initiatives in the district, including crime-prevention programs, career-training services, improvements in the built environment, and even an alternative high school for teenage mothers that operated out of a building on its corporate campus.[31]

The corporation also established a reputation for being concerned with the well-being of the city's growing Indigenous community. In the 1960s, for example, it empowered future AIM leader Dennis Banks to recruit Indigenous employees. As Smith and Warrior put it, "Honeywell seemed to like both Indians in general and Dennis Banks specifically," and the latter managed to recruit more than four hundred new employees during the course of his tenure with Honeywell.[32] Banks was also granted a paid leave of absence in 1968 in order to pursue his organizing work among the Twin Cities Indigenous community. While away from the job, however, Banks had a change of heart and decided that he was no longer interested in recruiting for a weapons manufacturer.[33] In hindsight, he felt that Honeywell's generosity was contingent on cooperation and noted that "once you turn around and start criticizing them and biting the hand that feeds you . . . they're not going to give you anymore."[34] Severing ties with Banks did not mark the end of Honeywell's engagement with the urban Indigenous community. Although direct recruiting waned in the years that followed Banks's departure, the corporation continued to provide some modest forms of support to area job seekers.

One such initiative is particularly noteworthy. In the early 1980s, a number of Honeywell executives pledged support for a nonprofit industrial-services enterprise called Phillips Works, which had a mandate to help "hard-to-employ" Phillips neighborhood residents earn a livelihood. The vast majority of those who would come to work at Phillips Works were Indigenous, and nearly all were heads of households who had been without work for more than a year.[35] With the help of Honeywell, the Dayton-Hudson Corporation, the Minneapolis Foundation, and a series of community funders, Phillips Works was able to marshal needed resources, equipment, and technical assistance. Starting as a small-scale bindery operation, the enterprise built on early success and expanded the scope of its activities to include light forms of manufacturing and assembly. As momentum accumulated, the enterprise adopted a for-profit model and continued to expand while maintaining its preference for employees who had difficulty finding work elsewhere.[36] Within five years, Phillips Works had outgrown its initial worksite and began making plans to relocate to a much larger space in an East Franklin Avenue facility, newly built and operated by the American Indian Business Development Corporation (AIBDC). According to Phillips Works's leadership, none of this would have been possible without Honeywell's considerable support. In particular, the corporation was praised for outsourcing a series of manufacturing contracts that now formed the core of the community enterprise's growing activities. "Our business would not have happened without Honeywell," one of Phillips Works principals told the *Star-Tribune* at the height of the organization's expansion.[37]

In spite of these auspicious beginnings, Phillips Works's connection to Honeywell soon became a public-relations problem. In 1986, several news outlets revealed that Phillips Works's manufacturing division (Light Manufacturing) was involved in the production of two of Honeywell's most controversial weapons, ADAM and RAAM. The president of Light Manufacturing acknowledged that the division's work included the inspection of a 3-inch by 5-inch metal component of an antipersonnel mine and the recycling of plastic tubes related to other weapons work, but noted that the company did not handle any explosives.[38] More than half of Light Manufacturing's annual revenues came from Honeywell contracts, she pointed out, stressing that the promise of future defense work was a critical means of establishing needed credibility with financial institutions. "Banks like military contracts," she told the *Star-Tribune*, ". . . they know those payments come in and they're fairly secure. Those contracts pay on a regular basis."[39]

These revelations precipitated something of a local uproar. Phillips Works had won initial praise as a difference maker but was now linked to the production of one of Honeywell's most reviled product lines. By the spring of 1987, that association was already threatening to translate into real consequences. Jim Heltzer, executive director of the Minneapolis Community Development Agency, was one of the first public officials to trouble these connections. Light Manufacturing was slated to occupy more than half of a building in which the city had invested $1.7 million as part of its inner-city economic development efforts. Heltzer worried that it might be inappropriate to use public money slated for inner-city development to subsidize weapons work.[40]

Public opinion on the matter seemed to break into two broad camps. Those who felt that Heltzer's concerns were misplaced cited a number of reasons why Phillips Works should continue to receive public support, in spite of its connections to Honeywell. Most of the arguments raised in support of this position were captured in a *Star-Tribune* editorial that sought to demonstrate why Heltzer's objections were off base. "Both Honeywell and the Phillips company are engaged in work that is legal and honorable, even if considered immoral by a portion of the community." Municipal authorities have an obligation to do everything in their power to bring needed jobs to a downtrodden neighborhood, the editors felt. The community enterprise's efforts were providing key opportunities for low-income people to edify themselves through meaningful work, it explained. "Helping Phillips Works Light Manufacturing would give only slight aid to Honeywell and the Pentagon," but "far greater benefit would flow to a blighted area of the city and to low-income Minneapolis residents seeking to improve their lives through work." It also argued that there was a local precedent for such subsidies, citing previous rounds of municipal investment in the "research" activities of Honeywell and the FMC Corporation. "Declining to help the Phillips firm, especially after aiding FMC and Honeywell, would convey an unfortunate double standard: Workers with higher incomes and better educations can benefit from defense contracts, occasionally with city assistance, but low-income people do not deserve the same."[41]

Those who questioned the desirability of municipal support for Light Manufacturing's weapons work made a number of compelling counterpoints. In the first place, they contested the view that Honeywell's land-mine work was in any way "honorable." Twin Cities journalist Mordecai Specktor reminded readers of the *Star-Tribune* that "Honeywell's cluster bombs have killed and maimed civilians in Southeast Asia and Lebanon."[42] He noted that locally built land mines could soon be used again, perhaps in ongoing conflicts in Central America. It was thus plausible, he continued, that a weapon produced by "poor Minnesotans" would wind up being employed to maim or kill "poor Salvadorans or Guatemalans" in the not-so-distant future.[43] In the words of one *Star-Tribune* reader, this was the "Faustian bargain" being offered to "hard-to-employ" Phillips workers.[44]

Critical voices also raised questions about Honeywell's motivations. As Specktor pointed out, the corporation had long been the target of mass demonstrations and was in need of avenues that would allow it to "maintain a positive face in the community."[45] These investments, he argued, were part of a shrewd ploy to entangle "murderous profits" with the "misfortune of jobless inner-city residents." Moreover, this was a moment when the Reagan administration and its congressional allies were pursuing major new investments in military research *and* exacting painful retrenchments of the existing social infrastructure.[46] Specktor argued that Honeywell was playing on this dynamic: "While peace activists argue that federal military spending forces cuts in social programs, Honeywell is able to present a façade of social concern by creating jobs in the four- to eight-dollar range for several dozen indigent Phillips residents." There must be a "better choice" than working on "weapons of war or going without," he concluded, and future discussions on the matter need to be conducted "with sensitivity towards those caught in the middle."[47] In making these points, critics of Honeywell's entanglements with Phillips Works pointed to the fundamental inequity at the heart of this controversy. They observed that Honeywell was acting from a position of considerable strength, seeing an opportunity to cloak its reviled weapons work in a mantle of community assistance.

It is worth remembering that the corporation's land-mine work was very profitable. Between 1985 and 1995, Honeywell and its spinoff enterprise Alliant Techsystems (now ATK) won Department of Defense land-mine contracts worth more than $336 million.[48] Thus, although Honeywell executives may well have "deplore[d] war" and military violence, they were also the immediate beneficiaries of it. As Honeywell's critics pointed out, those making decisions at the corporation had a very different set of interests than those working on land-mine production for Phillips Works. Indeed, those forced to make the "Faustian bargain" on an inner-city production line were motivated by a different set of factors than their counterparts in Honeywell boardrooms and policy circles charged with military decision making. Against the clichéd idea of a shared national "interest," the Phillips Works controversy reminds us that the spoils and suffering of American state violence are far from equally distributed.

What these critics did not articulate was the way in which a longer history of violence also animated this controversy. To understand Indigenous economic insecurity in Phillips, it is necessary to extend analyses beyond immediate economic circumstances and make links between contemporary hardship and the long-standing hierarchical politics of the settler colonial relation. The preponderance of Indigenous insecurity in this neighborhood at this time is inseparable from the long history of racialized social organization through which material security, prosperity, and political freedom were funneled to settler Americans and denied to Indigenous people. This is the contextual backdrop of the "Faustian bargain" that Phillips Works employees were forced to make. Honeywell's support did not merely create opportunities for a group of "poor" people. Rather, it did so for a group of "poor" people with a particular relationship to the deployment of state violence, a group of people whose economic marginality was inseparable from patterns of structured inequity that alienated Indigenous communities from the immense prosperity of settler society. There is a cruel irony here. Honeywell's minor efforts to mitigate the consequences of that history had the effect of implicating "hard-to-employ" workers in new rounds of state violence, exacted, for the most part, against marginalized people in other parts of the world.

In the end, the Phillips Works initiative probably only resulted in a few dozen jobs and the completion of a tiny fraction of Honeywell's significant defense contracting work. Nevertheless, this series of events is instructive. It is a reminder that the enduring violence of the settler colonial relation is never articulated in a sociopolitical vacuum.

Eric Almond's "Our Neighborhood's Impact on the World" was published in *The Alley* in January 1986. Cartoon by Eric Almond. Courtesy of *The Alley*.

American Violence and Migration to South Minneapolis

The well-worn idea that the United States is a "country of immigrants"—a phrase adopted and adapted by figures as diverse as Paul Ryan and Steve Earle—obscures the immense diversity of immigrant experience. Those who have traveled by land from Honduras or El Salvador in recent years, for example, have little in common with those who left Britain in the seventeenth and eighteenth centuries to be part of building a new society in the American colonies. I don't have the space here to consider important debates about the distinction between "settler" and "migrant," but I find compelling Mahmood Mamdani's suggestion that the key point of distinction is that settlers, unlike migrants, "are made by conquest, not just immigration."[49] Or, to put it differently, "settlers," according to Lorenzo Veracini, "are unique migrants" that "conquer as well as move across space."[50] While it should go without saying that contemporary migrants to the United States arrive on contested land, the degree to which they benefit from that fact is a legitimate matter of debate. Disentangling and contextualizing the history of immigration to what is now the United States is thus critical to making sense of who, precisely, are the primary beneficiaries of American conquest, past and present.

The ethnic and cultural diversity of American urban regions—including the Twin Cities—is inextricably linked to histories of outwardly projected state violence. There is some truth to the cliché that migrants come to the United States and other industrialized countries in order to "seek a better life," but the question of why people need to leave their homes to find that "better life" is usually left unexamined. The broader social and political context that precipitates migration is absent in most mainstream considerations of destination cities throughout the "developed" world. To include such questions in analyses of multicultural Western urban centers is to complicate what is at stake in uncritical celebrations of diversity and openness.

The Honeywell incident is far from the only instance in which the outward projection of American violence has had distinct local implications. The benefits and injuries born of the pursuit of American "interests" through violent means have shaped other outcomes on the inner-city Southside, including the migratory flows that transformed its ethnic composition.

It is no coincidence that substantial Indigenous, Hmong, and Somali communities emerged in Phillips during these decades, if temporarily in some cases. The significant proportion of these groups that settled in and around the Phillips neighborhood in the second half of the twentieth century did so for a variety of reasons. One of them is that few other neighborhoods offered affordable housing and opportunities for new arrivals to live among their counterparts while establishing initial networks for survival.

Indigenous residents of the Twin Cities numbered a few hundred before the Second World War, but the opportunities sparked by wartime mobilization created conditions in which that population would grow to an estimated six thousand by the end of hostilities in Europe and Asia.[51] The urban Indigenous community continued to expand in the years that followed, particularly in the Phillips neighborhood, where by 1990 the number of Indigenous residents was more than six times greater than it was in any other neighborhood.

The inner-city Southside was also an initial point of settlement for many of the large number of Hmong (primarily Laotian) people who moved to the Twin Cities in the aftermath of the Vietnam War, mostly as refugees. In the United States, refugee settlement is primarily administered by third-party voluntary agencies (VOLAGs) that make agreements with the State Department to facilitate the settlement of a given number of people in a particular community and commit to provide initial services. Minneapolis is home to a number of very active VOLAGs that sought to accommodate Hmong refugees in the aftermath of hostilities in Southeast Asia. As a result, the urban region emerged as a key hub of the global Hmong diaspora. Today, Minneapolis claims to be home to the largest Hmong population outside Laos.[52]

Upon their arrival in the Twin Cities, Hmong refugees tended to secure housing in low-income inner-city neighborhoods, often in public-housing projects, before moving to other parts of the city after they had reached a certain degree of stability.[53] Several hundred Hmong families settled in the Phillips neighborhood between 1979 and 1981, initiating a wave of Southeast Asian migration to the district that would peak in 1990, the same year that people of color first constituted a demographic majority of neighborhood residents.[54]

The Twin Cities have also been home to the largest community of Somali migrants in the United States since the early 1990s. Like the Hmong before them, many of the first Somali people to come to Minneapolis did so as refugees sponsored by Twin Cities' VOLAGs. The community has grown considerably in the period since and recent census estimates suggest it could well exceed thirty thousand.[55]

The Southside of Minneapolis has remained an important geographic center for Somali Minnesotans. Phillips and other Southside neighborhoods are home to a significant Somali population and a number of Somali businesses, including the Karmel Mall on Pillsbury Avenue and various grocery stores and remittance shops along East Franklin Avenue in the north. Perhaps the most robust center of inner-city Somali residential life is the Riverside Plaza housing estate in the nearby Cedar–Riverside neighborhood. This Corbusier-inspired complex—composed of a series of concrete high-rises and made iconic by its appearance in the opening sequence of the sixth season of the *Mary Tyler Moore Show*—is described as the residential heart of an area that is sometimes dubbed "Little Mogadishu."[56] Many of the businesses on the adjacent section of Cedar Avenue cater to a Somali and East African clientele.

Conventional narrations of how and why these three groups came to Minneapolis generally stress the desire of newcomers to seek deliverance from hardship in the place they departed. In the late 1960s, for example, the *Minneapolis Tribune* summarized the causes of Indigenous relocation to the Twin Cities as follows: "Indians began migrating to the cities after World War II to escape reservation poverty and seek a better life."[57] In the early 1980s, the *New York Times* summarized the cause of accelerated Hmong migration to the United States as follows: "About 35,000 Hmong are now living in the United States. Most of them fled their homeland after it was overrun in 1975 by the Pathet Lao."[58] More recently, a *New York Times*

The Riverside Plaza housing complex in the Cedar–Riverside neighborhood, 1974.
Courtesy of University of Minnesota Archives, University of Minnesota–Twin Cities.

profile on the Somali community in Minneapolis summarized the cause of their migration to the United States as follows:

The country they had fled, on the eastern tip of Africa, was embroiled in a civil war that had left it without a functioning government since 1991.

The anarchy reached American televisions two years later, when warlords shot down two Black Hawk helicopters, killing 18 United States soldiers. By then, tens of thousands of Somalis had died and a mass exodus had begun.

A generation of Somalis grew up in the overcrowded refugee camps of northern Kenya, where malaria, scorpion infestations and hunger took their toll. Tales of America sustained them.

Clean water was said to flow freely in kitchens, and simple jobs like plucking chickens paid handsomely.[59]

There is nothing particularly egregious about the *content* of these synoptic interpretations, all of which are typical of a much broader pattern of explanation. It is a matter of empirical fact that many reservations were in dire economic shape in the period that followed 1945, that the victory of the Pathet Lao in 1975 was dangerous for those associated with the other side of the conflict, and that the collapse of the Somali central government in 1991 amplified civil strife. What mainstream American interpretations like the ones just listed tend to exclude, however, is the degree to which American state violence was (and is) explicitly complicit in producing the existential vulnerabilities that foregrounded each of these mass relocations.

To interpret migratory hubs like Minneapolis strictly as zones of refuge is thus to risk obscuring a key point. The security and abundance that define Western destination cities has often been achieved at the expense of the places that those seeking deliverance have left. Acknowledging this basic point poses a challenge to the self-congratulatory tendency to interpret cities in the Global North as the benign beneficiaries of migratory flows. The production of American peace and prosperity is often bound up with the production of vulnerability and immiseration elsewhere.

In their most perverse form, exculpatory interpretations decontextualize migratory movements to the United States. They define them as a consequence of insecurities that were produced by the social disorganization, internal strife, and underdevelopment of the migrants' places of origin. Achille Mbembe's description of Western interpretations of the African continent as a "vast dark cave where every benchmark and distinction come together in total confusion, and the rifts of a tragic and unhappy human history stand revealed . . . a bottomless abyss where everything is noise, yawning gap, and primordial chaos" hints at what I mean.[60] When the insecurity of "foreign" places is understood as the product of the failure of "foreign" people, the degree to which the pursuit of American (and other) "interests" has contributed to the production of that insecurity need not be explored. The exculpatory logic that allows American cities to be interpreted as places of deliverance *from* insecurity (rather than the producers and beneficiaries of it) ought to be challenged, in other words.

In each of the contexts just alluded to, the American state's pursuit of its own "interests" and/or a sense of American entitlement to enter and act in lands *occupied by other people* precipitated extraordinary deployments of military violence. In each case, American intervention resulted in the alienation of resident groups from earlier patterns of land use and contributed to the production of conditions of extraordinary hardship and insecurity. American violence, in other words, was complicit in driving forms of mass migration into places like Minneapolis. Although the political contexts that drove the growth of distinct and diverse Indigenous, Hmong, and Somali communities on the Southside of Minneapolis cannot be conflated, all were at least partly driven by the deployment of American state violence. In the interest of elucidation, it is worth considering this point in each context.

The postwar relocation of Indigenous people to Minneapolis is frequently interpreted as a socioeconomic response to the devastation of reservation economies, as the *Star-Tribune* editorial cited earlier suggests. Chronicling reservation destitution seems to have been a good scoop in the world of postwar Minnesota journalism and various multiarticle exposés in Twin Cities newspapers chronicled the difficulties of reservation life in lurid detail. *Tribune* writer Carl Rowan's 1957 visits to a series of Upper Midwest reservations, for example, offered evidence that an epidemic of reservation poverty was driving migration to urban environments. Reporting from one reservation in the "north woods" of Minnesota, Rowan found residents wandering "almost frantically," "looking for the rabbit or squirrel that will mean the difference between eating Sunday dinner and fasting."[61] Reporting from reservations in the "lonely prairies" of North and South Dakota, Rowan found a bitter human geography composed of fruitless landscapes dotted with "a thousand tarpaper shacks, leaning away from bitter winds . . . their roofs sagging under the winter snow."[62]

Less than a decade later, another *Tribune* reporter, Sam Newlund, visited seven regional reservations and concluded that "poverty is still the rule, prosperity the exception." Indeed, Newlund had no trouble "finding poor people on [the] Indian reservations" of the Upper Midwest and his reporting provided anecdotal support for a series of grim national statistics, including reservation unemployment rates that were more than seven times greater than the national average, reservation housing stocks that were more than 90 percent unfit, and an average life expectancy that was only two-thirds that of the general population.[63] Newlund reported that even on the Red Lake Reservation, sometimes regarded as the "best off" of Minnesota's Indigenous communities, it was still tough to cobble together a basic living.[64] He noted that some adults might be able to find seasonal work in pulp cutting, fishing, or wild-rice harvesting but less than 10 percent of the population as a whole was able to secure steady year-round work. Several years later, a special supplement published by the *Minneapolis Star* reiterated these impressions, noting that urban migration was being driven in part by reservation economies that offered limited land, limited resources, and were taxed by a growing population.[65]

The circumstances that these reporters described were not new. In Minnesota, as elsewhere, the processes of settler colonial territorialization through which the American state seized, partitioned, and reimagined vast swaths of the North American continent had devastating consequences for Indigenous communities. In Minnesota and other jurisdictions, lands set aside for reservations were the ones least desired by settler colonists. Lands that proved lucrative at a later stage were sometimes alienated from Indigenous communities through dubious agreements, as in the case of the White Earth Reservation, where precious timber stands were lost through the double-dealing of lumber interests in league with the state.[66]

Although certain mythologies persist about the peacefulness with which this transformation was accomplished, the historical record reveals that a sustained pattern of violence coordinated and perpetuated against Indigenous peoples by various branches of the U.S. government was central to it.[67] The process by which Indigenous communities were established on remote reservations disrupted existing patterns of quotidian existence and made self-sufficiency extremely challenging.[68] This history of violence and the long shadows that it has cast are at the center of the reservation poverty that, alongside other factors, precipitated large-scale relocation to cities such as Minneapolis.

The migration of Hmong people to the Twin Cities also corresponds to this broad pattern. Throughout the period of French colonial rule in Indochina, most ethnic Hmong subsisted as agriculturalists in the relative isolation of the northern stretches of Laos, Thailand, and Vietnam. The defeat of French colonialism in the 1950s precipitated dramatic change, however, and the emergence of groups committed to achieving projects of communist liberation refigured regional politics.

In Laos, a period of prolonged conflict was inaugurated as forces allied with the Royal Lao Government clashed with forces allied with the revolutionary Pathet Lao. While several attempts to forge unity governments were brokered, all were eventually scuttled—not least because the United States understood communist advances in the region as an affront to its "interests" and made dogged efforts to repel them.

The 1954 Geneva Accords limited the legal right of foreign powers to assert influence in the region, but American operatives shirked these dictates in order to support anticommunist efforts. American interventions amplified regional violence, in part by training and outfitting the covert Armée Clandestine from the 1950s on.[69] In the early 1960s, the CIA brokered a deal with Vang Pao, a key figure in the Royal Lao Army, and began working with him to train a local guerrilla force capable of fighting Pathet Lao.

Throughout the 1960s and 1970s, the United States provided military aid to the anticommunist campaign by disguising it as U.S. Agency for International Development (USAID) grants. "The Laos war was overseen by the US ambassador, run by the CIA, and supported by the US military—all without the consent and knowledge of Congress."[70] As broader American efforts in the region were amplified and spilled into the Laos–Vietnam border region in the early

1970s, an estimated twenty thousand Hmong fought alongside American forces and provided "critical aid" in reconnaissance on (and disruption of) the Trường Sơn, or Ho Chi Minh Trail. But by 1975, anticommunist forces in Laos were facing certain defeat and the U.S.-backed campaign came to an abrupt end with the evacuation of American forces and a small Laotian elite. The vast majority of Hmong who had fought as allies of the United States were left abandoned by their sponsors in a perilous theater of war.

Those left behind were not only alienated from their agricultural territories. They also faced retribution from their victorious enemies after years of catastrophic fighting. In this context of abandonment, many hurried to find their way out.[71] "If the communists see you were with the Americans, they kill you," recounted one evacuee who later settled in the Phillips neighborhood.[72] Like so many others, he was forced to make a harrowing journey out of Laos. His escape demanded that he undertake a punishing trek through a vast wilderness, endure months of privation, witness the execution of several members of his traveling party, and complete a final death-defying crossing of the Mekong River into Thai territory.

The migration of Somali people to the Twin Cities also bears the imprint of American intervention and abandonment. Of course, the United States was not the first overseas power to pursue its "interests" in the regions that are home to ethnic Somalis. There is a long history of meddling in these parts of the Horn of Africa and the legacies of outside interventionism continue to have important effects. While formal decolonization was achieved by anticolonial independence movements in the 1960s, the traditional territories of Somali people remain fragmented. Indeed, the successful achievement of Somali independence in 1960 united a collection of coastal areas. But at the end of this process, Haile Selassie's Ethiopian empire retained control of the Ogaden region (sometimes called "Western Somalia") and this geographic "fact on the ground" would endure as a source of conflict in the region.

Thus, the termination of European control in the region did not signal the end of outside intervention so much as the start of a new chapter. The Horn of Africa would prove fertile ground for Cold War powers to pursue their "interests" through proxy conflict. In Somalia, as in many other parts of the continent, Cold War maneuvering had devastating local consequences, "scorch[ing] the young hopes of Africa's independence struggle like seedlings in a drought," as Chinua Achebe puts it.[73] The Ethiopian empire, meanwhile, received immense support from the United States until Selassie was deposed in 1974. The emperor's administration received half of U.S. aid to sub-Saharan Africa between 1953 and 1973.[74]

The fall of Selassie brought considerable transformation to the region, and his leftist successors declared their allegiance to the socialist camp. In this context, the Soviet Union hoped that a socialist alliance in the Horn would allow it to exert considerable power over parts of the Middle East and control shipping corridors with access to the Indian Ocean.[75] Such an alliance would never come to fruition, however, and conflict over the contested Ogaden region flared up in the mid-1970s, bringing Somalia and Ethiopia into a short but brutal war. In this context, the Somali state transferred allegiance to the United States while Ethiopia remained allied with the Communist bloc. The war initiated a period of extraordinary violence and intensified proxy conflict, as the two superpowers lavished their local allies with weaponry and support. The Carter administration provided considerable military and economic aid to Somalia, while the Soviet Union did the same on the other side of the border.[76]

The Ogaden war devastated Somalia's small economy, in spite of the ample spending of the government's American sponsors. The country's external debt tripled to nearly three hundred million dollars between 1976 and 1979 and mushroomed to about two billion by 1990, as the Somali state "began its final descent into chaos."[77] Discontent with President Siad Barre's administration in Mogadishu transformed into armed revolt in the late 1980s and would continue to intensify until the government lost control of the capital in 1991. The vacuum left by Barre's ouster created a series of conflicts throughout Somalia as various factions fought for control. By 1992, the spiraling crisis had resulted in famine in various parts of the country and mass displacement began to follow. Refugee camps in neighboring Kenya were set up to house Somalis who crossed the border in "desperate physical condition."[78] Reporting for the *New York Times* in the months that followed Barre's ouster, Jane Perez observed that "abandonment" was evident in the Horn of Africa.[79] "Ethiopia and Somalia, which were at the center of the tussle for influence on the African continent in the 1970s, now lie devastated, orphans of the post–cold war era," she wrote. With the ouster of Barre, "a long-rotting structure came crashing down, and Somalia has not had a functioning government since," writes journalist Christian Parenti.[80] "Worse yet," he continues, "its war and constant instability have infected the entire region" as "the flow of weapons, ammunition, contraband, and armed men across borders has created a lawless zone."

Here again, the violent pursuit of American "interests" (alongside and against the Soviet Union, in this case) contributed to a monumental human catastrophe. Somali people have been alienated from their traditional territories and postintervention abandonment has once again driven a crisis of displacement as millions of Somalis have been forced to seek refuge elsewhere. The considerable growth of the Twin Cities Somali community is directly connected to the radical instability of contemporary Somalia, a set of conditions that the United States is complicit in having created.

In rather direct ways, then, these three patterns of displacement and relocation were precipitated by the violent pursuit of American "interests." This fact complicates the portrayal of Minneapolis as a site of refuge and challenges the comforting fiction that people move to places like the Twin Cities simply because they are seeking a "better life." It demands that tough questions be asked about the material histories of predation on which that "better life" is built.

*

Of course, Minneapolis will continue to be celebrated for its diversity, but it is critical to ask what sort of relationships make that diversity possible. Militarism is productive of space even where its most visceral effects are not observable, and Minneapolis is no exception. It has been shaped by the outward projection of American violence. Indeed, the city can, in a certain light, be understood as a "military geography," assuming that we interpret that term broadly to include the diverse spatial effects of militarism.[81] Geographer Stephen Flusty and his colleagues insist that contemporary research needs to extend beyond well studied "'spaces of exception' where bodies are subject to 'extraordinary rendition' and 'enhanced interrogation,'" in order to focus on the "unexceptional spaces of metropolitan cores, colonized edges, and sites like superbases and homeless shelters where cores and peripheries irrupt deep within one another's hearts."[82]

At this stage, it is worth returning to the contradiction described at the beginning of this chapter. While cities such as Minneapolis are lauded for their social amenities, economic buoyancy, civic ambition, and multicultural density, it is critical to interrogate the relations that make these conditions possible and sustainable. The celebration of the prosperity and diversity of "progressive" Western cities often belies the degree to which those advantages are contingent on a predatory position within a global power circuitry.

The experience of Indigenous peoples in the United States and other settler colonial societies are a reminder that the politics of violently securing prosperity for some is first and foremost a domestic agenda. Indeed, the sustained articulation of the settler colonial relation intersects with other forms of violence and critics of settler colonial national projects ought to pay close heed to the ways in which processes of settler colonization were and are bound up with broader global flows and other forms racialized violence.[83]

Epilogue

In the spring of 1988, Ronald Reagan addressed an audience of students and faculty at Moscow State University beneath an immense bust of Vladimir Lenin. The president's remarks were pointed but diplomatic, mixing contempt for central planning with a gentle optimism that the United States might yet make a "friend" out of a longtime adversary.

The broader Moscow summit, of which Reagan's speech was a small part, was not always so successful at diffusing mutual animosity through diplomatic niceties. On the day before his university address, Reagan provoked the ire of his hosts by meeting with Soviet dissidents at Spaso House, the residence of the U.S. ambassador. The Soviet press retaliated by publishing a series of articles depicting the United States as "a contrasting land of technological marvels, poverty, hunger and repression."[1] Soviet television, meanwhile, aired a press conference held by Indigenous activists who had come to Moscow from the United States to draw attention to a range of grievances and demand a meeting with the president.[2]

Following Regan's Moscow State University speech, one student put the Indigenous delegation's appeal explicitly to the Gipper. During a brief question period, the student asked the president if he would make an effort to meet with the activists, if not in Moscow then back in the United States. Reagan was sheepish at first. He told the student that he had not been aware of any meeting requests but noted noncommittally that he would be happy to engage. Then he pivoted, assumed a more cocksure tone, and seized the opportunity to contest Soviet claims that the treatment of Indigenous people in the United States revealed the hypocrisy of American sermonizing about "human rights." He offered an improvised interpretation of the colonial history of his country:

> Let me tell you just a little something about the American Indian in our land. We have provided millions of acres of land for what are called preservations—or reservations, I should say. They, from the beginning, announced that they wanted to maintain their way of life, as they had always lived there in the deserts and the plains and so forth. And we set up these reservations so they could, and have the Bureau of Indian Affairs to help take care of them. At the same time we provide education for them— schools on the reservations. And they're free also to leave the reservations and be American citizens among the rest of us, and many do. Some still prefer, however, that way—that early way of life. And we've done everything we can to meet their demands as to how they want to live. Maybe we made a mistake. Maybe we should not have humored them in that wanting to stay in that kind of primitive lifestyle. Maybe we should have said, no, come join us; be citizens along with the rest of us. As I say, many have; many have been very successful.[3]

Not surprisingly, Reagan's tidy sweep was criticized at home by a small group of analysts who rejected his sanitized and condescending presentation of a violent history. His primary transgression, they noted, was to suggest that Indigenous people had been "humored" in being allowed to cling to "primitive" forms of life.[4] The literary scholar Kenneth Lincoln described the remarks as an "ethnocentric whitewash," reminding his readers that the Bureau of Indian Affairs (BIA) was not a government agency intended to "take care" of Indigenous people but one that emerged first as a branch of the U.S Department of War, that reservations were never intended to be oases for cultural survival and more often resembled "wasteland tokens for outright theft and betrayal," and that American citizenship, far from something that had been rebuffed by reservation residents pursuing an "early way of life," had only been extended to Indigenous Americans for about six decades.[5] The president's off-the-cuff history lesson was, in other words, steeped in revisionist fantasy.

Ronald Reagan speaks beneath a bust of Lenin at Moscow State University during a 1988 visit. Courtesy of the U.S. National Archives.

In spite of its glaring inaccuracies, Reagan's sketch should not be dismissed as the "avuncular musings" of an out-of-touch chauvinist nor misrepresented as the strategic posturing of a seasoned cold warrior.[6] Distilled to its elemental core, Reagan's interpretation recapitulates a narrative of American innocence that has had an enduring place in both pop cultural and academic interpretations of the history of the United States.[7]

While such presentations do not always disavow historical violence *tout court,* they routinely insist that the American experience of continental territorialization has been animated by a fundamentally *different* logic than the territorial conquests of European empires. The perseverance of this and other "legitimizing myths" hinges, in part, on the view that the United States was and is an anti-imperialist polity, that it is a political community forged through the crucible of a revolt *against* empire that has eschewed imperialist ambitions of its own.[8]

This nationalist apologetics has proved remarkably durable. Frederick Turner's late-nineteenth-century vision of the frontier of westward expansion as a place where post-European identities were constructed was steeped in this thinking, reimagining American expansionism as a mode of emancipation rather than conquest.[9] But this conceit did not vanish with the "closing" of the frontier, and American interpretations of inherent national "greatness"— apparently born of a "unique and somehow unrepeatable" revolution *against* empire—have "remained constant," dictating and obscuring the realities of historical and contemporary forms of American imperial practice, as Edward Said observes.[10] That Reagan's remarks elicited only a minor blowback, driven primarily by the leadership of Indigenous advocacy organizations, is a testament to the enduring potency of this exculpatory thinking.

The idea that the state of Minnesota was born of dispossession is hardly a matter of serious historical debate. This fact is supported by a rich evidentiary record, which is easily accessed by anybody who desires to examine it. Yet, while non-Indigenous observers sometimes acknowledge this troubling past, they rarely suggest that historical patterns of dispossession have anything to do with contemporary social arrangements.

This book challenges historical and contemporary mythologies of American innocence by tracking some of the ways that a colonial relationship grounded in a hierarchical politics of dispossession has endured as a dimension of social and political life. By drawing on a range of examples from Minneapolis—and especially the postwar dynamics of its Southside Phillips neighborhood—it demonstrates some of the ways that this politics has persisted.

To observe that the settler colonial relation continues is to observe that it must be actively confronted in the politics of the present.

Acknowledgments

Settler Colonial City began as a PhD dissertation in the Department of Geography at York University in Toronto. I am indebted to Patricia K. Wood, my academic mentor, for her intellectual guidance and support. Only now, after I have begun to supervise graduate students myself, can I appreciate her skill at assessing the differences between forests and trees. At York I also benefited from the intellectual guidance of Stefan Kipfer and William Jenkins (who were members of my committee), Valerie Preston, Phillip Kelly, Ranu Basu, and Nik Theodore (who were my teachers), and Peter Brogan (who was my office mate and inimitable fellow traveler). At the University of Minnesota, I owe thanks to Bruce Braun, who hosted me as a research visitor (during the 2011–12 academic year and again during the summer of 2013) and was a key figure in cultivating the dynamic intellectual atmosphere that prevailed in the Department of Geography at that time. I continue to benefit from the friendship of a brilliant group of people I met while I was spending time in Minnesota, including Melissa Olson, Sara Holiday Nelson, Randall Cohn, Bill Lindeke, Laura Cesafsky, Charmaine Chua, Jessi Lehman, Kai Bosworth, Paul Jackson, Joe Getzoff, Morgan Adamson, Peter Crandall, Julia Corwin, and Lalit Batra. Thanks also to my partner, Stacy Douglas, who uprooted her life to join me in the Twin Cities and wrote much of her own PhD dissertation on wobbly tables in South Minneapolis coffee shops. In recent years, I have had the opportunity to learn from a range of brilliant colleagues and collaborators. In particular, I thank Heather Dorries, Robert Henry, Tyler McCreary, and Julie Tomiak, who taught me so much during the course of the multiyear project that became *Settler City Limits*. Thanks also to Evelyn Peters, Libby Porter, Michael Simpson, and my colleagues at Carleton University in Ottawa, especially Natalie Pressburger, Scott Mitchell, Patrizia Gentile, Emilie Cameron, Jennifer Ridgely,

Jill Wigle, Pablo Mendez, Karen Hébert, Sheryl-Ann Simpson, Chris Webb, and the late Doug King.

While most of the material in *Settler Colonial City* is based on evidence gathered in archival collections, this book was also indelibly shaped by conversations I had with the people who agreed to meet with me during the research process. Only a handful of these interviews are cited in the text, but the insights of these interlocutors were a key source of context, inspiration, and provocation. This project would not have been possible without their wisdom and generosity.

I also owe a debt of gratitude to Kristian Tvedten, my editor at the University of Minnesota Press. His interventions have been very helpful. Thanks also to Brad Herried, David Thorstad, Rachel Moeller, Laura Westlund, Anne Wrenn, and Émélie Desrochers-Turgeon.

An earlier version of chapter 1 was previously published in 2016 as "Metropolitan Transformation and the Colonial Relation: The Making of an 'Indian Neighborhood' in Postwar Minneapolis" in a special issue of *Middle West Review*. Several of the theoretical points that I elaborate in the Introduction were considered in "What Is a Settler-Colonial City?" published in *Geography Compass* in 2017. My brief considerations of the life of Thomas Barlow Walker in the Introduction are extracted from a larger elaboration on that topic published as "Settler Colonial Urbanism" in an issue of *Settler Colonial Studies* in 2016. Several points developed in chapters 1 and 3 appeared initially in "Comparative Settler Colonial Urbanisms" in a chapter in the collection *Settler City Limits,* published by the University of Manitoba Press in 2019.

This research was made possible by support from the Department of Geography at York University, the Faculty of Arts and Social Sciences at Carleton University, the Social Sciences and Humanities Research Council of Canada, the Fulbright Foundation, and the Ontario Ministry of Training, Colleges, and Universities.

Notes

Preface

1. Gilmore, *Golden Gulag*, 247.
2. *New York Times*, "Virus Has Cost More Than 2.5 Million Years of Potential Life, Study Finds." By April 2021, researchers were estimating that more than 20 million years of life had been lost globally due to Covid-19. See Pifarré i Arolas et al., "Years of Life Lost to COVID-19 in 81 Countries."
3. Smith, "The Revolutionary Imperative," 51.
4. Buchanan, Bui, and Patel, "Black Lives Matter May Be the Largest Movement in U.S. History."
5. In late September 2020, the *New York Times* reported that many Minneapolis city council members were quietly retreating from their promise to defund the city's police department. At the time of writing, the situation remains fluid. See Herndon, "How a Pledge to Dismantle the Minneapolis Police Collapsed."
6. Derickson, "Let This Radicalize Us."

Introduction

1. Sawyer, "After Outcry and Protests, Walker Art Center Will Remove 'Scaffold' Sculpture."
2. For an in-depth treatment of the relationship between Thomas Barlow Walker's life and the settler colonization of Minnesota, see Hugill, "Settler Colonial Urbanism."
3. *Minnesota Journal*, "TB Walker Reputed to Be Richest Man in Minnesota."
4. Smith, *The New Urban Frontier*, xvi. See also Limerick, *The Legacy of Conquest*.
5. The phrase "organized forgetting" is borrowed from Blomley, "Law, Property, and the Geography of Violence," 128. On the "active 'forgetting' of historical geographies of urban areas as Indigenous," see also Tomiak, "Contesting the Settler City."
6. Peters, "'Urban' and 'Aboriginal': An Impossible Contradiction?"; Deloria, *Indians in Unexpected Places*; Thrush, *Native Seattle*, especially 8–11.

7. For more on the *back then, out there* framing, see Hugill, "Settler Colonial Urbanism," and Tomiak et al., "Introduction."
8. Coulthard, *Red Skin, White Masks,* 7.
9. Lipsitz, *How Racism Takes Place.*
10. See Hugill, "Settler Colonial Urbanism."
11. Schuyler, "Glimpses of Western Architecture."
12. For classic examples, see Carney, *Minnesota: The Star of the North;* Blegen, *Minnesota: A History of the State.*
13. See Cowen, "Following the Infrastructures of Empire," for a particularly illuminating discussion of this process as project of infrastructural investment.
14. Again, Ruth Wilson Gilmore's materialist definition of racism as the production of group-differentiated exposure to vulnerability and premature death is particularly apt here. See Gilmore, *Golden Gulag,* 28.
15. Piterberg, *The Returns of Zionism,* 57.
16. Césaire, *Discourse on Colonialism,* 39.
17. Coates, *Between the World and Me,* 151.
18. For foundational examples, see Banivanua-Mar and Edmonds, *Making Settler Colonial Space;* Bateman and Pilkington, *Studies in Settler Colonialism;* Brown, "The Logic of Settler Accumulation in a Landscape of Perpetual Vanishing"; Coulthard, *Red Skin, White Masks;* Edmonds, "Unpacking Settler Colonialism's Urban Strategies"; Elkins and Pedersen, *Settler Colonialism in the Twentieth Century;* Goldstein, "Where the Nation Takes Place"; Mackey, *Unsettled Expectations;* Stasiulis and Yuval-Davis, *Unsettling Settler Societies;* Veracini, "Introducing Settler Colonial Studies"; Veracini, *Settler Colonialism;* Veracini, *The Settler Colonial Present;* Veracini, "Settler Colonialism as a Distinct Mode of Domination"; Wolfe, *Settler Colonialism and the Transformation of Anthropology;* Wolfe, "Settler Colonialism and the Elimination of the Native."
19. Wolfe, "Settler Colonialism and the Elimination of the Native," 388.
20. Battell Lowman, Barker, and Rollo, "Settler Colonialism and the Consolidation of Canada in the Twentieth Century"; LaDuke and Cowen, "Beyond Windigo Infrastucture"; Mackey *Unsettled Expectations;* Veracini, "Settler Collective, Founding Violence and Disavowal"; Wolfe, "Settler Colonialism and the Elimination of the Native."
21. Wolfe, "Settler Colonialism and the Elimination of the Native," 387.
22. Edmonds, "Unpacking Settler Colonialism's Urban Strategies," 5.
23. Richardson, "Some Observations on 'Decolonizing' the University." See also Treuer, *The Heartbeat of Wounded Knee.*

24. Blatman-Thomas and Porter, "Placing Property"; Coulthard, *Red Skin, White Masks*; Daschuk, *Clearing the Plains*; Dempsey, Gould, and Sunberg, "Changing Land Tenure, Defining Subjects"; Gutiérrez Nájera and Maldonado, "Transnational Settler Colonial Formations and Global Capital"; Lawrence, *"Real" Indians and Others*; Milloy, *A National Crime*; Pasternak, "How Capitalism Will Save Colonialism"; Pasternak and Dafnos, "How Does a Settler State Secure the Circuitry of Capital?"; Povinelli, *The Cunning of Recognition*; Simpson, "Whither Settler Colonialism?"; Wolfe, "Settler Colonialism and the Elimination of the Native."
25. Simpson, *Mohawk Interruptus*, 7–8. See also Blomley, *Unsettling the City*, 109.
26. Porter and Yiftachel, "Urbanizing Settler-Colonial Studies," 3.
27. For a particularly persuasive example of settler colonialism's instability, see the first chapter ("Siege") of Nick Estes's *Our History Is the Future*.
28. Wingerd, *North Country*, xix.
29. Westerman and White, *Mni Sota Makoce*, 3. See also Waziyatawin, *What Does Justice Look Like?* 17–21.
30. Westerman and White, *Mni Sota Makoce*, 3.
31. Wingerd, *North Country*, xix.
32. It is beyond the scope of this Introduction to offer an in-depth accounting of what these patterns entailed, but that does not mean that they are not worth considering in their specificity. I share Mishuana Goeman's view that detailed materialist accounts are a key defense against the presumptions, oversimplifications, and romanticizations that so often animate narratives about Indigenous relationships to land. See Goeman, *Mark My Words*, 28. See also Grandinetti, "Urban Aloha 'Aina," 228.
33. Meyer, *The White Earth Tragedy*, 9.
34. Ibid., 17.
35. Waziyatawin, *What Does Justice Look Like?* 26.
36. Adelman and Aron, "From Borderlands to Borders," 816, 839.
37. Wingerd, *North Country*, xvi.
38. Waziyatawin, *What Does Justice Look Like?* 31.
39. Meyer, *History of the Santee Sioux*, 87.
40. Waziyatawin, *What Does Justice Look Like?* 50–61.
41. Ibid., 60–61.
42. Ibid., 38.
43. Meinig, *The Shaping of America*, 100.
44. See Hall, *American Empire and the Fourth World*, 427–69.
45. Hall, *Earth into Property*, 466.
46. Child, *Holding Our World Together*, 141.
47. LaGrand, *Indian Metropolis*, 47.

48. For a detailed and authoritative account of the termination and relocation initiatives, see Fixico, *Termination and Relocation*.

49. Hall, *American Empire and the Fourth World*, 467.

50. Carpio, *Indigenous Albuquerque*, 10.

51. Iverson, *We Are Still Here*, 123.

52. Child and White, "'I've Done My Share'"; Snipp, "American Indians and Alaska Natives in Urban Environments," 176.

53. Snipp, "American Indians and Alaska Natives," 177.

54. Child and White, "'I've Done My Share,'" 197.

55. Shoemaker, "Indians and Ethnic Choices."

56. *Minneapolis Tribune*, "The Plight of the Urban Indian."

57. Broker, *Night Flying Woman*, 1–7.

58. Rowan, "The Plight of the Upper Midwest Indian."

59. *Minneapolis Tribune*, "The Plight of the Urban Indian," 6.

60. Alfred and Corntassel, "Being Indigenous," 601.

61. See Nesterak, "The 'Wall of Forgotten Natives' Returns with Call for Greater Response to Homelessness."

62. Abu-Lughod, "Tale of Two Cities"; Alsayyad, *Forms of Dominance*; Home, *Of Planting and Planning*; Home, "Shaping Cities of the Global South"; King, *Colonial Urban Development*; Legg, *Spaces of Colonialism*; Ross and Telkamp, *Colonial Cities*; Simon, "Third World Colonial Cities in Context"; Driver and Gilbert, "Heart of Empire?"; Kipfer "Decolonization in the Heart of Empire."

63. Ross and Telkamp, *Colonial Cities*.

64. Abu-Lughod, "Tale of Two Cities"; Abu-Lughod, *Rabbat*; Fanon, *The Wretched of the Earth*; King, *Colonial Urban Development*.

65. Baloy, "Spectacles and Specters"; Barry and Agyeman, "On Belonging and Becoming in the Settler-Colonial City"; Blatman-Thomas, "Reciprocal Repossession"; Blatman-Thomas and Porter, "Placing Property"; Barraclough, "Wrangling Settler Colonialism in the Urban U.S. West"; Bledsoe, McCreary, and Wright, "Theorizing Diverse Economies in the Context of Racial Capitalism"; Brown, "Experiments in Regional Settler Colonization"; Cowen, "Following the Infrastructures of Empire"; Dorries, "Welcome to Winnipeg"; Dorries and Harjo, "Beyond Safety"; Dorries, Hugill, and Tomiak, "Racial Capitalism and the Production of Settler Colonial Cities"; Dorries et al., *Settler City Limits*; Estes, "Anti-Indian Common Sense"; Edmonds, "Unpacking Settler Colonialism's Urban Strategies"; Gilad, "Is Settler Colonial History Urban History?"; Grandinetti, "Urban Aloha 'Aina"; Grunow, "Cultivating Settler Colonial Space in Korea"; Hugill, "Comparative Settler Colonial Urbanisms"; Hugill, "Settler Colonial Urbanism"; Hugill, "Metropolitan Transformation and the Colonial Relation"; Hugill "What Is a Settler-Colonial City?"; Hugill and

Toews, "Born Again Urbanism"; Mays, "Pontiac's Ghost in the Motor City"; McClintock, "Urban Agriculture, Racial Capitalism, and Resistance in the Settler-Colonial City"; Milner, "Devaluation, Erasure, and Replacement"; Miller, "Temporal Analysis of Displacement"; Monteith, "Markets and Monarchs"; Nagam, "Digging Up Indigenous History in Toronto's Cityscape"; Noterman, "Taking Back Vacant Property"; Kipfer, "Pushing the Limits of Urban Research"; Porter, Jackson, and Johnson, "Remaking Imperial Power in the City"; Porter and Yiftachel, "Urbanizing Settler Colonial Studies"; Ramirez, "Take the Houses Back/Take the Land"; Rhook, "What's in a Grid?"; Simpson and Bagelman, "Decolonizing Urban Political Ecologies"; Simpson, "Fossil Urbanism"; Tedesco and Bagelman, "The 'Missing' Politics of Whiteness and Rightful Presence in the Settler Colonial City"; Thornton, "Settling Sapporo"; Todd, "Decolonizing Prairie Public Art"; Toews, *Stolen City*; Tomiak, "Unsettling Ottawa"; Tomiak, "Contesting the Settler City"; Tomiak, "Contested Entitlement"; Tomiak et al., "Introduction"; Veracini, "Suburbia, Settler Colonialism, and the World Turned Inside Out."

66. Belich, *Replenishing the Earth*.
67. Tuck and Yang, "Decolonization Is Not a Metaphor," 5.
68. For interesting reflections on the limits of drawing sharp lines of distinction between colonial projects that are characterized by either exploitation or dispossession, see Kelly, "The Rest of Us"; Englert, "Settlers, Workers, and the Logic of Accumulation by Dispossession."
69. Deloria, *Indians in Unexpected Places*; Peters, "Three Myths about Aboriginals in Cities"; Peters and Andersen, *Indigenous in the City*; Suarez, "Indigenizing Minneapolis"; Thrush, *Native Seattle*; Toews, *Stolen City*; Wilson and Peters, "'You Can Make a Place for It.'"
70. Wolfe, "Settler Colonialism and the Elimination of the Native."
71. Barker, "The Contemporary Reality of Canadian Imperialism"; Byrd, *The Transit of Empire*; Estes, *Our History Is the Future*; Mawani, "Law, Settler Colonialism, and 'the Forgotten Space' of Maritime Worlds"; Perry, *On the Edge of Empire*; Tuck and Yang, "Decolonization Is Not a Metaphor"; Walcott, "The Problem of the Human."
72. Weber, "Gentiles Preferred."
73. Tomiak et al., "Introduction."
74. For an exceptionally compelling example of this kind of analysis, see Perry, *Aqueduct*.
75. Cronon, *Nature's Metropolis*, 264.
76. Ibid.

77. Greer, "Commons and Enclosure in the Colonization of North America," 372. Greer uses the metaphor of a "quilt of native commons" to suggest that a diverse range of territorial arrangements existed in the "real" America "where Europeans came to establish their colonies." By stressing that the continent contained a diverse range of human societies, each governed by its own set of "land-use" rules, he challenges the Lockean view of America as a "universal commons completely open to all."

78. Western, "Undoing the Colonial City?"

79. Veracini, *The Settler Colonial Present*, 1.

80. Toews, *Stolen City*, 19.

81. Wolfe, "Settler Colonialism and the Elimination of the Native," 406.

82. These adjustments and transformations are not always "spectacular." For an instructive example of how settler colonial inequity persists in commonplace ("even banal") practices in contemporary Minnesota, see Smiles, "'. . . to the Grave.'"

83. Berg, "Banal Naming, Neoliberalism, and Landscapes of Dispossession," 13.

84. See Waziyatawin, *What Does Justice Look Like?*; Suarez, "Indigenizing Minneapolis."

85. Tomiak et al., "Introduction," 6. See also Blomely, *Unsettling the City*; Child, *Holding Our World Together*; Dorries, "Welcome to Winnipeg'"; Estes, "Anti-Indian Common Sense"; Henry, "'I Claim in the Name of . . .'"; Lobo, "Urban Clan Mothers"; Peters, Stock, and Werner, *Rooster Town*; Peters and Andersen, *Indigenous in the City*; Ramirez, *Native Hubs*; Smith, "Talisi through the Lens"; Suarez, "Indigenizing Minneapolis"; Toews, *Stolen City*; Tomiak, "Contested Entitlement."

86. Child, *Holding Our World Together*; Suarez, "Indigenizing Minneapolis."

87. See Burley, "Rooster Town"; Keeler, "Indigenous Suburbs"; Peters, Stock, and Werner, *Rooster Town*; Toews, *Stolen City*.

88. Keeler, "Indigenous Suburbs," 27–73.

89. See, for example, Perry, *Aqueduct*; Wood, "The 'Sarcee War'"; Stanger-Ross, "Municipal Colonialism in Vancouver."

90. See Coulthard, *Red Skin, White Masks*; Denoon, "Understanding Settler Societies"; Wolfe, *Settler Colonialism and the Transformation of Anthropology*; Wolfe, "Settler Colonialism and the Elimination the Native"; Veracini, *Settler Colonialism*; Veracini, *The Settler Colonial Present*.

91. For empirical examples, see Carter, *Lost Harvests*; Harris, *Making Native Space*.

92. Porter and Yiftachel, "Urbanizing Settler-Colonial Studies," 177.

93. Coulthard, *Red Skin, White Masks*, 125.
94. Blatman-Thomas and Porter, "Placing Property," 33.
95. Meriam, *The Problem with Indian Administration*.
96. Keeler, "Indigenous Suburbs."
97. For a comparative study of this process in the region, see Dorries et al., *Settler City Limits*.
98. Piterberg, *The Returns of Zionism*, 55. See also Piterberg, "Settlers and Their States."
99. Alfred and Corntassel, "Being Indigenous," 601.
100. Rowse, "The Reforming State, the Concerned Public, and Indigenous Political Actors," 66.
101. Ibid., 69.
102. Tuck, "Suspending Damage," 412.
103. Macoun and Strakosch, "The Ethical Demands of Settler Colonial Theory," 435.
104. Snelgrove, Dhamoon, and Corntassel, "Unsettling Settler Colonialism," 9. See also Bhandar and Ziadah, "Acts and Omissions."
105. See, for example, Alfred and Corntassel, "Being Indigenous"; Borrows, *Recovering Canada*; Corntassel, "Re-Envisioning Resurgence"; Coulthard, *Red Skins, White Masks*; Gaudry, "Researching the Resurgence"; The Kino-nda-niimi Collective, *The Winter We Danced*; Simpson, *Mohawk Interruptus*; Simpson, *Dancing on Our Turtle's Back*; Simpson, "Indigenous Resurgence and Co-Resistance"; Simpson, *As We Have Always Done*; Simpson, *Lighting the Eighth Fire*; Tomiak et al., "Introduction," 8.
106. Daigle and Ramírez, "Decolonial Geographies," 80.
107. For more on these discussions, see Bledsoe, McCreary, and Wright, "Theorizing Diverse Economies in the Context of Racial Capitalism"; Bonds and Inwood, "Beyond White Privilege"; Day, *Alien Capital*; Dorries, Hugill, and Tomiak, "Racial Capitalism and the Production of Settler Colonial Cities"; McClintock, "Urban Agriculture, Racial Capitalism, and Resistance in the Settler Colonial City"; Simpson, Walcott, and Coulthard, "Idle No More and Black Lives Matter"; Toews, *Stolen City*; Walcott, "The Problem of the Human"; Wang, *Carceral Capitalism* (especially chapter 1); Yusoff, *A Billion Black Anthropocenes or None*.
108. Daigle and Ramírez, "Decolonial Geographies," 80.
109. Veracini, *Settler Colonialism*, 12.
110. It is worth pointing out that research on the politics of settler colonization has often extended beyond the now-familiar examples of Canada, the United States, and Australia. On the failure of settler colonial theory to grapple with key examples of settler colonization in the African context (especially in South Africa, Southern Rhodesia [now Zimbabwe], Kenya, and Algeria), see

Kelly, "The Rest of Us," 269. For examples of the deployment of the settler colonial framework in Palestine/Israel, see Barakat, "Writing/Righting Palestine Studies"; Blatman-Thomas, "Commuting for Rights"; Getzoff, "Zionist Frontiers"; Lloyd, "Settler Colonialism and the State of Exception"; Morgensen, "Queer Settler Colonialism in Canada and Israel"; Pappé, "Shetl Colonialism"; Piterberg, *The Returns of Zionism*; Rouhana and Sabbagh-Khoury, "Settler-Colonial Citizenship"; Salaita, *Inter/ Nationalism*; Salmanca et al., "Past Is Present"; Shihade, "Settler Colonialism and Conflict"; Veracini, "The Other Shift"; Veracini, "What Can Settler Colonial Studies Offer to an Interpretation of the Conflict in Israel–Palestine?" For efforts to think through the complexities of applying the settler colonial framework to Latin American contexts, see Castellanos, "Introduction"; Goebel, "Settler Colonialism in Postcolonial Latin America"; Gott, "Latin America as White Settler Society"; Gutiérrez Nájera and Maldonado, "Transnational Settler Colonial Formations and Global Capital"; Speed, "Structures of Settler Capitalism in Abya Yala."

111. Mawani, "Law, Settler Colonialism, and the 'Forgotten Space' of Maritime Worlds."
112. Day, *Alien Capital,* 18–25.
113. Ibid., 17.
114. Tomiak et al., "Introduction," 2–4.
115. Ibid., 2.
116. See Barnd, *Native Space*; Barraclough, "Wrangling Settler Colonialism in the Urban U.S. West"; Tomiak, "Contesting the Settler City"; Tomiak, "Contested Entitlement."
117. Tomiak et al., "Introduction," 2; see also Tomiak, "Contesting the Settler City," 928.

1. Urban Change and the Settler Colonial Relation
1. Rowan, "The Plight of the Upper Midwest Indian."
2. Teaford, *The Metropolitan Revolution.*
3. Panitch and Gindin, *The Making of Global Capitalism,* 81.
4. Delton, *Making Minnesota Liberal,* 24.
5. Panitch and Gindin, *The Making of Global Capitalism,* 82.
6. Ibid., 83.
7. Saunders, "Surburbia Booms as 'Blue Collar' Workers Arrive."
8. McNeil and Engelke, *The Great Acceleration,* 66.
9. Katz, *Why Don't American Cities Burn?* 30.
10. Adams and VanDrasek, *Minneapolis–St. Paul,* 90.
11. Martin and Goddard, *Past Choices/Present Landscapes,* 5.
12. Reichard, "Mayor Hubert H. Humphrey," 59.
13. Martin and Goddard, *Past Choices/Present Landscapes,* 13.

14. Ibid., 5.
15. Freund, *Colored Property*; Hirsch, *Making the Second Ghetto*; Katznelson, *When Affirmative Action Was White*; Jackson, *Crabgrass Frontier*.
16. See mappingprejudice.org.
17. Lipsitz, *How Racism Takes Place*, 27. Lipsitz also points out that those who benefited most directly from such arrangements have often been the quickest to point to chronically underfunded inner-city public-housing projects as proof that government support for housing cannot work.
18. Mohl, "Planned Destruction," 287.
19. Adams and VanDrasek, *Minneapolis–St. Paul*, 94.
20. First National Bank of Minneapolis, *Implosion in Minneapolis*, 15.
21. Rupar, "'Racist' Twin Cities Maps Make Point about Interstate Highways."
22. Marks, "I-35W Disrupted Minority Community, Boxed-In Phillips."
23. Ibid.
24. Ibid.
25. Model City Policy and Planning Committee, *Problem Analysis*.
26. Katz, *Why Don't American Cities Burn?* 38.
27. Millet, "Ghost of the Gateway," 114.
28. Hirschoff and Hart, *Down and Out*, 10.
29. Ibid., 23.
30. Lightfoot, *Down on Skid Row*.
31. Dahl, "Does Franklin Avenue Have a Future?" 8; Martin and Goddard, *Past Choices/Present Landscapes*, 66–67.
32. Lightfoot, *Down on Skid Row*.
33. Hirschoff and Hart, *Down and Out*, 51.
34. Katz, *Why Don't American Cities Burn?* 38.
35. Katz, *The Undeserving Poor*, 162.
36. City of Minneapolis, "Neighborhood Profiles."
37. Phillips Neighborhood Improvement Association, *Phillips Comprehensive Neighborhood Plan*.
38. The term "organized abandonment" is borrowed from Ruth Wilson Gilmore. See Kumanyika, "Ruth Wilson Gilmore Makes the Case for Abolition."
39. Sugrue, *The Origins of the Urban Crisis*, 4.
40. Todd, "A Better Day in the Neighborhood."
41. Adams, VanDrasek, and Lambert, *The Path of Urban Decline*, 37.
42. Todd, "A Better Day in the Neighborhood."
43. Model City Policy and Planning Committee, *Problem Analysis*.
44. City of Minneapolis, "City of Minneapolis Neighborhoods."
45. Compton, "1990 Census."

46. Goetz, Chapple, and Lukermann, "The Rise and Fall of Fair Share Housing," 253.
47. Model City Policy and Planning Committee, *Problem Analysis*, 6.
48. Fixico, *The Urban Indian Experience in America*, 9.
49. See Drinnon, *Keeper of Concentration Camps*.
50. Iverson, *We Are Still Here*, 132.
51. Fixico, *The Urban Indian Experience in America*, 4.
52. Davis, *Survival Schools*, 23.
53. Neils, *Reservation to City*, 32.
54. It is also worth noting that reservation affiliation was not the only thing that brought people together in the city. Urban Indigenous people sometimes knew each other as a result of their experiences in regional institutions that had an impact on the lives of certain generations of Indigenous people—Indian boarding schools, for example. Dennis Banks, who grew up on the Leech Lake Reservation in northern Minnesota, recalled feeling at home in Minneapolis because many of his friends from the Pipestone Boarding School were there (Banks, in discussion with the author, Federal Dam, Minnesota, July 15, 2012).
55. Davis, *Survival Schools*, 26.
56. Ibid. The emergence of an Indigenous neighborhood on the Southside of Minneapolis poses an important challenge to Susan Lobo's suggestion that residential concentration has not been a dominant feature of urban Indigenous life in the United States (Lobo, "Urban Clan Mothers," 505–6). Her research suggests that Indigenous people who moved to American cities have rarely clustered in "ethnically homogenous geographic locations, unless they are historically established villages or communities that have been engulfed by the expanding metropolis." For this reason, "Indian urban communities differ substantially from more visible ethnic-based neighborhoods," she contends. In her estimation, then, the urban Indigenous experience has often been one of dispersal. Accordingly, urban Indigenous forms of togetherness tend to defy commonsense conceptualizations of community as geographically concentrated. Indeed, she contends that urban Indigenous geographies are perhaps better understood as a network of relationships spread widely over the space of the city. The evidence from Minneapolis suggests that we should be cautious about assuming the universal applicability of Lobo's assertion, however.
57. See Vizenor *Interior Landscapes*, 185–98.
58. See Suarez, "Indigenizing Minneapolis."
59. Committee on Urban Indians, *Public Forum before the Committee on Urban Indians in Minneapolis–St. Paul*, 68.

60. Ibid., 146.
61. League of Women Voters of Minnesota, *Indians in Minnesota*, 2d ed., 108.
62. CWC Indian Committee, *The Minneapolis Indian in Minnesota*, quoted in League of Women Voters of Minneapolis, *Indians in Minneapolis*, 55.
63. League of Women Voters of Minneapolis, *Indians in Minneapolis*, 55.
64. League of Women Voters of Minnesota, *Indians in Minnesota*, 2d ed., 109.
65. Ibid.
66. Phillips Neighborhood Improvement Association, *Phillips Comprehensive Neighborhood Plan*.
67. Minneapolis Department of Civil Rights complaint files are available only from the period 1968 to 1977.
68. Minneapolis was not the only city where Indigenous renters encountered this tactic; see Hugill, "Comparative Settler Colonial Urbanisms."
69. Minneapolis Department of Civil Rights, Case File 68-*.
70. Ibid.
71. Minneapolis Department of Civil Rights, Case File 69–17.
72. Minneapolis Department of Civil Rights, Case File 72–93.
73. Lipsitz, *How Racism Takes Place*, 2.
74. Vizenor, "Indian's Lot," B1.
75. R. M. Johnson, letter to Gerald Vizenor (Gerald Vizenor Papers).
76. Ibid.
77. Disgusted Taxpayer, letter to Gerald Vizenor (Gerald Vizenor Papers).
78. Nelson, "Racist Remarks Not a Right, Court Rules," B1.
79. Ibid.
80. League of Women Voters of Minneapolis, *Indians in Minneapolis*, 36.
81. Lipsitz, *How Racism Takes Place*, 3.
82. See Drinnon, *Facing West*; King, *The Inconvenient Indian*; Chavers, *Racism in Indian Country*.
83. I am using the expression "in place" in Tim Cresswell's sense (Cresswell, *In Place/Out of Place*).
84. Lipsitz, *How Racism Takes Place*, 36.
85. Schulman, *The Gentrification of the Mind*, 27.
86. On the new geography of American poverty, see *The Economist*, "American Poverty Is Moving from the Cities to the Suburbs"; Kneebone, "The Changing Geography of US Poverty"; Misra, "Confronting the Myths of Suburban Poverty."
87. See Hunt's comments in Holmes, Hunt, and Piedalue, "Violence, Colonialism, and Space," 550.
88. Peters, "Aboriginal Public Policy in Urban Areas," 11.

89. Suarez, "Indigenizing Minneapolis" (pagination forthcoming).
90. Tomiak et al., "Introduction," 3.
91. Ibid.
92. Kipfer, "Pushing the Limits of Urban Research," 2.

2. Liberal Antiracism as Political Dead End

1. *Minneapolis Tribune,* "Plight of the Urban Indian."
2. Harrington, *The Other America,* 1–2.
3. Harrington did not consider Indigenous poverty in the first edition of *The Other America.* He apologized for that omission in 1971. See Usner, *Indian Work,* 77.
4. Ebbott and White Bear Lake League of Women Voters, Letter to Local Chapters of the League of Women Voters of Minnesota (Elizabeth Ebbott Research Files).
5. See Ebbott's annotated copy of Rowan's "The Plight of the Upper Midwest Indian" (Elizabeth Ebbott Research Files).
6. Young, *In the Public Interest,* 4.
7. League of Women Voters, "Why Join the League of Women Voters?" 38.
8. League of Women Voters, "The League's Legislative Program," 47.
9. Young, *In the Public Interest,* 4.
10. Ebbott and White Bear Lake League of Women Voters, Letter to Local Chapters of the League of Women Voters of Minnesota (Elizabeth Ebbott Research Files).
11. For example, the powerful federal judge (and former congressman) Edward J. Devitt wrote to Ebbott while he was in the midst of preparing landmark rulings that would affirm the rights of Ojibwe people to hunt, fish, and harvest rice without the interference of the state. "I have paged through it," Devitt wrote in a letter of thanks. "It looks like a splendid work and should be particularly helpful to me in obtaining background knowledge about legal and factual issues involved in my Indian fishing and ricing cases." Ebbott also received letters of congratulations from significant figures in "Indian" administration, including the acting deputy commissioner of the federal Department of the Interior and other high-ranking government officials. Her correspondence also suggests a working relationship with Senator Walter Mondale, who wrote to Ebbott after hearing that a second edition would be published and noted that the earlier edition had impressed his colleagues on the Special Subcommittee on Indian Education in Washington and that he had had it reprinted in the formal hearing records.
12. Janski, "Letter to the Editor."
13. Banks, Letter to Janski (Elizabeth Ebbott Research Files).

14. Gloria Phillips, "Indians at Convention" (Elizabeth Ebbott Research Files).

15. Robert Bonine, Letter to Elizabeth Ebbott (Elizabeth Ebbott Research Files).

16. League of Women Voters of Minnesota, *Indians in Minnesota*, 1st ed., 33, 37, 45, 49.

17. League of Women Voters of Minneapolis, Indians in Minneapolis, 1.

18. Kotke, "U Program for People Minds Their Business"; Katznelson, "Was the Great Society a Lost Opportunity?" 196.

19. Training Center for Community Programs, "Untitled Grant Report" (TCCP Program Files).

20. Ibid.

21. Katznelson, "Was the Great Society a Lost Opportunity?" 202.

22. Training Center for Community Programs, "New Grant to U of M Continues Training Center for Community Programs" (TCCP Program Files).

23. It is not clear whether *Modern Minnesota Ojibwa* was ever published.

24. Training Center for Community Programs, "Harkins Directs Training Center for Community Programs" (TCCP Program Files).

25. Kotke, "U Program for People Minds Their Business."

26. See, for example, Gibbons et al., *Indian Americans in Southside Minneapolis*; Harkins and Woods, *Attitudes of Minneapolis Agency Personnel toward Urban Indians*; Harkins and Woods, *The Social Programs and Political Styles of Minneapolis Indians*; Skovbroten and Wolens, *Indians in the Urban Slum*; Woods and Harkins, *Indian Employment in Minneapolis*; Woods and Harkins, *A Review of Recent Research on Minneapolis Indians*.

27. On these assumptions, see Gray, *Liberalism*; Goldberg, *Racist Culture*; Hedges, *Death of the Liberal Class*.

28. Goldberg, *Racist Culture*, 5.

29. Ibid.

30. Ibid.

31. Gray, *Liberalism*, xii.

32. Goldberg, *Racist Culture*, 5.

33. Isserman and Kazin, *America Divided*, 48.

34. Fraser and Gerstle, *The Rise and Fall of the New Deal Order.* See also Katz, *The Undeserving Poor*, 113–19.

35. Hedges, *Death of the Liberal Class*, 11; emphasis added.

36. Williams, *Keywords*, 181.

37. Hartz, *The Liberal Tradition in America*, 259.

38. Goldberg, *Racist Culture*, 8.

39. Ebbott and White Bear Lake League of Women Voters, Letter to

Local Chapters of the League of Women Voters of Minnesota (Elizabeth Ebbott Research Files).

40. Delton, *Making Minnesota Liberal,* 22.
41. Ibid., xvi; Valelly, *Radicalism in the States.*
42. Delton, *Making Minnesota Liberal,* 23–25.
43. Eagleton, "Why Ideas No Longer Matter."
44. Delton, *Making Minnesota Liberal,* 21.
45. Johnson, "Special Message to the Congress Proposing a Nationwide War on the Sources of Poverty."
46. Isserman, "Michael Harrington."
47. Training Center for Community Programs, "Untitled Grant Report" (TCCP Program Files).
48. Isserman, "Michael Harrington."
49. Training Center for Community Programs, "Untitled Grant Report" (TCCP Program Files).
50. League of Women Voters of Minneapolis, *Indians in Minneapolis,* 108.
51. Training Center for Community Programs, "Untitled Grant Report" (TCCP Program Files).
52. Ibid.
53. Ebbott and White Bear Lake League of Women Voters, Letter to Local Chapters of the League of Women Voters of Minnesota (Elizabeth Ebbott Research Files).
54. Danforth, "The Division of Indian Work," 2.
55. Kitagawa, "Racial and Cultural Relations in the Ministry to the American Indians," 2.
56. Cross, "Indian Church Is on Road to Integration."
57. Brunette, "The Minneapolis Urban Indian Community," 10.
58. Newlund, "Indian 'Red Power' Now Emerging."
59. Ibid.
60. Jessop, *State Power,* 123.
61. Ibid., 125.
62. Lipsitz, *How Racism Takes Place,* 36.
63. Coulthard, *Red Skin, White Masks,* 35. Of course, their efforts should not be dismissed *tout court.* Certainly, the social-democratic policies that both groups supported, if fully implemented, would have gone a considerable way toward alleviating some of the immediate material suffering that was shouldered by Indigenous people. Daniel Cobb has shown, for example, that a number of Great Society initiatives, particularly the Community Action Programs, had significant impacts in a range of Indigenous communities (see Cobb, "Philosophy of an Indian War"). Importantly, this flawed approach and circumscribed ambition tell us something about the failures of state-centric postwar liberalism more generally. Because liberal reformers

did not substantially challenge the fundamental bases of poverty and deprivation, they failed to achieve their already muted ambitions. "Neither the War on Poverty nor Great Society slowed or reversed the impact of urban redevelopment and racial segregation on the nation's cities," observes Michael Katz (*The Undeserving Poor,* 163). The cumulative effect of this failure was that many of the social achievements of the postwar era proved vulnerable to retrenchment in the significantly more conservative political climate of the 1970s and 1980s. Importantly, too, the failures of 1960s liberalism came to serve as an important symbol for the forces of the new right. By the early 1980s, neoconservatives were increasingly citing problems with 1960s antipoverty efforts as incontrovertible proof that redistributive forms of statecraft were doomed to failure, trapping the impoverished in cycles of dependency rather than providing them with opportunities to secure their own well-being. In this context, it was possible for the leading figure of American neoliberalism, Ronald Reagan, to declare that postwar efforts to defeat the "sources of poverty" had been an abject failure in practice. "I guess you could say, poverty won the war," he gloated in a 1986 radio address (Reagan, "Radio Address to the Nation on Welfare Reform").

64. Ebbott, for example, was fond of repeating the mantra that those interested in helping Indigenous people ought to remember "two basic facts": first that "Indians want to be Indians," and second that "Indians want to control their own lives." (See Elizabeth Ebbott Research Files.)

65. League of Women Voters of Minneapolis, *Indians in Minneapolis,* 108.

66. Goldberg, *Racist Culture,* 5.

67. Bruyneel, "The American Liberal Colonial Tradition," 316.

68. Ebbott, "The Indian Problem" (Elizabeth Ebbott Research Files).

69. Ebbott and White Bear Lake League of Women Voters, Letter to Local Chapters of the League of Women Voters of Minnesota (Elizabeth Ebbott Research Files).

70. Mackey, "The Apologizer's Apology."

71. It is worth noting that while Indigenous activists have routinely made similar demands—insisting that Indigenous people be adequately housed, be able to access state benefits, not have to fear police violence, for example—they have often done so in ways that insisted on the ongoing nature of colonial violence.

72. Simpson, "The Ruse of Consent and the Anatomy of 'Refusal,'" 22.

73. Piterberg, *The Returns of Zionism,* 56–57.

74. Ibid., 57; emphasis in the original.

3. Cops and Counterpatrols

1. Human Rights Watch, *Shielded from Justice.*
2. Ibid. See also Specktor, "City and County Decline to Charge Police in Squad Car Trunk Incident."
3. Specktor, "City and County Decline to Charge Police in Squad Car Trunk Incident."
4. Furst, "2 Officers Suspended after Putting Indians in the Trunk."
5. See, for example, National Council on Indian Opportunity, *Public Forum before the Committee on Urban Indians*; League of Women Voters of Minnesota, *Indians in Minnesota,* 2d ed.; Cohen, "The Indian Patrol in Minneapolis" (dissertation); Westermeyer, "Indian Powerlessness in Minnesota"; Minnesota Human Rights Commission, *Police Brutality, Minneapolis Public Hearing #2*; Robertson, "Man Beaten by Police"; Parker, "What Happened to Les Robinson?"; Indergaard, "Urban Renewal and the American Indian Movement in Minneapolis"; Diaz, "200 March to Protest Crime against Indians"; Akard, "Wocante Tinza"; Tai and Jeter, "Minorities"; Brunette, "The Minneapolis Urban Indian Community"; Couture, "The American Indian Movement"; Banks and Erdoes, *Ojibwa Warrior*; Bellecourt and Lurie, *The Thunder before the Storm*; Birong, "The Influence of Police Brutality on the American Indian Movement's Establishment in Minneapolis"; D'Arcus, "The Urban Geography of Red Power"; Davis, *Survival Schools*; Bancroft and Waterman Wittstock, *We Are Still Here.*
6. Comack, *Racialized Policing,* 15.
7. Ibid.; Comack, "Policing Racialized Spaces"; Comack et al., *Indians Wear Red.*
8. Comack, *Racialized Policing,* 17–18.
9. Holmes and Smith, *Race and Police Brutality,* 8.
10. See especially Minneapolis Department of Civil Rights, Case Files, 1967–77; Minnesota Human Rights Commission, *Police Brutality, Minneapolis Public Hearing #2.*
11. The evidence suggests that the MPD aggressively targeted the customers of a shifting range of East Franklin Avenue establishments, including Bud's Bar, the Coral, the Bear's Den, the Brite Spot, the Anchor, and Mr. Arthur's.
12. Minnesota Human Rights Commission, *Police Brutality, Minneapolis Public Hearing #2,* 15.
13. Banks and Erdoes, *Ojibwa Warrior,* 59.
14. Cohen, "The Indian Patrol in Minneapolis" (dissertation), 62–66.
15. League of Women Voters of Minneapolis, *Indians in Minneapolis,* 51.
16. League of Women Voters of Minnesota, *Indians in Minnesota,* 2d ed., 139.

17. Indergaard, "Urban Renewal and the American Indian Movement," 44–45.
18. Perry, *Policing Race and Place in Indian Country,* 23.
19. League of Women Voters of Minneapolis, *The Police and the Community.*
20. United States Commission on Civil Rights, *Bridging the Gap,* quoted in Davis, *Survival Schools,* 27.
21. See, for example, League of Women Voters of Minneapolis, *Indians in Minneapolis*; Woods, *Rural and City Indians in Minnesota Prisons.* More recent analysis suggests that Minnesota's Indigenous population remains decidedly overrepresented among the incarcerated; see Ahtone, "A Cross to Bear"; Ahtone, "Native American Gangs Series"; Wagner, *Native Americans Are Overrepresented in Minnesota's Prisons and Jails.*
22. League of Women Voters of Minnesota, *Indians in Minnesota,* 3d ed., 146.
23. Benjamin and Kim, *American Indians and the Criminal Justice System in Minnesota.*
24. Indergaard, "Urban Renewal and the American Indian Movement," 45.
25. Ebbott, Rosenblatt, and the League of Women Voters of Minnesota, *Indians in Minnesota,* 4th ed.
26. Guerry, "Minnesota Prisons Begin Tracking Tribal Affiliations of Native American Inmates."
27. The phrase "machinery of enforcement" is borrowed from Schulman, *Gentrification of the Mind,* 27.
28. Hovik, "Urban Indians Must Conquer Problems of 'Alien' Culture."
29. See Peters, "'Urban' and 'Aboriginal'"; Hugill "Comparative Settler Colonialisms."
30. Community Welfare Council Indian Committee, *The Minnesota Indian in Minneapolis.*
31. Governor's Human Rights Commission, *Minnesota's Indian Citizens,* 42–43.
32. Woods, *Rural and City Indians in Minnesota Prisons,* 1.
33. League of Women Voters of Minneapolis, *Indians in Minneapolis,* 49.
34. Community Welfare Council Indian Committee, *The Minnesota Indian in Minneapolis,* 4.
35. Meeting Minutes, League of Women Voters of Minnesota Pre-Legislative Conference (Elizabeth Ebbott Research Files).
36. Drilling, *Problems with Alcohol among Urban Indians in Minneapolis.*
37. Harding, "The Media, Aboriginal People, and Common Sense"; McCue, "What It Takes for Aboriginal People to Make the News."
38. Westermeyer, "'The Drunken Indian,'" 29.

39. Vizenor, *Manifest Manners,* 30–31. See also Fixico, *The Urban Indian Experience,* 86–106.
40. Vizenor, *Manifest Manners,* 29.
41. *The Alley,* "Police/Community Relations."
42. Hall and O'Shea, "Common-Sense Neoliberalism," 8.
43. Estes, "Anti-Indian Common Sense," 49.
44. Rifkin, *Settler Common Sense,* xv.
45. Ibid., xvi.
46. Fanon, *Black Skin, White Masks,* 91.
47. Neugebauer, "First Nations People and Law Enforcement," quoted in Perry, *Policing Race and Place,* 49.
48. *The Alley,* "Police/Community Relations," 8.
49. Ibid.
50. Ibid.
51. Wacquant, "Three Pernicious Premises in the Study of the American Ghetto," 344.
52. For thorough consideration of Indigenous organizing in the years before 1965, see Child, *Holding Our World Together*; Shoemaker, "Urban Indians and Ethnic Choices"; Suarez, "Indigenizing Minneapolis."
53. Davis, *Survival Schools,* 30.
54. Importantly, too, AIM's work was shaped by a much broader group of people than most histories generally acknowledge. Brenda Child argues, for example, that a disproportionate focus on AIM's male leaders has obscured the critical organizing role played by women (Child, *Holding Our World Together,* 139–60). In this vein, see also Davis, *Survival Schools,* and Estes, *Our History Is the Future,* 180–81.
55. Mitchell, "Aldermanic Campaign Speech, Ward 6" (Gerald Vizenor Papers).
56. Ibid.
57. Needham, "Police Brutality, an American Indian Problem."
58. Shellum, "Lawyer Hall Urges Indians to Be Politically Active."
59. Ibid.
60. Banks and Erdoes, *Ojibwa Warrior,* 61.
61. Ibid., 62.
62. Ibid.
63. Bancroft and Waterman Wittstock, *We Are Still Here,* 4. This interpretation is not shared universally among members of the Minneapolis Indigenous community. Vizenor, for example, is particularly critical of AIM's early work: "The serious issue was police harassment, but the method of trailing police cars in expensive convertibles became an extravagant satire. The rhetoric was colonial oppression, the press coverage was excellent then,

and thousands of dollars of guilt money rolled in from church groups . . ." (Vizenor, "Dennis of Wounded Knee," 55).

64. Anderson, "Indian Patrol's First Night Quiet"; Banks and Erdoes, *Ojibwa Warrior*, 63.

65. Banks, Bellecourt, and Mitchell had all experienced the unevenness of the criminal justice system firsthand. In Banks's telling, his politicization and subsequent desire to build some form of organization came from his experience in Stillwater prison, where he served time for burglary between 1966 and 1968. It was here that Banks first began to develop an analysis of systemic racism, initially through a friendship that he developed with another inmate, Tom Jones. Through the course of their conversations, Jones had encouraged Banks to pay close attention to the disproportionate number of Indigenous inmates serving time for petty crimes. As Banks remembers: "[Tom asked me], 'How many people are here on capital crimes?' I said, 'Probably about three.' I was working in the athletic department [and] I had a clipboard to go around . . . [and] I'd go around asking people whether they wanted to sign up for basketball, baseball. But I was looking more for Native people and so I went through A block, B block, C block . . . A, B, C, D, E. . . . and so I knew all the Indians in there. And eventually I knew what they were in there for. We'd talk. Three people were in there for capital crimes. But the rest of them—the rest of us—they we're in there for burglary, there was ten guys, they were up there for pickpocketing, cashing bad checks . . . So, when Tom [started] asking me . . . how many people were there for capital crimes, I said, 'Well, I know, Tom.' He said, 'Well, let's think about it.' And so all the real petty crimes was about that [gesturing large] and the felony crimes were like that [gesturing small]. The prison population was a thousand people. The number of Native people was [maybe] 520, 525 . . . We were like not even 1 percent [of the broader population] and yet here we make up 50 percent of the prison population. And he was saying, 'Do the math, Dennis, do the math'" (Banks, in discussion with the author, Federal Dam, Minnesota, July 15, 2012). For Banks, these realizations, coupled with a growing awareness of the upheaval occurring outside of the prison, first fomented his political ambitions. "I would read the papers and see that demonstrations about civil rights and the Vietnam war were going on all over the country. I realized I desperately wanted to be part of a movement for Indian people," he recalls (Banks and Erodes, *Ojibwa Warrior*, 60). George Mitchell, Banks's fellow leaflet distributor and childhood friend (from the Pipestone Indian boarding school), had already had considerable

political experience by the time he was helping coordinate what would become the American Indian Movement.

66. Anderson "Indian Patrol's First Night Quiet."

67. Cohen, "The Indian Patrol in Minneapolis" (dissertation), 62–66.

68. Ibid.; Birong, "The Influence of Police Brutality on the American Indian Movement's Establishment."

69. Minnesota Human Rights Commission, *Police Brutality, Minneapolis Public Hearing #2*, 15.

70. For examples, see Minnesota Human Rights Commission, *Police Brutality, Minneapolis Public Hearing #2*; Akard, "Wocante Tinza"; Matthiessen, *In the Spirit of Crazy Horse*; Means and Wolf, *Where White Men Fear to Tread*; Banks and Erdoes, *Ojibwa Warrior*; Birong, "The Influence of Police Brutality on the American Indian Movement's Establishment."

71. Cohen, "The Indian Patrol in Minneapolis" (article), 779.

72. Akard, "Wocante Tinza"; Marable, *Race, Reform, and Rebellion*; Calfee, "Prevailing Winds"; Banks and Erdoes, *Ojibwa Warrior*; Birong, "The Influence of Police Brutality on the American Indian Movement's Establishment."

73. Black Panther Party for Self-Defense, "What We Believe."

74. Marable, *Race, Reform, and Rebellion*, 107.

75. Banks and Erdoes, *Ojibwa Warrior*, 63.

76. *Capital Sunday Magazine*, "Indian Power." For a similar statement, see also Edmonds, "Indians to Patrol Franklin Av. to Deter 'Harassment' by Police."

77. Marable, *Race, Reform, and Rebellion*, 155.

78. Ibid., 123.

79. Austin, *Up against the Wall*, 32.

80. Ibid., 26.

81. For an example of research that emphasizes the centrality of the BPP's influence on AIM, see D'Arcus, "The Urban Geography of Red Power," 1250.

82. For an informative account of the "disturbances" that broke on the Northside's Plymouth Avenue in the period, see Vizenor, "1966," 20–21.

83. Davis, *Overcoming*, 162–64.

84. Cohen, "The Indian Patrol in Minneapolis" (dissertation), 190–93. The police had initially opposed these patrols, but they would later win police endorsement (although that relationship would eventually deteriorate).

85. Cohen, "The Indian Patrol in Minneapolis" (article), 781.

86. Edmonds, "Indians to Patrol Franklin Av. to Deter 'Harassment' by Police."

87. Matthiessen, *In the Spirit of Crazy Horse,* 36.
88. Clyde Bellecourt, in discussion with author, Minneapolis, Minnesota, May 15, 2012.
89. Cohen, "The Indian Patrol in Minneapolis" (dissertation), 49.
90. American Indian Movement of Minneapolis, "American Indian News, 1970–1971."
91. Cohen, "The Indian Patrol in Minneapolis" (dissertation), 71.
92. Ibid.
93. Vizenor, "Dennis of Wounded Knee," 55.

4. Land Mines at Home and Abroad

1. Miller, "America's Most Literate Cities"; Albo, "Gayest Cities in America"; *Bicycling Magazine,* "America's Most Bicycle-Friendly Cities."
2. City of Minneapolis, "Diverse Minneapolis."
3. Ibid.
4. Nickrand, "Minneapolis's White Lie."
5. Williams, "Quietly, Indians Reshape Cities and Reservations."
6. Minneapolis Foundation, *A New Age of Immigrants.*
7. Furst, "Twin Cities Jobless Gap Worst in Nation"; Gilbert, "Twin Cities Again Leads Nation in Black, White Unemployment Gap."
8. Institute on Metropolitan Opportunity, *Twin Cities in Crisis.*
9. Taylor, *African Americans in Minnesota,* 80. As in other American cities, the view that police consistently target Black men with unwarranted stops has been a source of considerable political tension in Minneapolis. In recent years, local activists organizing under the banner Black Lives Matter have drawn attention to municipal ordinances that criminalize conduct such as "lurking, loitering, and spitting on sidewalks," which they say are consistently employed to "profile, cite, and harass people of color." See Black Lives Matter Minneapolis, "Black Lives Matter Minneapolis."
10. Kipfer and Goonewardena, "Colonization and the New Imperialism," 3.
11. Massey, "A Counterhegemonic Relationality of Place," 4. See also Massey, "A Global Sense of Place"; Jacobs, "Urban Geographies I."
12. Harvey, *Seventeen Contradictions and the End of Capitalism,* 1.
13. Ibid.
14. For a particularly sharp assessment of this contradiction (written in the context of the revolts that followed the murder of George Floyd), see Derickson, "Let This Radicalize Us."
15. Flusty et al., "Interventions in Banal Neoimperialism." See also

Inwood and Bonds, "Confronting White Supremacy and a Militaristic Pedagogy in the U.S. Settler Colonial State."
16. Walcott, "The Problem of the Human," 96–101.
17. Panitch and Gindin, *The Making of Global Capitalism,* 19. In spite of this distinction, it is worth pointing out that the United States does have a history of overseas imperialism that has sometimes closely mirrored the classic model; see, for example, Smith, *American Empire*; Immerwahr, *How to Hide an Empire.*
18. Panitch and Gindin, *The Making of Global Capitalism,* 1.
19. United States Department of Defense, "Defense Budget Overview."
20. Stein, "U.S. Military Budget Inches Closer to $1 Trillion Mark, as Concerns over Federal Deficit Grow."
21. For a critical discussion of this literature, see Cowen, *The Deadly Life of Logistics,* 6–8.
22. Blum, *Rogue State,* 16.
23. Marks, "Honeywell," 10–11.
24. Ibid.
25. Smith and Warrior, *Like a Hurricane,* 130.
26. HP's coalition partners included Clergy and Laity Concerned, Educators for Social Responsibility, Friends for a Non-Violent World, Minnesota Council for Soviet-American Friendship, the Children's Campaign for Nuclear Disarmament, Minnesota Freeze Campaign, Minnesota War Resisters, Northern Sun Alliance, Women Against Military Madness, Phillips People for Survival, Physicians for Social Responsibility, and the Women's International League for Social Responsibility, among others.
27. Oakes, "13 Juveniles among 140 Arrested at Honeywell Protest."
28. Ibid., B1.
29. Klauda, "Panel Discusses Nuclear Concerns with Teens," B9.
30. Inskip, "Business Executives Look for Ways to Help the Hard-to-Employ." On Minnesota's tradition of corporate philanthropy, see Pratt and Spencer, "Dynamics of Corporate Philanthropy in Minnesota."
31. *New York Times,* "Some Dismay in Honeywell's Hometown."
32. Smith and Warrior, *Like a Hurricane,* 130.
33. Ibid.
34. Ibid.
35. Inskip, "In Phillips, a Job Program That Works," A15.
36. Ibid.
37. Ibid.
38. McGrath, "Subsidies May Aid Defense Contractor," B1.
39. Ibid.
40. Ibid.
41. *Minneapolis Star-Tribune,* "Building Better Lives with Land Mines," A18.

42. Specktor, "Military Spending Spurs Controversy among Neighbors."

43. It is worth noting that the various "counterinsurgency" programs carried out and supported by the American state during the 1980s were the source of considerable controversy among Indigenous radicals in the United States, particularly in the American Indian Movement. Opinion was split over the Nicaraguan revolution. Some argued that the Sandinistas posed a serious threat to the survival and well-being of the Miskito peoples while others supported the revolution's toppling of the U.S.-backed Somoza regime. See Simpson and Smith, *Theorizing Native Studies*, 17–18; Dunbar-Ortiz, *Blood on the Border*.

44. Stiegler, "Letter to the Editor," A10.

45. Specktor, "Military Spending Spurs Controversy among Neighbors," 19A.

46. Schneider and Merle, "Reagan's Defense Buildup Bridged Military Eras, Huge Budgets Brought Life Back to Industry," 1E.

47. Specktor, "Military Spending Spurs Controversy among Neighbors," 19A.

48. Human Rights Watch, *Exposing the Source*.

49. Mamdani, "When Does the Settler Become a Native?" 1. For more on the debate about the distinction between "settler" and "migrant," see Lawrence and Dua, "Decolonizing Antiracism," and Sharma and Wright, "Decolonizing Resistance, Challenging Colonial States." See also Day, *Alien Capital*, 18–25.

50. Veracini, *The Settler Colonial Present*, 41.

51. Shoemaker, "Indians and Ethnic Choices," 434.

52. City of Minneapolis, "Diverse Minneapolis."

53. Vang, *Hmong in Minnesota*.

54. Compton, "1990 Census."

55. Williams, "New Census Data."

56. Elliott, "A Call to Jihad, Answered in America."

57. *Minneapolis Tribune*, "The Plight of the Urban Indian."

58. King, "Nightmares Suspected in Bed Deaths of 18 Laotians."

59. Elliott, "A Call to Jihad, Answered in America."

60. Mbembe, *On the Postcolony*, 3.

61. Rowan, "The Plight of the Upper Midwest Indian."

62. Ibid.

63. Newlund, "Community Action Program Helps Indians Help Themselves."

64. Newlund, "Reservations Offer Little Regular Work."

65. *Minneapolis Star*, "Indians Are Drawn from Reservations by the Job Opportunities of the Cities."

66. Meyer, *The White Earth Tragedy*; Youngbear-Tibbets, "Without Due Process."

67. For an extensive treatment of the broader mythology, see Grandin, *The End of the Myth.*

68. Graves, Ebbott, and the League of Women Voters of Minnesota, *Indians in Minnesota,* 5th ed., 11–15.

69. Blum, *Killing Hope,* 141.

70. Vang, *Hmong in Minnesota,* 2.

71. Ibid., 6.

72. Waligora, "Story of Survival."

73. Achebe, *Africa's Tarnished Name,* 50.

74. Parenti, *Tropic of Chaos,* 78.

75. Ibid., 80.

76. Jackson, "The Carter Administration and Somalia."

77. Parenti, *Tropic of Chaos,* 83.

78. Hyndman, "A Post–Cold War Geography of Forced Migration in Kenya and Somalia," 109.

79. Perez, "After the Cold War."

80. Parenti, *Tropic of Chaos,* 83–84.

81. For a comprehensive discussion of "military geographies," see Woodward, "From Military Geography to Militarism's Geographies."

82. Flusty et al., "Interventions in Banal Neoimperialism," 619.

83. See, for example, Weizman, "The War of Streets and Houses"; Cowen, *The Deadly Life of Logistics,* 184–90; Mawani, "Law, Settler Colonialism, and the 'Forgotten Space' of Maritime Worlds."

Epilogue

1. Gillette, "Reagan Meets 96 Soviet Dissidents."

2. Goldstein, "Reagan Meets Soviet Dissidents, Promises More Work in Human Rights Area."

3. Reagan, "Remarks and a Question-and-Answer Session with the Students and Faculty at Moscow State University."

4. Dorris, "The Cowboy and the Indians"; de Lama, "Reagan Says No Regrets on Indian Remarks"; Stevens, "Reagan View of Indians Called 'Ignorant'"; Venables, "Letter to the Editor."

5. Lincoln, *Indi'n Humor,* 123.

6. For a brilliant set of reflections on the cunning politics that undergirded Reagan's "folksy" way of speaking, including what often appeared to be "random avuncular musings," see Didion, *Miami,* chapter 16.

7. Hietala, *Manifest Design*; Smith, *American Empire*; Tyrrell, "American Exceptionalism in an Age of International History."

8. Hietala, *Manifest Design,* 256.

9. Turner, *The Frontier in American History,* 23.

10. Said, *Culture and Imperialism,* 8–9.

Bibliography

Abu-Lughod, Janet. *Rabbat: Urban Apartheid in Morocco.* Princeton, N.J.: Princeton University Press, 1981.

———. "Tale of Two Cities: The Origins of Modern Cairo." *Comparative Studies in Society and History* 7 (1965): 429–57.

Achebe, Chinua. *Africa's Tarnished Name.* London: Penguin Books, 2018.

Adams, John, and Barbara VanDrasek. *Minneapolis–St. Paul: People, Place, and Public Life.* Minneapolis: University of Minnesota Press, 1993.

Adams, John, Barbara VanDrasek, and Laura Lambert. *The Path of Urban Decline: What the 1990 Census Says about Minnesota.* Minneapolis: Center for Urban and Regional Affairs, 1995.

Adelman, Jeremy, and Stephen Aron. "From Borderlands to Borders: Empires, Nation-States, and the Peoples in between in North American History." *American Historical Review* 104 (1999): 814–41.

Ahtone, Tristan. "A Cross to Bear: James Cross Knows Why Native American Kids Join Gangs." *Al-Jazeera America,* January 19, 2015. http://projects.aljazeera.com/2015/01/native-gangs/.

———. "Native American Gangs Series." *Al-Jazeera English,* January 19–23, 2015. http://projects.aljazeera.com/2015/01/native-gangs/.

Akard, William K. "Wocante Tinza: A History of the American Indian Movement." PhD dissertation, Ball State University, 1987.

Albo, Mike. "Gayest Cities in America." *Advocate,* January 12, 2011. http://www.advocate.com/travel/2011/01/12/gayest-cities-america -february-2011?page=full.

Alfred, Taiaiake, and Jeff Corntassel. "Being Indigenous: Resurgences against Contemporary Colonialism." *Government and Opposition* 40 (2005): 597–614.

The Alley. "Police/Community Relations: The Residents, the Police." *The Alley,* January 1976.

Alsayyad, Nezar. *Forms of Dominance: On the Architecture and Urbanism of the Colonial Enterprise.* Brookfield, Conn.: Avebury, 1992.

American Indian Movement of Minneapolis. "American Indian News, 1970–1971." Microform, Minnesota Historical Society Archives, St. Paul.

Anderson, Brian. "Indian Patrol's First Night Quiet; Seeking Harassment by Police." *Minneapolis Tribune,* August 25, 1968.

Artforum. "Dakota Nation Demands Removal of Sculpture at Walker Art Center." *Artforum,* May 29, 2017. https://www.artforum.com /news/dakota-nation-demands-removal-of-sculpture-at-walker -art-center-68759.

Austin, Curtis. *Up against the Wall: Violence in the Making and Unmaking of the Black Panther Party.* Fayetteville: University of Arkansas Press, 2006.

Baloy, Natalie. "Spectacles and Specters: Settler Colonial Spaces in Vancouver." *Settler Colonial Studies* 6 (2016): 209–34.

Bancroft, Dick, and Laura Waterman Wittstock. *We Are Still Here: A Photographic History of the American Indian Movement.* St. Paul: Minnesota Historical Society Press, 2013.

Banivanua-Mar, Tracey, and Penelope Edmonds. *Making Settler Colonial Space: Perspectives on Race, Place, and Identity.* Houndmills and New York: Palgrave-Macmillan, 2010.

Banks, Dennis, and Richard Erdoes. *Ojibwa Warrior: Dennis Banks and the Rise of the American Indian Movement.* Norman: University of Oklahoma Press, 2004.

Barakat, Rana. "Writing/Righting Palestine Studies: Settler Colonialism, Indigenous Sovereignty and Resisting the Ghost(s) of History." *Settler Colonial Studies* 8 (2018): 349–63.

Barker, Adam. "The Contemporary Reality of Canadian Imperialism: Settler Colonialism and the Hybrid Colonial State." *American Indian Quarterly* 33 (2009): 325–51.

Barnd, Natchee Blu. *Native Space: Geographic Strategies to Unsettle Settler Colonialism.* Corvallis: Oregon State University Press, 2017.

Barraclough, Laura. "Wrangling Settler Colonialism in the Urban U.S. West: Indigenous and Mexican American Struggles for Social Justice." *Annals of the American Association of Geographers* 108 (2018): 513–23.

Barry, Janice, and Julian Agyeman. "On Belonging and Becoming in the Settler-Colonial City: Co-Produced Futurities, Placemaking, and Urban Planning in the United States." *Journal of Race, Ethnicity, and the City* (2020). https://doi.org/10.1080/26884674.2020 .1793703.

Bateman, Fiona, and Lionel Pilkington. *Studies in Settler Colonialism: Politics, Identity, and Culture.* Houndmills and New York: Palgrave-Macmillan, 2011.

Battell Lowman, Emma, Adam J. Barker, and Toby Rollo. "Settler Colonialism and the Consolidation of Canada in the Twentieth Century." In *The Routledge Handbook of the History of Settler Colonialism,* ed. Lorenzo Veracini and Edward Cavanagh, 153–68. New York: Taylor and Francis, 2016.

Belich, James. *Replenishing the Earth: The Settler Revolution and the Rise of the Anglo-World, 1783–1939.* Oxford and New York: Oxford University Press, 2011.

Bellecourt, Clyde, and John Lurie. *The Thunder before the Storm: The Autobiography of Clyde Bellecourt.* St. Paul: Minnesota Historical Society Press, 2016.

Benjamin, Roger, and Choong Nam Kim. *American Indians and the Criminal Justice System in Minnesota.* Minneapolis: Center for Urban and Regional Affairs, University of Minnesota, 1979.

Berg, Lawrence. "Banal Naming, Neoliberalism, and Landscapes of Dispossession." *ACME* 10 (2011): 13–22.

Bhandar, Brenna, and Rafeef Ziadah. "Acts and Omissions: Framing Settler Colonialism in Palestine Studies." *Jadaliyya,* January 14, 2016. https://www.jadaliyya.com/Details/32857.

Bicycling Magazine. "America's Most Bicycle-Friendly Cities." Bicycling .com, 2011. http://www.bicycling.com/news/featured-stories /bicyclings-top-50.

Birong, Christine. "The Influence of Police Brutality on the American Indian Movement's Establishment in Minneapolis, 1968–1969." MA thesis, University of Arizona, 2009.

Black Lives Matter Minneapolis. "Black Lives Matter Minneapolis." Facebook, January 2015. https://www.facebook.com/BlackLives MatterMinneapolis.

Black Panther Party for Self-Defense. "What We Believe." *Black Panther* 1 (1967).

Blatman-Thomas, Naama. "Commuting for Rights: Circular Mobilities and Regional Identities of Palestinians in a Jewish-Israeli Town." *Geoforum* 78 (2017): 22–32.

———. "Reciprocal Repossession: Property as Land in Urban Australia." *Antipode* 51 (2019): 1395–1415.

Blatman-Thomas, Naama, and Libby Porter. "Placing Property: Theorizing the Urban from Settler Colonial Cities." *International Journal of Urban and Regional Research* 43 (2019): 30–45.

Bledsoe, Adam, Tyler McCreary, and Willie Wright. "Theorizing Diverse Economies in the Context of Racial Capitalism." *Geoforum,* published online July 15, 2019. https://doi.org/10.1016/j.geoforum.2019.07.004.

Blegen, Theodore Christian. *Minnesota: A History of the State.* Minneapolis: University of Minnesota Press, 1963.

Blomley, Nicholas. "Law, Property, and the Geography of Violence: The Frontier, the Survey, and the Grid." *Annals of the Association of American Geographers* 93 (2003): 121–41.

———. *Unsettling the City: Urban Land and the Politics of Property.* London and New York: Routledge, 2004.

Blum, William. *Killing Hope: U.S. Military and CIA Interventions since World War II.* London: Zed Books, 2003.

———. *Rogue State: A Guide to the World's Only Superpower.* 2d ed. London: Zed Books, 2012.

Bonds, Anne, and Joshua Inwood. "Beyond White Privilege: Geographies of White Supremacy and Settler Colonialism." *Progress in Human Geography* 40 (2016): 715–33.

Borrows, John. *Recovering Canada: The Resurgence of Indigenous Law.* Toronto: University of Toronto Press, 2002.

Broker, Ignatia. *Night Flying Woman: An Ojibway Narrative.* St. Paul: Minnesota Historical Society Press, 1983.

Brown, Nicholas A. "Experiments in Regional Settler Colonization: Pursuing Justice and Producing Scale through the Montana Study." In *Settler City Limits: Indigenous Resurgence and Colonial Violence in the Urban Prairie West,* ed. Heather Dorries, Robert Henry, David Hugill, Tyler McCreary, and Julie Tomiak, 118–50. Winnipeg: University of Manitoba Press, 2019.

———. "The Logic of Settler Accumulation in a Landscape of Perpetual Vanishing." *Settler Colonial Studies* 4 (2013): 1–26.

Brunette, Pauline. "The Minneapolis Urban Indian Community." *Hennepin County History* 49 (1990): 4–15.

Bruyneel, Kevin. "The American Liberal Colonial Tradition." *Settler Colonial Studies* 3 (2013): 311–21.

Buchanan, Larry, Quoctrung Bui, and Jugal K. Patel. "Black Lives Matter May Be the Largest Movement in U.S. History." *New York Times,* July 3, 2020.

Buff, Rachel. *Immigration and the Political Economy of Home: West Indian Brooklyn and American Indian Minneapolis, 1945–1992.* Berkeley: University of California Press, 2001.

Burley, David. "Rooster Town: Winnipeg's Lost Métis Suburb, 1900–60." *Urban History Review* 42 (2013): 3–25.

Byrd, Jodi. *The Transit of Empire: Indigenous Critiques of Colonialism.* Minneapolis: University of Minnesota Press, 2011.

Calfee, David Kent. "Prevailing Winds: Radical Activism and the American Indian Movement." MA thesis, East Tennessee State University, 2002.

Capital Sunday Magazine. "Indian Power: We Will Probably Have to Come to the Brink of Rioting." *Capital Sunday Magazine, St. Paul Pioneer Press,* October 1968.

Carney, Mary Vance. *Minnesota: The Star of the North.* Boston and New York: D. C. Heath and Company, 1920.

Carpio, Myla Vincente. *Indigenous Albuquerque.* Lubbock: Texas Technical Press, 2011.

Carter, Sarah. *Lost Harvests: Prairie Indian Reserve Farmers and Government Policy.* Montreal and Kingston: McGill–Queen's University Press, 1990.

Castellanos, M. Bianet. "Introduction: Settler Colonialism in Latin America." *American Quarterly* 69 (2017): 777–81.

Césaire, Aimé. *Discourse on Colonialism.* New York: Monthly Review Press, 2000.

Chavers, Dean. *Racism in Indian Country.* New York: Peter Lang, 2009.

Child, Brenda. *Holding Our World Together: Ojibwe Women and the Survival of Community.* New York: Viking, 2012.

Child, Brenda, and Karris White. "'I've Done My Share': Ojibwe People and World War II." *Minnesota History* 61 (2009): 196–207.

City of Minneapolis. "City of Minneapolis Neighborhoods." Minneapolis.org. http://www.minneapolismn.gov/residents/neighbor hoods/index.htm.

———. "Diverse Minneapolis." Minneapolis.org. http://www.minneapolis .org/visitor/diverse-minneapolis.

Coates, Ta-Nehisi. *Between the World and Me.* New York: Spiegel and Grau, 2015.

Cobb, Daniel. "Philosophy of an Indian War: Indian Community Action in the Johnson Administration's War on Indian Poverty, 1964–1968." *American Indian Culture and Research Journal* 22 (1968): 71–102.

Cohen, Fay. "The Indian Patrol in Minneapolis: Social Control and Social Change in an Urban Context." PhD dissertation, University of Minnesota, 1973.

———. "The Indian Patrol in Minneapolis: Social Control and Social Change in an Urban Context." *Law and Society Review* 7 (1972): 779–86.

Comack, Elizabeth. "Policing Racialized Spaces." In *Settler City Limits: Indigenous Resurgence and Colonial Violence in the Urban Prairie West,* ed. Heather Dorries, Robert Henry, David Hugill, Tyler McCreary, and Julie Tomiak, 175–95. Winnipeg: University of Manitoba Press, 2019.

———. *Racialized Policing: Aboriginal People's Encounters with the Police.* Halifax and Winnipeg: Fernwood Publishing, 2012.

Comack, Elizabeth, Lawrence Deane, Larry Morrissette, and Jim Silver. *Indians Wear Red: Colonialism, Resistance, and Aboriginal Street Gangs.* Halifax and Winnipeg: Fernwood Publishing, 2013.

Committee on Urban Indians. *Public Forum before the Committee on Urban Indians in Minneapolis–St. Paul,* March 18–19, 1969.

Community Welfare Council Indian Committee. *The Minnesota Indian in Minneapolis.* Minneapolis: Community Welfare Council of Hennepin County, 1956.

Compton, Steve. "1990 Census: People of Color Now Majority in Phillips." *The Alley,* May 1991.

Corntassel, Jeff. "Re-Envisioning Resurgence: Indigenous Pathways to

Decolonization and Sustainable Self-Determination." *Decolonization: Indigeneity, Education, and Society* 1 (2012): 86–101.

Coulthard, Glen. *Red Skin, White Masks: Rejecting the Colonial Politics of Recognition.* Minneapolis: University of Minnesota Press, 2014.

Couture, Steven L. "The American Indian Movement: A Historical Perspective." PhD dissertation, St. Thomas University, 1996.

Cowen, Deborah. *The Deadly Life of Logistics: Mapping Violence in Global Trade.* Minneapolis: University of Minnesota Press, 2014.

———. "Following the Infrastructures of Empire: Notes on Cities, Settler Colonialism, and Method." *Urban Geography,* published online November 26, 2019. https://doi.org/10.1080/02723638.2019.1677990.

Cresswell, Tim. *In Place/Out of Place: Geography, Ideology, and Transgression.* Minneapolis: University of Minnesota Press, 1996.

Cronon, William. *Nature's Metropolis: Chicago and the Great West.* New York: W. W. Norton, 1991.

Cross, Mercer. "Indian Church Is on Road to Integration." *Minneapolis Tribune,* December 2, 1957.

Dahl, Dick. "Does Franklin Avenue Have a Future? When the Problems Are Poverty, Unemployment, Alcoholism, and Empty Buildings, What Are the Solutions?" *City Pages,* August 10, 1983, 7–11.

Daigle, Michelle, and Margaret Marietta Ramirez. "Decolonial Geographies." In *Keywords in Radical Geography: Antipode at 50,* ed. *Antipode* Editorial Collective. Hoboken, N.J., and Oxford: Wiley-Blackwell, 2019.

Danforth, Pauline. "The Division of Indian Work: Reflecting on the Past, Shaping the Future." Unpublished manuscript, May 2012.

Danzinger, Edmund Jefferson. *Survival and Regeneration: Detroit's American Indian Community.* Detroit: Wayne State University Press, 1991.

D'Arcus, Bruce. "The Urban Geography of Red Power: The American Indian Movement in Minneapolis Saint Paul 1968–70." *Urban Studies* 47 (2010): 1241–55.

Daschuk, James. *Clearing the Plains: Disease, Politics of Starvation, and the Loss of Aboriginal Life.* Regina: University of Regina Press, 2013.

Davis, Julie. *Survival Schools: The American Indian Movement and Community Education in the Twin Cities.* Minneapolis: University of Minnesota Press, 2013.

Day, Iyko. *Alien Capital: Asian Racialization and the Logic of Settler Colonial Capitalism.* Durham, N.C.: Duke University Press, 2016.

de Lama, George. "Reagan Says No Regrets on Indian Remarks." *Chicago Tribune,* June 10, 1988.

Deloria, Phillip. *Indians in Unexpected Places.* Lawrence: University Press of Kansas, 2004.

Delton, Jennifer. *Making Minnesota Liberal: Civil Rights and the Transformation of the Democratic Party.* Minneapolis: University of Minnesota Press, 2002.

Dempsey, Jessica, Kevin Gould, and Juanita Sunberg. "Changing Land Tenure, Defining Subjects: Neoliberalism and Property Regimes on Native Reserves." In *Rethinking the Great White North: Race, Nature, and the Historical Geographies of Whiteness in Canada,* ed. Andrew Baldwin, Laura Cameron, and Audrey Kobayashi, 233–57. Vancouver: University of British Columbia Press, 2012.

Denoon, Donald. "Understanding Settler Societies." *Historical Studies* 18 (1979): 511–27.

Derickson, Kate. "Let This Radicalize Us: After the Minneapolis Uprising." Verso Books Blog, June 9, 2020. https://www.versobooks.com/blogs/4741-let-this-radicalize-us-after-the-minneapolis-uprising.

Diaz, Kevin. "200 March to Protest Crime against Indians." *Minneapolis Star-Tribune,* November 27, 1986.

Didion, Joan. *Miami.* New York: Simon and Schuster, 1987.

Dorries, Heather. "'Welcome to Winnipeg': Making Settler-Colonial Urban Space in 'Canada's Most Racist City.'" In *Settler City Limits: Indigenous Resurgence and Colonial Violence in the Urban Prairie West,* ed. Heather Dorries, Robert Henry, David Hugill, Tyler McCreary, and Julie Tomiak, 25–43. Winnipeg: University of Manitoba Press, 2019.

Dorries, Heather, and Laura Harjo. "Beyond Safety: Refusing Colonial Violence through Indigenous Feminist Planning." *Journal of Planning Education and Research,* published online January 11, 2020. https://doi.org/10.1177/0739456X19894382.

Dorries, Heather, Robert Henry, David Hugill, Tyler McCreary, and Julie Tomiak, eds. *Settler City Limits: Indigenous Resurgence and Colonial Violence in the Urban Prairie West.* Winnipeg: University of Manitoba Press, 2019.

Dorries, Heather, David Hugill, and Julie Tomiak. "Racial Capitalism and the Production of Settler Colonial Cities." *Geoforum,* published online August 19, 2019. https://doi.org/10.1016/j.geoforum.2019.07.016.

Dorris, Michael. "The Cowboy and the Indians: Reagan's Patronizing Remarks Add Insult to Injury." *Los Angeles Times,* June 12, 1988.

Drilling, Vern. *Problems with Alcohol among Urban Indians in Minneapolis.* Minneapolis: Training Center for Community Programs, 1970.

Drinnon, Richard. *Facing West: The Metaphysics of Indian-Hating and Empire-Building.* Norman: University of Oklahoma Press, 2009.

———. *Keeper of Concentration Camps: Dillon S. Myer and American Racism.* Berkeley: University of California Press, 1989.

Driver, Felix, and David Gilbert. "Heart of Empire? Landscape, Space, and Performance in Imperial London." *Environment and Planning D: Society and Space* 16 (1998): 11–28.

Dunbar-Ortiz, Roxanne. *Blood on the Border: A Memoir of the Contra War.* Cambridge: South End Press, 2005.

Durant, Sam. "A Statement from Sam Durant." Walker Art Center, May 29, 2017. https://walkerart.org/magazine/a-statement-from -sam-durant-05-29-17.

Eagleton, Terry. "Why Ideas No Longer Matter." *Guardian,* March 23, 2004.

Earth Guardians. "Letter from Graci Horne." Facebook, May 27, 2017. https://www.facebook.com/EarthGuardiansNY/posts/from-sasha -brown-please-share-the-following-letter-from-graci-horne -with-instruc/645053702355337/.

Ebbott, Elizabeth. Research Files, 1955–1986. Minnesota Historical Society Archives, St. Paul.

Ebbott, Elizabeth, Judith Rosenblatt, and the League of Women Voters of Minnesota. *Indians in Minnesota,* 4th ed. St. Paul: League of Women Voters, 1985.

The Economist. "American Poverty Is Moving from the Cities to the Suburbs." *The Economist,* September 26, 2019. https://www .economist.com/special-report/2019/09/26/american-poverty -is-moving-from-the-cities-to-the-suburbs.

Edmonds, Penelope. "Unpacking Settler Colonialism's Urban Strategies: Indigenous People in Victoria British Columbia, and the Transition to a Settler-Colonial City." *Urban History Review* 38 (2010): 4–20.

Edmonds, Rick. "Indians to Patrol Franklin Av. to Deter 'Harassment' by Police." *Minneapolis Tribune,* August 20, 1968.

Eldred, Sheila. "Walker Art Center's Reckoning with 'Scaffold' Isn't Over Yet." *New York Times,* September 13, 2017. https://www.nytimes .com/2017/09/13/arts/design/walker-art-center-scaffold.html.

Elkins, Caroline, and Susan Pedersen. *Settler Colonialism in the Twentieth Century: Projects, Practices, Legacies.* New York: Routledge, 2005.

Elliott, Andrea. "A Call to Jihad, Answered in America." *New York Times,* July 11, 2009.

Englert, Sai. "Settlers, Workers, and the Logic of Accumulation by Dispossession." *Antipode* 52 (2020): 1647–66.

Estes, Nick. "Anti-Indian Common Sense: Border Town Violence and Resistance in Mni Luzahan." In *Settler City Limits: Indigenous Resurgence and Colonial Violence in the Urban Prairie West,* ed. Heather Dorries, Robert Henry, David Hugill, Tyler McCreary, and Julie Tomiak, 44–89. Winnipeg: University of Manitoba Press, 2019.

———. *Our History Is the Future.* New York and London: Verso Books, 2019.

Fanon, Frantz. *Black Skin, White Masks.* New York: Grove Press, 2008.

———. *The Wretched of the Earth.* New York: Grove Press, 2004.

First National Bank of Minneapolis. *Implosion in Minneapolis: An Invitation to Share in This Dynamic Market.* Minneapolis: First National Bank of Minneapolis, 1962.

Fixico, Donald. *Termination and Relocation: Federal Indian Policy, 1945–1960.* Albuquerque: University of New Mexico Press, 1990.

———. *The Urban Indian Experience in America.* Albuquerque: University of New Mexico Press, 2000.

Flusty, Steven, Jason Dittmer, Emily Gilbert, and Merje Kuus. "Interventions in Banal Neoimperialism." *Political Geography* 27 (2008): 617–29.

Fraser, Steve, and Gary Gerstle, eds. *The Rise and Fall of the New Deal Order, 1930–1980.* Princeton, N.J.: Princeton University Press, 1989.

Freund, David. *Colored Property: State Policy and White Racial Politics in Suburban America.* Chicago: University of Chicago Press, 2007.

Furst, Randy. "Twin Cities Jobless Gap Worst in the Nation." *Minneapolis Star-Tribune,* March 25, 2011.

———. "2 Officers Suspended after Putting Indians in the Trunk." *Minneapolis Star-Tribune,* April 23, 1993.

Gaudry, Adam. "Researching the Resurgence: Insurgent Research and Community-Engaged Methodologies in Twenty-first Century Academic Inquiry." In *Research as Resistance: Revisiting Critical, Indigenous, and Anti-Oppressive Approaches,* 2d ed., ed. Leslie Brown and Susan Strega. Toronto: Canadian Scholars' Press, 2015.

Getzoff, Joseph. "Zionist Frontiers: David Ben-Gurion, Labor Zionism, and Transnational Circulations of Settler Development." *Settler Colonial Studies* 10 (2020): 74–93.

Gibbons, Richard, Linda Keintz, Sharon Lemke, Carol Mellom, Dianne Rochel, Amy Silberberg, Henry Ladislaus Sledz, and Georgia Smith. *Indian Americans in Southside Minneapolis: Additional Field Notes from the Urban Slum.* Minneapolis: Training Center for Community Programs, University of Minnesota, 1970.

Gilad, Efrat. "Is Settler Colonial History Urban History?" Global Urban History Blog, February 10, 2020. https://globalurbanhistory.com /2020/02/10/is-settler-colonial-history-urban-history/.

Gilbert, Curtis. "Twin Cities Again Leads Nation in Black, White Unemployment Gap." Minnesota Public Radio News, July 3, 2012. http://www.mprnews.org/story/2012/07/03/labor-unemployment-gap.

Gillette, Robert. "Reagan Meets 96 Soviet Dissidents: He Praises Their Courage, Says 'I Came to Give You Strength.'" *Los Angeles Times,* May 31, 1988.

Gilmore, Ruth Wilson. *Golden Gulag: Prisons, Surplus, Crisis, and Opposition in Globalizing California.* Berkeley: University of California Press, 2007.

Goebel, Michael. "Settler Colonialism in Postcolonial Latin America." In *The Routledge Handbook of the History of Settler Colonialism,* ed. Edward Cavanagh and Lorenzo Veracini, 139–52. London: Routledge, 2016.

Goeman, Mishuana. *Mark My Words: Native Women Mapping Our Nations.* Minneapolis: University of Minnesota Press, 2013.

Goetz, Edward, Karen Chapple, and Barbara Lukermann. "The Rise and Fall of Fair Share Housing: Lessons from the Twin Cities." In *The Geography of Opportunity: Race and Housing Choice in Metropolitan America,* ed. Xavier de Souza Briggs and William Julius Williams, 247–65. Washington, D.C.: Brookings Institution, 2005.

Goldberg, David Theo. *Racist Culture: Philosophy and the Politics of Meaning.* Oxford and Malden, Mass.: Blackwell, 1993.

Goldstein, Alyosha. "Where the Nation Takes Place: Proprietary Regimes, Antistatism, and U.S. Settler Colonialism." *South Atlantic Quarterly* 107 (2008): 833–61.

Goldstein, Steve. "Reagan Meets Soviet Dissidents, Promises More Work in Human Rights Area." *Philadelphia Inquirer,* May 31, 1988.

Gott, Richard. "Latin America as White Settler Society." *Bulletin of Latin American Research* 26 (2007): 169–289.

Governor's Human Rights Commission. *Minnesota's Indian Citizens: Yesterday and Today.* St. Paul: State of Minnesota, 1965.

Grandin, Greg. *The End of the Myth: From the Frontier to the Border Wall in the Mind of America.* New York: Metropolitan Books, 2019.

Grandinetti, Tina. "Urban Aloha 'Aina: Kaka'ako and a Decolonized Right to the City." *Settler Colonial Studies* 9 (2019): 227–46.

Graves, Kathy Davis, Elizabeth Ebbott, and League of Women Voters of Minnesota. *Indians in Minnesota.* 5th ed. Minneapolis: University of Minnesota Press, 2006.

Gray, John. *Liberalism.* Minneapolis: University of Minnesota Press, 1995.

Greer, Allan. "Commons and Enclosure in the Colonization of North America." *American Historical Review* 117 (2012): 365–86.

Grunow, Tristan. "Cultivating Settler Colonial Space in Korea: Public Works and the Urban Environment under Japanese Rule." *International Journal of Korean History* 25 (2020): 85–119.

Guerry, Matthew. "Minnesota Prisons Begin Tracking Tribal Affiliations of Native American Inmates." *Twin Cities Pioneer Press,* February 26, 2020.

Gutiérrez Nájera, Lourdes, and Korinta Maldonado. "Transnational Settler Colonial Formations and Global Capital: A Consideration of Indigenous Mexican Migrants." *American Quarterly* 69 (2017): 809–21.

Hall, Anthony. *American Empire and the Fourth World: The Bowl with One Spoon.*, Vol. 1. Montreal and Kingston: McGill–Queens University Press, 2003.

———. *Earth into Property: The Bowl with One Spoon.* Vol. 2. Montreal and Kingston: McGill–Queen's University Press, 2010.

Hall, Stuart, and Allan O'Shea. "Common-Sense Neoliberalism." *Soundings* 55 (2013): 8–24.

Harding, Robert. "The Media, Aboriginal People, and Common Sense." *Canadian Journal of Native Studies* 25 (2005): 311–35.

Harkins, Arthur, and Richard Woods. *Attitudes of Minneapolis Agency Personnel toward Urban Indians.* Minneapolis: Training Center for Community Programs, University of Minnesota, 1968.

———. *The Social Programs and Political Styles of Minneapolis Indians: An Interim Report.* Minneapolis: Training Center for Community Programs, University of Minnesota, 1969.

Harrington, Michael. *The Other America: Poverty in the United States.* New York: Touchstone, 1997 [1962].

Harris, Cole. *Making Native Space: Colonialism, Resistance, and Reserves in British Columbia.* Vancouver: University of British Columbia Press, 2003.

Hartz, Louis. *The Liberal Tradition in America: An Interpretation of American Political Thought since the Revolution.* San Diego: Harcourt Brace Jovanovich, 1991 [1955].

Harvey, David. *Seventeen Contradictions and the End of Capitalism.* Oxford and New York: Oxford University Press, 2014.

Hedges, Chris. *Death of the Liberal Class.* Toronto: Vintage Canada, 2011.

Henry, Robert. "'I Claim in the Name of . . .': Indigenous Street Gangs and Politics of Recognition in Prairie Cities." In *Settler City Limits: Indigenous Resurgence and Colonial Violence in the Urban Prairie West,* ed. Heather Dorries, Robert Henry, David Hugill, Tyler McCreary, and Julie Tomiak, 222–47. Winnipeg: University of Manitoba Press, 2019.

Herndon, Astead W. "How a Pledge to Dismantle the Minneapolis Police Collapsed." *New York Times,* September 26, 2020.

Hietala, Thomas. *Manifest Design: American Exceptionalism and Empire.* Ithaca, N.Y.: Cornell University Press, 2003.

Hirsch, Arnold. *Making the Second Ghetto: Race and Housing in Chicago, 1940–1960.* Chicago: University of Chicago Press, 1998.

Hirschoff, Edwin, and Joseph Hart. *Down and Out: The Life and Death of Minneapolis's Skid Row.* Minneapolis: University of Minnesota Press, 2002.

Holmes, Cindy, Sarah Hunt, and Amy Piedalue. "Violence, Colonialism, and Space: Towards a Decolonizing Dialogue." *ACME: An International E-Journal for Critical Geographers* 14 (2014): 539–70.

Holmes, Malcolm, and Brad Smith. *Race and Police Brutality: Roots of an Urban Dilemma.* Albany: State University of New York Press, 2008.

Home, Robert. *Of Planting and Planning: The Making of British Colonial Cities.* London: Routledge, 1997.

———. "Shaping Cities of the Global South: Legal Histories of Planning and Colonialism." In *The Routledge Handbook on Cities of the Global South,* ed. Susan Parnell and Sophie Oldfield. London and New York: Routledge, 2014.

Hovik, Suzanne. "Urban Indians Must Conquer Problems of 'Alien' Culture. *Minneapolis Star,* April 3, 1968.

Hugill, David. "Comparative Settler Colonial Urbanisms: Racism and the Making of Inner-City Winnipeg and Minneapolis, 1940–1975." In *Settler City Limits: Indigenous Resurgence and Colonial Violence in the Urban Prairie West,* ed. Heather Dorries, Robert Henry, David Hugill, Tyler McCreary, and Julie Tomiak, 70–91. Winnipeg: University of Manitoba Press, 2019.

———. "Metropolitan Transformation and the Colonial Relation: The Making of an 'Indian Neighborhood' in Postwar Minneapolis." *Middle West Review* 2 (2016): 169–200.

———. "Settler Colonial Urbanism: Notes from Minneapolis and the Life of Thomas Barlow Walker." *Settler Colonial Studies* 6 (2016): 265–78.

———. "What Is a Settler-Colonial City?" *Geography Compass* 11 (2017): 1–11.

Hugill, David, and Owen Toews. "Born Again Urbanism: New Missionary Incursions, Aboriginal Resistance, and Barriers to Rebuilding Relationships in Winnipeg's North End." *Human Geography* 7 (2014): 69–83.

Human Rights Watch. *Exposing the Source: U.S. Companies and the Production of Antipersonnel Mines.* New York: Human Rights Watch, 1997. http://www.hrw.org/reports/1997/gen2/General2.htm.

———. *Shielded from Justice: Police Brutality and Accountability in the United States.* New York: Human Rights Watch, July 1, 1998. http://www.hrw.org/reports/1998/07/01/shielded-justice.

Hyndman, Jennifer. "A Post–Cold War Geography of Forced Migration in Kenya and Somalia." *Professional Geographer* 51 (1999): 104–14.

Immerwahr, Daniel. *How to Hide an Empire: A History of the Greater United States.* New York: Farrar, Straus and Giroux, 2019.

Indergaard, Michael. "Urban Renewal and the American Indian Movement in Minneapolis: A Case Study in Political Economy and the Urban Indian." MA thesis, Michigan State University, 1983.

Inskip, Leonard. "Business Executives Look for Ways to Help the Hard-to-Employ." *Minneapolis Star-Tribune,* January 26, 1986.

———. "In Phillips, a Job Program That Works." *Minneapolis Star-Tribune,* March 12, 1986.

Institute on Metropolitan Opportunity. *Twin Cities in Crisis: Unequal Treatment of Communities of Color in Mortgage Lending.* Minneapolis: University of Minnesota Law School, 2014.

Intercepted. "Ruth Wilson Gilmore Makes the Case for Abolition." *Intercept,* June 10, 2020. https://theintercept.com/2020/06/10/ruth-wilson-gilmore-makes-the-case-for-abolition/.

Inwood, Joshua, and Anne Bonds. "Confronting White Supremacy and a Militaristic Pedagogy in the U.S. Settler Colonial State." *Annals of the American Association of Geographers* 106 (2016): 521–29.

Isserman, Maurice. "Michael Harrington: Warrior on Poverty." *New York Times,* June 19, 2009.

Isserman, Maurice, and Michael Kazin. *America Divided: The Civil War of the 1960s.* New York: Oxford University Press, 2000.

Iverson, Peter. *We Are Still Here: American Indians in the Twentieth Century.* Wheeling, Ill.: Harlan Davidson Press, 1998.

Jackson, Donna. "The Carter Administration and Somalia." *Diplomatic History* 31 (2007): 703–21.

Jackson, Kenneth. *Crabgrass Frontier: The Suburbanization of the United States.* Oxford and New York: Oxford University Press, 1985.

Jacobs, Jane M. "Urban Geographies I: Still Thinking Relationally." *Progress in Human Geography* 36 (2012): 412–22.

Janski, Irene. Letter to the Editor. *Minneapolis Tribune,* March 29, 1970.

Jessop, Bob. *State Power: A Strategic-Relational Approach.* Cambridge: Polity, 2007.

Johnson, Lyndon. "Special Message to the Congress Proposing a Nationwide War on the Sources of Poverty." Presidential Address, March 16, 1964, published online by The American Presidency Project, University of California, Santa Barbara. http://www.presidency.ucsb.edu/ws/?pid=26109.

Katz, Michael. *The Undeserving Poor: America's Enduring Confrontation with Poverty.* 2d ed. New York: Oxford University Press, 2013.

———. *Why Don't American Cities Burn?* Philadelphia: University of Pennsylvania Press, 2011.

Katznelson, Ira. "Was the Great Society a Lost Opportunity?" In *The Rise and Fall of the New Deal Order,* ed. Steve Fraser and Gary Gerstle, 195–205. Princeton, N.J.: Princeton University Press, 1989.

———. *When Affirmative Action Was White: An Untold History of Racial Inequality in Twentieth-Century America.* New York: W. W. Norton, 2006.

Keeler, Kasey. "Indigenous Suburbs: Settler Colonialism, Housing Policy, and American Indians in Suburbia." PhD dissertation, University of Minnesota, 2016.

Kelly, Robin D. G. "The Rest of Us: Rethinking Settler and Native." *American Quarterly* 69 (2017): 267–76.

King, Anthony D. *Colonial Urban Development: Culture, Social Power, and Environment.* London and Boston: Routledge and Kegan Paul, 1976.

———. "Postcolonial Cities." In *International Encyclopedia of Human Geography,* ed. Robert Kitchin and Nigel Thrift. Amsterdam: Elsevier, 2009.

———. *Urbanism, Colonialism, and the World-Economy.* London and New York: Routledge, 1990.

King, Thomas. *The Inconvenient Indian: A Curious Account of Native People in North America.* Minneapolis: University of Minnesota Press, 2013.

King, Wayne. "Nightmares Suspected in Bed Deaths of 18 Laotians." *New York Times,* May 10, 1981.

The Kino-nda-niimi Collective, eds. *The Winter We Danced: Voices from the Past, the Future, and the Idle No More Movement.* Winnipeg: ARP Books, 2014.

Kipfer, Stefan. "Decolonization in the Heart of Empire: Some Fanonian Echoes in France Today." *Antipode* 43 (2011): 1155–80.

———. "Pushing the Limits of Urban Research: Urbanization, Pipelines, and Counter-Colonial Politics." *Environment and Planning D: Society and Space* 36 (2018): 474–93.

Kipfer, Stefan, and Kanishka Goonewardena. "Colonization and the New Imperialism: On the Meaning of Urbicide Today." *Theory and Event* 10 (2007): 1–39.

Kitagawa, Daisuke. "Racial and Cultural Relations in the Ministry to the American Indians: A Case Study of One Aspect of the Sociology of Christian Missions." *Occasional Bulletin of the Missionary Research Library* 4 (1953): 1–15.

Klauda, Paul. "Panel Discusses Nuclear Concerns with Teens." *Minneapolis Star-Tribune,* June 22, 1986.

Kneebone, Elizabeth. "The Changing Geography of US Poverty." Brookings.edu, February 15, 2017. https://www.brookings.edu /testimonies/the-changing-geography-of-us-poverty/.

Kotke, Lee. "U Program for People Minds Their Business." *Minneapolis Tribune,* January 7, 1968.

Kumanyika, Chenjerai, guest host. "Ruth Wilson Gilmore Makes the Case for Abolition." Intercepted (podcast), January 10, 2020. https://theintercept.com/2020/06/10/ruth-wilson-gilmore-makes -the-case-for-abolition/.

LaDuke, Winona, and Deborah Cowen. "Beyond Windigo Infrastructure." *South Atlantic Quarterly* 119 (2020): 243–68.

LaGrand, James. *Indian Metropolis: Native Americans in Chicago, 1945–1975.* Urbana: University of Illinois Press, 2002.

Lawrence, Bonita. *"Real" Indians and Others: Mixed-Blood Urban Native Peoples and Indigenous Nationhood.* Vancouver: University of British Columbia Press, 2004.

Lawrence, Bonita, and Enakshi Dua. "Decolonizing Antiracism." *Social Justice* 32 (2005): 120–43.

League of Women Voters. "The League's Legislative Program." In *For the Public Record: A Documentary History of the League of Women Voters,* ed. Barbara Stuhler, 46–48. Westport, Conn.: Greenwood Press, 2000.

———. "Why Join the League of Women Voters?" In *For the Public Record: A Documentary History of the League of Women Voters,* ed. Barbara Stuhler, 37–38. Westport, Conn.: Greenwood Press, 2000.

League of Women Voters of Minneapolis. *Indians in Minneapolis.* Minneapolis: League of Women Voters of Minneapolis, 1968.

———. *The Police and the Community.* Minneapolis: League of Women Voters of Minneapolis, 1968.

League of Women Voters of Minnesota. *Indians in Minnesota.* 1st ed. Minneapolis: League of Women Voters of Minnesota, 1962.

———. *Indians in Minnesota.* 2d ed. Minneapolis: League of Women Voters of Minnesota, 1971.

———. *Indians in Minnesota.* 3d ed. Minneapolis: League of Women Voters of Minnesota, 1974.

Legg, Stephen. *Spaces of Colonialism: Delhi's Urban Governmentalities.* Oxford and Malden, Mass.: Blackwell Publishers, 2007.

Lightfoot, John. *Down on Skid Row.* Twin Cities Public Television, 1998.

Limerick, Patricia N. *The Legacy of Conquest: The Unbroken Past of the American West.* New York: W. W. Norton, 1987.

Lincoln, Kenneth. *Indi'n Humor: Bicultural Play in Native America.* New York: Oxford University Press, 1993.

Lipsitz, George. *How Racism Takes Place.* Philadelphia: Temple University Press, 2011.

Lloyd, David. "Settler Colonialism and the State of Exception: The Example of Palestine/Israel." *Settler Colonial Studies* 2 (2012): 59–80.

Lobo, Susan. "Urban Clan Mothers: Key Households in Cities." *American Indian Quarterly* 27 (2003): 505–22.

Mackey, Eva. "The Apologizer's Apology." In *Reconciling Canada: Historical Injustices and the Contemporary Culture of Redress,* ed. Jennifer Henderson and Pauline Wakeham. Toronto and Buffalo: University of Toronto Press, 2013.

———. *Unsettled Expectations: Uncertainty, Land, and Settler Decoloniza-tion.* Halifax and Winnipeg: Fernwood Publishing, 2016.

Macoun, Alissa, and Elizabeth Strakosch. "The Ethical Demands of Settler Colonial Theory." *Settler Colonial Studies* 3 (2013): 426–33.

Mamdani, Mahmood. "When Does a Settler Become a Native? Reflections of the Colonial Roots of Citizenship in Equatorial and South Africa." Unpublished lecture, University of Cape Town, May 13, 1998. https://citizenshiprightsafrica.org/wp-content/uploads/1998/05/mamdani-1998-inaugural-lecture.pdf.

Marable, Manning. *Race, Reform, and Rebellion: The Second Reconstruction in Black America, 1945–1990.* Jackson and London: University Press of Mississippi, 1991.

Marks, Wizard. "Honeywell: From the Damper Flapper to a Corporate Giant in 105 Years." *The Alley,* July 1990.

———. "I-35W Disrupted Minority Community, Boxed-In Phillips." *The Alley,* August 1990.

Martin, Judith, and Anthony Goddard. *Past Choices/Present Landscapes: The Impact of Urban Renewal on the Twin Cities.* Minneapolis: Center for Urban and Regional Affairs, University of Minnesota, 1989.

Massey, Doreen. "A Counterhegemonic Relationality of Place." In *Mobile Urbanism: Cities and Policymaking in the Global Age,* ed. Eugene McCann and Kevin Ward, 1–14. Minneapolis: University of Minnesota Press, 2011.

———. "A Global Sense of Place." *Marxism Today* 38 (1991): 24–29.

Matthiessen, Peter. *In the Spirit of Crazy Horse.* New York: Viking, 1991.

Mawani, Renisa. "Law, Settler Colonialism, and 'the Forgotten Space' of Maritime Worlds." *Annual Review of Law and Social Science* 12 (2016): 107–31.

Mays, Kyle. "Pontiac's Ghost in the Motor City: Indigeneity and the Discursive Construction of Modern Detroit." *Middle West Review* 2 (2016): 115–42.

Mbembe, Achille. *On the Postcolony.* Berkeley: University of California Press, 2001.

McClintock, Nathan. "Urban Agriculture, Racial Capitalism, and Resistance in the Settler-Colonial City." *Geography Compass* 12 (2018): 1–16.

McCue, Duncan. "What It Takes for Aboriginal People to Make the News." *CBC News,* January 29, 2014. http://www.cbc.ca/1.2514466.

McGrath, Dennis. "Subsidies May Aid Defense Contractor." *Minneapolis Star-Tribune,* June 4, 1987.

McNeill, J. R., and Peter Engleke. *The Great Acceleration: An Environmental History of the Anthropocene since 1945.* Cambridge: Belknap Press, 2016.

Means, Russell, and Marvin Wolf. *Where White Men Fear to Tread: The Autobiography of Russell Means.* New York: St. Martin's Press, 1995.

Meinig, Donald. *The Shaping of America: A Geographical Perspective on 500 Years of History.* Volume 2, *Continental America, 1800–1867.* New Haven and London: Yale University Press, 1993.

Meriam, Lewis. *The Problem with Indian Administration.* New York: Institute for Government Research, 1928.

Meyer, Melissa L. *The White Earth Tragedy: Ethnicity and Dispossession at a Minnesota Anishinaabe Reservation, 1889–1920.* Lincoln: University of Nebraska Press, 1994.

Meyer, Roy Willard. *History of the Santee Sioux: United States Indian Policy on Trial.* Lincoln: University of Nebraska Press, 1993.

Miller, Douglas. *Indians on the Move: Native American Mobility and Urbanization in the Twentieth Century.* Chapel Hill: University of North Carolina Press, 2019.

Miller, Jessica Ty. "Temporal Analysis of Displacement: Racial Capitalism and Settler Colonial Urban Space." *Geoforum* (2020). https://doi.org/10.1016/j.geoforum.2020.08.005.

Miller, John. "America's Most Literate Cities." America's Most Literate Cities Study, Central Connecticut State University, 2007. http://web.ccsu.edu/americasmostliteratecities.

Millett, Larry. "Ghost of the Gateway: The Metropolitan Building, Minneapolis." *Minnesota History* 53 (1992): 112–15.

Milloy, John. *A National Crime: The Canadian Government and the Residential School System, 1879–1986.* Winnipeg: University of Manitoba Press, 1999.

Milner, Eva Lucy. "Devaluation, Erasure, and Replacement: Urban Frontiers and the Reproduction of Settler Colonial Urbanism in Tel Aviv." *Environment and Planning D: Society and Space* 38 (2020): 267–86.

Minneapolis Department of Civil Rights. Case Files, 1967–1977. Minnesota Historical Society Archive, St. Paul.

Minneapolis Foundation. *A New Age of Immigrants: Making Immigration Work for Minnesota.* Minneapolis: Minneapolis Foundation, 2010.

Minneapolis Star. "Indians Are Drawn from Reservations by the Job Opportunities of the Cities." September 20, 1969.

Minneapolis Star-Tribune. "Building Better Lives with Land Mines." June 6, 1987.

Minneapolis Tribune. "The Plight of the Urban Indian." April 11, 1968.

Minnesota Human Rights Commission. *Police Brutality, Minneapolis Public Hearing #2,* June 25, 1975, Minneapolis.

Minnesota Journal. "TB Walker Reputed to Be Richest Man in Minnesota." In *Sketches of the Life of Honorable TB Walker,* ed. Platt B. Walker, 64. Minneapolis: Lumberman Publishing Company, 1907.

Misra, Tanvi. "Confronting the Myths of Suburban Poverty." *Citylab,*
July 6, 2017. https://www.citylab.com/solutions/2017/07
/confronting-the-myths-about-suburban-poverty/532680/.

Mitchell, George. "Aldermanic Campaign Speech, Ward 6." Gerald
Vizenor Papers. Date unknown, 1967.

Model City Policy and Planning Committee. *Problem Analysis: Goals,
Objectives, Strategies.* Minneapolis: Minneapolis Model City Program, 1971.

Mohl, Raymond. "Planned Destruction: The Interstates and Central
City Housing." In *The Making of Urban America,* 3d ed., ed. Ray-
mond Mohl and Roger Biles, 287–302. Lanham, Md.: Rowan and
Littlefield, 2012.

Monteith, William. "Markets and Monarchs: Indigenous Urbanism in
Postcolonial Kampala." *Settler Colonial Studies* 9 (2019): 247–65.

Morgensen, Scott Lauria. "Queer Settler Colonialism in Canada and
Israel: Articulating Two-Spirit and Palestinian Queer Critiques."
Settler Colonial Studies 2 (2012): 167–90.

Nagam, Julie. "Digging Up Indigenous History in Toronto's Cityscape."
Canadian Dimension 43 (2009).

National Council on Indian Opportunity. *Public Forum before the Committee on Urban Indians in Minneapolis–St. Paul, Minnesota, March
18–19, 1969.* Washington, D.C.: National Council on Indian Opportunity, 1969.

Needham, Marvin. "Police Brutality, an American Indian Problem."
Unpublished manuscript, 1967.

Neils, Elaine. *Reservation to City: Indian Migration and Federal Relocation.* Chicago: University of Chicago Department of Geography,
1971.

Nelson, Bruce. "Racist Remarks Not a Right, Court Rules." *Minneapolis
Star-Tribune,* December 12, 1980.

Nesterak, Max. "The 'Wall of Forgotten Natives' Returns with Call
for Greater Response to Homelessness." *Minnesota Reformer,*
September 4, 2020.

Neugebauer, Robynne. "First Nations Peoples and Law Enforcement:
Community Perspectives on Police Response." In *Criminal
Injustice: Racism in the Criminal Justice System,* ed. Robynne
Neugebauer, 109–28. Toronto: Canadian Scholars' Press, 2000.

Newlund, Sam. "Community Action Program Helps Indians Help
Themselves." *Minneapolis Tribune,* July 8, 1966.

———. "Indian 'Red Power' Now Emerging; Minority Asks Share in
Government Jobs." *Minneapolis Tribune,* October 23, 1966.

———. "Reservations Offer Little Regular Work; Isolation from Com-
merce, Poor Farms Are Factors." *Minneapolis Tribune,* July 15,
1966.

New York Times. "Some Dismay in Honeywell's Hometown." *New York Times,* June 8, 1999.

Nickrand, Jessica. "Minneapolis's White Lie." *Atlantic,* February 21, 2015. http://www.theatlantic.com/business/archive/2015/02/minneapoliss-white-lie/385702/.

Nightingale, Carl. *Segregation: A Global History of Divided Cities.* Chicago: University of Chicago Press, 2012.

Noterman, Elsa. "Taking Back Vacant Property." *Urban Geography,* published online March 26, 2020. https://doi.org/10.1080/02723638.2020.1743519.

Oakes, Larry. "13 Juveniles among 140 Arrested at Honeywell Protest," *Minneapolis Star-Tribune,* April 18, 1986.

Panitch, Leo, and Sam Gindin. *The Making of Global Capitalism: The Political Economy of American Empire.* London and New York: Verso, 2012.

Pappé, Illan. "Shetl Colonialism: First and Last Impressions of Indigeneity by Colonised Colonisers." *Settler Colonial Studies* 2 (2012): 39–58.

Parenti, Christian. *Tropic of Chaos: Climate Change and the New Geography of Violence.* New York: Nation Books, 2011.

Parker, Steve. "What Happened to Les Robinson? Alleged Brutality Case." *The Alley,* July 1980.

Pasternak, Shiri. "How Capitalism Will Save Colonialism: The Privatization of Reserve Lands in Canada." *Antipode* 47 (2015): 179–96.

Pasternak, Shiri, and Tia Dafnos. "How Does a Settler State Secure the Circuitry of Capital?" *Environment and Planning D; Society and Space* 36 (2018): 739–57.

Perez, Jane. "After the Cold War: Views from Africa; Stranded by Superpowers, Africa Seeks an Identity." *New York Times,* May 17, 1992.

Perry, Adele. *Aqueduct: Colonialism, Resources, and the Histories We Remember.* Winnipeg: ARP Books, 2016.

———. *On the Edge of Empire: Gender, Race, and the Making of British Columbia, 1849–1871.* Toronto: University of Toronto Press, 2001.

Perry, Barbara. *Policing Race and Place in Indian Country: Over- and Underenforcement.* Lanham, Md.: Lexington Books, 2009.

Peters, Evelyn. "Aboriginal Public Policy in Urban Areas: An Introduction." In *Urban Aboriginal Policy Making in Canadian Municipalities,* ed. Evelyn Peters, 3–32. Kingston and Montreal: McGill–Queen's University Press, 2011.

———. "Three Myths about Aboriginals in Cities." Presentation to the Canadian Federation for the Humanities and Social Sciences, Ottawa, March 25, 2004.

———. "'Urban' and 'Aboriginal': An Impossible Contradiction?" In *City*

Lives and City Forms: Critical Research and Canadian Urbanism.
Toronto and Buffalo: University of Toronto Press, 1996.

Peters, Evelyn, and Chris Andersen, eds. *Indigenous in the City: Contemporary Identities and Cultural Innovation.* Vancouver: University of British Columbia Press, 2014.

Peters, Evelyn, Matthew Stock, and Adrian Werner. *Rooster Town: The
History of an Urban Métis Community, 1901–1961.* Winnipeg: University of Manitoba Press, 2018.

Phillips Neighborhood Improvement Association. *Phillips Comprehensive Neighborhood Plan: Inventory and Analysis.* Minneapolis: Phillips Neighborhood Improvement Association, 1979.

Pifarré i Arolas, Héctor, Enrique Acosta, Guillem López-Casasnovas,
Adeline Lo, Catia Nicodemo, Tim Riffe, and Mikko Myrskylä.
"Years of Life Lost to COVID-19 in 81 Countries." *Scientific Reports*
11, 3504 (2021). https://doi.org/10.1038/s41598-021-83040-3.

Piterberg, Gabriel. *The Returns of Zionism: Myths, Politics, and Scholarship in Israel.* London and New York: Verso, 2008.

———. "Settlers and Their States." *New Left Review* 62 (2010): 115–24.

Porter, Libby, Sue Jackson, and Louise Johnson. "Remaking Imperial
Power in the City: The Case of the William Barak Building, Melbourne." *Environment and Planning D: Society and Space* 37 (2019):
1119–37.

Porter, Libby, and Oren Yiftachel. "Urbanizing Settler-Colonial Studies: Introduction to the Special Issue." *Settler Colonial Studies* 9
(2019): 177–86.

Povinelli, Elizabeth. *The Cunning of Recognition: Indigenous Alterities
and the Making of Australian Multiculturalism.* Durham, N.C.:
Duke University Press, 2002.

Pratt, John, and Edson Spencer. "Dynamics of Corporate Philanthropy
in Minnesota." *Daedalus: Journal of the American Academy of Arts
and Sciences* 129 (2000): 269–92.

Ramírez, Margaret Marietta. "Take the Houses Back/Take the Land
Back: Black and Indigenous Urban Futures in Oakland. *Urban
Geography,* published online March 16, 2020. https://doi.org
/10.1080/02723638.2020.1736440.

Ramirez, Renya K. *Native Hubs: Culture, Community, and Belonging in
Silicon Valley and Beyond.* Durham, N.C.: Duke University Press,
2007.

Reagan, Ronald. "Radio Address to the Nation on Welfare Reform."
Presidential Address, Santa Barbara, February 15, 1986, published online by the American Presidency Project, University
of California at Santa Barbara. http://www.presidency.ucsb.edu
/ws/?pid=36875.

———. "Remarks and a Question-and-Answer Session with the Students and Faculty at Moscow State University." Presidential Address, Moscow, Russia, May 31, 1988, published online by the Ronald Reagan Library and Museum. https://www.reaganlibrary.gov /archives/speech/remarks-and-question-and-answer-session -students-and-faculty-moscow-state.

Reichard, Gary. "Mayor Hubert H. Humphrey." *Minnesota History* 56 (1998): 50–67.

Rhook, Nadia. "What's in a Grid? Finding the Form of Settler Colonialism in Melbourne." Global Urban History Blog, February 11, 2016. https://globalurbanhistory.com/2016/02/11/whats-in-a-grid -finding-the-form-of-settler-colonialism-in-melbourne/#_ftnref1.

Richardson, Robbie. "Some Observations on 'Decolonizing' the University." *Los Angeles Review of Books,* July 6, 2021. https://www .lareviewofbooks.org/article/antiracism-in-the-contemporary -university/.

Rifkin, Mark. *Settler Common Sense: Queerness and Everyday Colonialism in the American Renaissance.* Minneapolis: University of Minnesota Press, 2014.

Robertson, Chuck. "Man Beaten by Police." *The Alley,* September 1976.

Ross, Robert, and Gerard Telkamp, eds. *Colonial Cities: Essays on Urbanism in a Colonial Context.* Dordrecht, the Netherlands: Martinus Nijhoff Publishers, 1985.

Rouhana, Nadim N., and Areej Sabbagh-Khoury. "Settler-Colonial Citizenship: Conceptualizing the Relationship between Israel and Its Palestinian Citizens." *Settler Colonial Studies* 5 (2015): 205–25.

Rowan, Carl. "The Plight of the Upper Midwest Indian: 'The First Are Last.'" *Minneapolis Tribune,* Special Supplement, February 17–March 3, 1957.

Rowse, Tim. "The Reforming State, the Concerned Public and Indigenous Political Actors." *Australian Journal of Politics and History* 56 (2010): 66–81.

Rupar, Aaron. "'Racist' Twin Cities Maps Make Point about Interstate Highways." *City Pages,* August 18, 2014. http://www.citypages .com/news/racist-twin-cities-maps-make-point-about-interstate -highways-images-6543145.

Said, Edward. *Culture and Imperialism.* New York: Vintage, 1994.

Salaita, Steven. *Inter/Nationalism: Decolonizing Native America and Palestine.* Minneapolis: University of Minnesota Press, 2016.

Salamanca, Omar Jabary, Mezno Qato, Kareem Rabie, and Sobhi Samour. "Past Is Present: Settler Colonialism in Palestine." *Settler Colonial Studies* 2 (2012): 1–8.

Saunders, Richard. "Suburbia Booms as 'Blue Collar' Workers Arrive." *Minneapolis Tribune,* January 10, 1960.

Sawyer, Liz. "After Outcry and Protests, Walker Art Center Will Remove 'Scaffold' Sculpture." *Minneapolis Star-Tribune,* May 28, 2017. https://www.startribune.com/walker-will-take-down-controversial-sculpture-after-protests/424820003/.

Schneider, Greg, and Renae Merle. "Reagan's Defense Buildup Bridged Military Eras, Huge Budgets Brought Life Back to Industry." *Washington Post,* June 9, 2004.

Schulman, Sarah. *The Gentrification of the Mind: Witness to a Lost Imagination.* Berkeley: University of California Press, 2012.

Schuyler, Montgomery. "Glimpses of Western Architecture." *Harper's New Monthly Magazine* 83 (1981): 736–55.

Sharma, Nandita, and Cynthia Wright. "Decolonizing Resistance, Challenging Colonial States." *Social Justice* 35 (2008–9): 120–38.

Shellum, Bernie. "Lawyer Hall Urges Indians to Be Politically Active." *Minneapolis Tribune,* February 27, 1967.

Shihade, Magid. "Settler Colonialism and Conflict: The Israeli State and Its Palestinian Subjects." *Settler Colonial Studies* 2 (2012): 108–23.

Shoemaker, Nancy. "Indians and Ethnic Choices: American Indian Organizations in Minneapolis, 1920–1950." *Western Historical Quarterly* 19 (1988): 431–47.

Simon, David. "Third World Colonial Cities in Context: Conceptual and Theoretical Approaches with Particular Reference to Africa." *Progress in Human Geography* 8 (1984): 66–81.

Simpson, Audra. *Mohawk Interruptus: Political Life across the Borders of Settler States.* Durham, N.C.: Duke University Press, 2014.

———. "The Ruse of Consent and the Anatomy of 'Refusal': Cases from Indigenous North America and Australia." *Postcolonial Studies* 20 (2017): 18–33.

———. "Whither Settler Colonialism?" *Settler Colonial Studies* 6 (2016): 438–45.

Simpson, Audra, and Andrea Smith. *Theorizing Native Studies.* Durham, N.C., and London: Duke University Press, 2014.

Simpson, Leanne Betasamosake. *As We Have Always Done: Indigenous Freedom through Radical Resistance.* Minneapolis: University of Minnesota Press, 2017.

———. *Dancing on Our Turtle's Back: Stories of Nishnaabeg Re-Creation, Resurgence, and a New Emergence.* Winnipeg: ARP Books, 2011.

———. "Indigenous Resurgence and Co-Resistance." *Critical Ethnic Studies* 2 (2016): 19–34.

———, ed. *Lighting the Eighth Fire: The Liberation, Resurgence, and Protection of Indigenous Nations.* Winnipeg: ARP Books, 2008.

Simpson, Leanne Betasamosake, Rinaldo Walcott, and Glen Coulthard. "Idle No More and Black Lives Matter: An Exchange." *Studies in Social Justice* 12 (2018): 75–89.

Simpson, Michael. "Fossil Urbanism: Fossil Fuel Flows, Settler Colonial Circulations, and the Production of Carbon Cities." *Urban Geography (2020)*. https://doi.org/10.1080/02723638.2020.1840206.

Simpson, Michael, and Jen Bagelman. "Decolonizing Urban Political Ecologies: The Production of Nature in Settler Colonial Cities." *Annals of the American Association of Geographers* 108 (2018): 558–68.

Skovbroten, Gary, and Joan Wolens. *Indians of the Urban Slum: Field Notes from Minneapolis*. Minneapolis: Training Center for Community Programs, University of Minnesota, 1970.

Smiles, Deondre. "'. . . to the Grave'—Autopsy, Settler Structures, and Indigenous Counter-Conduct." *Geoforum* 91 (2018): 141–50.

Smith, Lindsey Claire. "Talisi through the Lens: Locating Tulsa in the Films of Sterlin Harjo." In *Settler City Limits: Indigenous Resurgence and Colonial Violence in the Urban Prairie West*, ed. Heather Dorries, Robert Henry, David Hugill, Tyler McCreary, and Julie Tomiak, 251–70. Winnipeg: University of Manitoba Press, 2019.

Smith, Neil. *American Empire: Roosevelt's Geographers and the Prelude to Globalization*. Berkeley: University of California Press, 2003.

———. *The New Urban Frontier: Gentrification and the Revanchist City*. New York: Routledge, 1996.

———. "The Revolutionary Imperative." *Antipode* 41 (2009): 50–65.

Smith, Paul Chaat and Robert Warrior. *Like a Hurricane: The Indian Movement from Alcatraz to Wounded Knee*. New York: New Press, 1996.

Snelgrove, Corey, Rita Kaur Dhamoon, and Jeff Corntassel. "Unsettling Settler Colonialism: The Discourse and Politics of Settlers, and Solidarity with Indigenous Nations." *Decolonization: Indigeneity, Education, and Society* 3 (2014): 1–32.

Snipp, C. Matthew. "American Indians and Alaska Natives in Urban Environments." In *Indigenous in the City: Contemporary Identities and Cultural Innovation*, ed. Evelyn Peters and Chris Anderson, 173–92. Vancouver: University of British Columbia Press, 2013.

Sommers, Jeff, and Nicholas Blomley. "The Worst Block in Vancouver." In *Stan Douglas: Every Building on 100 West Hastings*, ed. Reid Shier, 18–58. Vancouver: Contemporary Art Gallery and Arsenal Pulp, 2002.

Specktor, Mordecai. "City and County Decline to Charge Police in Squad Car Trunk Incident." *The Circle*, June 1992.

———. "Military Spending Spurs Controversy among Neighbors." *Minneapolis Star-Tribune*, September 10, 1986.

Speed, Shannon. "Structures of Settler Capitalism in Abya Yala." *American Quarterly* 69 (2017): 783–90.

Stanger-Ross, Jordan. "Municipal Colonialism in Vancouver: City

Planning and the Conflict over Indian Reserves, 1928–1950s."
Canadian Historical Review 89 (2008): 541–80.

Stasiulis, Daiva, and Nira Yuval-Davis. *Unsettling Settler Societies: Articulations of Gender, Race, Ethnicity, and Class.* London and Thousand Oaks, Calif.: Sage, 1995.

Stein, Jeff. "U.S. Military Budget Inches Closer to $1 Trillion Mark, as Concerns over Federal Deficit Grow." *Washington Post,* June 19, 2018.

Stevens, Amy. "Reagan View of Indians Called 'Ignorant.'" *Los Angeles Times,* June 8, 1988.

Stiegler, Ben. "Letter to the Editor." *Minneapolis Star-Tribune,* November 24, 1968.

Stuhler, Barbara, ed. *For the Public Record: A Documentary History of the League of Women Voters.* New York and Westport, Conn.: Greenwood Press, 2000.

Suarez, Sasha. "Indigenizing Minneapolis: Building American Indian Community Infrastructure in the Mid-Twentieth Century." In *Indian Cities: Histories of Indigenous Urbanism,* ed. Kent Blansett, Cathleen D. Cahill, and Andrew Needham. Norman: University of Oklahoma Press, 2021.

Sugrue, Thomas. *The Origins of the Urban Crisis: Race and Inequality in Postwar Detroit.* Princeton, N.J.: Princeton University Press, 1999.

Tai, Wendy, and Jon Jeter. "Minorities: Police Abuse Rises/Bouza Denies Charges." *Minneapolis Star-Tribune,* September 27, 1988.

Taylor, David Vassar. *African Americans in Minnesota.* St. Paul: Minnesota Historical Society Press, 2002.

Teaford, Jon. *The Metropolitan Revolution: The Rise of Post-Urban America.* New York: Columbia University Press, 2006.

Tedesco, Delacey, and Jen Bagelman. "The 'Missing' Politics of Whiteness and Rightful Presence in the Settler Colonial City." *Millennium: Journal of International Studies* 45 (2017): 380–402.

Thompson, Derek. "The Miracle of Minneapolis." *The Atlantic,* February 16, 2015. http://www.theatlantic.com/magazine/archive/2015/03/the-miracle-of-minneapolis/384975/.

Thornton, Michael A. "Settling Sapporo: City and State in the Global Nineteenth Century." PhD dissertation, Harvard University, 2018.

Thrush, Coll. *Native Seattle: Histories from the Crossing-Over Place.* 2d ed. Seattle: University of Washington Press, 2007.

Todd, Richard M. "A Better Day in the Neighborhood: The Rise and Fall of Poverty Concentration in the Twin Cities," *Community Dividend* (Fall 2003). https://www.minneapolisfed.org/publications/community-dividend/a-better-day-in-the-neighborhood-the-rise-and-decline-of-poverty-concentration-in-the-twin-cities-19702000.

Todd, Zoe. "Decolonizing Prairie Public Art: The Further Adventures of the Ness Namew." In *Settler City Limits: Indigenous Resurgence and Colonial Violence in the Urban Prairie West,* ed. Heather Dorries, Robert Henry, David Hugill, Tyler McCreary, and Julie Tomiak, 289–309. Winnipeg: University of Manitoba Press, 2019.

Toews, Owen. *Stolen City: Racial Capitalism and the Making of Winnipeg.* Winnipeg: ARP Books, 2019.

Tomiak, Julie. "Contested Entitlement: The Kapyong Barracks, Treaty Rights, and Settler Colonialism in Winnipeg." In *Settler City Limits: Indigenous Resurgence and Colonial Violence in the Urban Prairie West,* ed. Heather Dorries, Robert Henry, David Hugill, Tyler McCreary, and Julie Tomiak, 95–117. Winnipeg: University of Manitoba Press, 2019.

———. "Contesting the Settler City: Indigenous Self-Determination, New Urban Reserves, and the Neoliberalization of Colonialism." *Antipode* 49 (2017): 928–45.

———. "Unsettling Ottawa: Settler Colonialism, Indigenous Resistance, and the Politics of Scale." *Canadian Journal of Urban Research* 25 (2016): 8–21.

Tomiak, Julie, Tyler McCreary, David Hugill, Robert Henry, and Heather Dorries. "Introduction." In *Settler City Limits: Indigenous Resurgence and Colonial Violence in the Urban Prairie West,* ed. Heather Dorries, Robert Henry, David Hugill, Tyler McCreary, and Julie Tomiak, 1–21. Winnipeg: University of Manitoba Press, 2019.

Training Center for Community Programs. Program Files 1966–1973, University Extension Records. University of Minnesota Archives, Andersen Library, Minneapolis.

Treuer, David. *The Heartbeat of Wounded Knee: Native America from 1890 to the Present.* New York: Riverhead Books, 2019.

Tuck, Eve. "Suspending Damage: A Letter to Communities." *Harvard Educational Review* 79 (2009): 409–27.

Tuck, Eve, and K. Wayne Yang. "Decolonization Is Not a Metaphor." *Decolonization: Indigeneity, Education, and Society* 1 (2012): 1–40.

Turner, Frederick Jackson. *The Frontier in American History.* Tucson: University of Arizona Press, 1986 [1947].

Tyrrell, Ian. "American Exceptionalism in an Age of International History." *American Historical Review* 96 (1991): 1031–55.

United States Commission on Civil Rights. *Bridging the Gap: The Twin Cities Native American Community, A Report.* Washington: U.S. Commission on Civil Rights, 1975.

United States Department of Defense. "Defense Budget Overview: United States Department of Defense Fiscal Year 2019 Budget Request." Washington, D.C.: Office of the Secretary of Defense

(Comptroller), 2018. https://dod.defense.gov/Portals/1/Documents
/pubs/FY2019-Budget-Request-Overview-Book.pdf.

Usner, Daniel. *Indian Work: Language and Livelihood in Native American History.* Cambridge: Harvard University Press, 2009.

Valelly, Richard. *Radicalism in the States: The Minnesota Farmer-Labor Party and the American Political Economy.* Chicago: University of Chicago Press, 1989.

Vang, Chia Youyee. *Hmong in Minnesota.* St. Paul: Minnesota Historical Society Press, 2008.

Venables, Robert. "Letter to the Editor: Reagan Remarks Insult American Indians." *New York Times,* June 23, 1988.

Veracini, Lorenzo. "Introducing Settler Colonial Studies," *Settler Colonial Studies* 1 (2011): 1–12.

——. "The Other Shift: Settler Colonialism, Israel, and the Occupation." *Journal of Palestine Studies* 42 (2013): 26–42.

——. "Settler Collective, Founding Violence, and Disavowal: The Settler Colonial Situation." *Journal of Intercultural Studies* 29 (2008): 363–79.

——. *The Settler Colonial Present.* Basingstoke: Palgrave-Macmillan, 2015.

——. *Settler Colonialism: A Theoretical Overview.* Basingstoke: Palgrave-Macmillan, 2010.

——. "Settler Colonialism as a Distinct Mode of Domination." In *The Routledge Handbook of the History of Settler Colonialism,* ed. Edward Cavanagh and Lorenzo Veracini, 1–8. London: Routledge, 2016.

——. "Suburbia, Settler Colonialism and the World Turned Inside Out." *Housing, Theory, and Society* 29 (2012): 339–57.

——. "What Can Settler Colonial Studies Offer to an Interpretation of the Conflict in Israel–Palestine?" *Settler Colonial Studies* 5 (2015): 268–71.

Viso, Olga. "Learning in Public: An Open Letter on Sam Durant's *Scaffold.*" Walker Art Center, May 26, 2017. https://walkerart.org/magazine/learning-in-public-an-open-letter-on-sam-durants-scaffold.

Vizenor, Gerald. "1966: 'Plymouth Avenue Is Going to Burn.'" *Twin Citian Magazine,* October 1966.

——. *Crossbloods: Bone Courts, Bingo, and Other Reports.* Minneapolis: University of Minnesota Press, 1990.

——. "Dennis of Wounded Knee." *American Indian Quarterly* 7 (1983): 51–65.

——. Gerald Vizenor Papers, 1950–1998. Minnesota Historical Society Archives. St. Paul.

——. "Indian's Lot: Rent, Ruins, and Roaches." *Minneapolis Tribune,* January 12, 1969.

———. *Interior Landscapes: Autobiographical Myths and Metaphors.* Albany: State University of New York Press, 2009.

———. *Manifest Manners: Narratives on Postindian Survivance.* London and Lincoln: University of Nebraska Press, 1999 [1994].

———. *Wordarrows: Indians and Whites in the Fur Trade.* Minneapolis: University of Minnesota Press, 1978.

Wacquant, Loïc. "Three Pernicious Premises in the Study of the American Ghetto." *International Journal of Urban and Regional Research* 21 (1997): 341–53.

Wagner, Peter. *Native Americans Are Overrepresented in Minnesota's Prisons and Jails.* Northampton, Mass.: Prison Policy Initiative, 2004. http://www.prisonpolicy.org/graphs/MN_Native.html.

Walcott, Rinaldo. "The Problem of the Human: Black Ontologies and 'the Coloniality of Our Being.'" In *Postcoloniality–Decoloniality–Black Critique: Joints and Fissures,* ed. Sabine Broeck and Carsten Junker. Frankfurt/New York: Campus Verlag, 2014.

Waligora, Bob. "Story of Survival." *The Alley,* March 1983.

Wang, Jackie. *Carceral Capitalism.* Los Angeles: Semiotext(e), 2018.

Waterman Wittstock, Laura. "Becoming a City of Shame." *Minneapolis Star-Tribune,* May 25, 1993.

Waziyatawin. *What Does Justice Look Like? The Struggle for Liberation in Dakota Homeland.* St. Paul: Living Justice Press, 2008.

Weber, Laura. "Gentiles Preferred: Minneapolis Jews and Employment 1920–1950." *Minnesota History* 52 (1991): 166–82.

Weizman, Eyal. "The War of Streets and Houses: Thomas Bugeaud." *Cabinet Magazine* (summer 2006). http://www.cabinetmagazine .org/issues/22/bugeaud.php.

Westerman, Gwen, and Bruce White. *Mni Sota Makoce: The Land of the Dakota.* St. Paul: Minnesota Historical Society Press, 2012.

Westermeyer, Joseph. "'The Drunken Indian': Myths and Realities." *Psychiatric Annals* 4 (1974): 29–31.

———. "Indian Powerless in Minnesota." *Society* 10 (1973): 45–52.

Western, John. "Undoing the Colonial City?" *Geographical Review* 75 (1985): 335–57.

White, Richard. *The Middle Ground: Indians, Empires, and the Republics in the Great Lakes Region, 1650–1815.* Cambridge: Cambridge University Press, 1991.

Williams, Chris. "New Census Data: Minnesota Somali Population Grows." *Minneapolis Star-Tribune,* October 27, 2011.

Williams, Raymond. *Keywords: A Vocabulary of Culture and Society,* rev. ed. New York: Oxford University Press, 1976.

Williams, Timothy. "Quietly, Indians Reshape Cities and Reservations." *New York Times,* April 13, 2013.

Wilson, Kathi, and Evelyn Peters. "'You Can Make a Place for It':

Remapping Urban First Nations Spaces of Identity." *Environment and Planning D: Society and Space* 23 (2005): 395–413.

Wingerd, Mary. *North Country: The Making of Minnesota.* Minneapolis: University of Minnesota Press, 2010.

Wolfe, Patrick. "Settler Colonialism and the Elimination of the Native." *Journal of Genocide Research* 8 (2006): 387–409.

———. *Settler Colonialism and the Transformation of Anthropology: The Politics and Poetics of an Ethnographic Event.* London and New York: Cassell, 1999.

Wood, Patricia. "The 'Sarcee War': Fragmented Citizenship and the City." *Space and Polity* 10 (2006): 229–42.

Woods, Richard. *Rural and City Indians in Minnesota Prisons.* Minneapolis: Training Center for Community Programs, University of Minnesota, 1970.

Woods, Richard, and Arthur Harkins. *Indian Employment in Minneapolis.* Minneapolis: Training Center for Community Programs, University of Minnesota, 1968.

———. *A Review of Recent Research on Minneapolis Indians: 1968–1969.* Minneapolis: Training Center for Community Programs, University of Minnesota, 1969.

Woodward, Rachel. "From Military Geography to Militarism's Geographies: Disciplinary Engagements with the Geographies of Militarism and Military Activities." *Progress in Human Geography* 29 (2005): 718–40.

Young, Louise. *In the Public Interest: The League of Women Voters, 1920–1970.* New York and Westport, Conn.: Greenwood Press, 1989.

Youngbear-Tibbets, Holly. "Without Due Process: The Alienation of Individual Trust Allotments of the White Earth Anishinaabeg." *American Indian Culture and Research Journal* 15 (1991): 93–138.

Yusoff, Kathryn. *A Billion Black Anthropocenes or None.* Minneapolis: University of Minnesota Press, 2018.

Index

abolition, viii, 1

accumulation, 17, 35; land, 7; martial, 119; primitive, 117; strategies, 16, 24, 29

activism, 67, 69–72, 78, 80, 82, 83, 102, 103, 105, 106, 109–11, 121, 127, 143, 165n71, 171n9; African American, 110; AIM, 71, 72, 107, 111–13; government, 36

advantage, ix, x, 4, 5, 7, 44, 89, 141, 147; structured, 3, 34, 55, 56, 59, 60; white, 37, 54, 55. *See also* disadvantage; immunity

Africa, 80, 133, 134, 138–40, 157n110; East Africa, 132

African American, ix, 34, 44, 45, 55, 104, 108, 109, 110, 116; community, 110, 116; ghettos, 61, 102, 108, 110

Alfred, Taiaiake, 15, 26

alienation, 19, 97, 98, 135; territorial, 8, 12, 46

Alley, The, 95, 101, 129

Almond, Eric, 95, 129

American: capitalism, 120; conquest, 130; defense, 121; expansionism, 146; hegemony, 119; innocence, 146, 147; "interests," 118, 131, 134, 135, 140; military, 119, 138; prosperity, 119, 134; taxpayers, 119

American empire, 5, 115, 118, 120, 128, 130, 131, 134, 135, 137, 138

American Housing Act, 39

American Indian Cultural Corridor, xi, 49

American Indian Movement (AIM), 71, 72, 91, 102, 107–13, 124, 166n5, 168n54, 168n63, 169n65, 170n81, 173n43

Anishinaabe, 9, 47, 61

anti-Black, 27, 92

antibrutality, 103,104

anticapitalist, 76

anticolonial, 27, 138

anti-imperialist, 146

antiracism, 30, 65, 66, 67, 75, 77, 78, 83–85. *See also* liberal; racism

Area Denial Artillery Munition (ADAM). *See* land mines

assimilation, 8, 13, 46, 81; assimilationism, 82, 83, 88; assimilationist, 47; assimilative, 86

Banks, Dennis, 71, 105, 108, 110, 124, 126, 160n54

Bdote, x, 11

Bellecourt, Clyde, 91, 105, 107, 111–13, 169n65, 171n88

Black Lives Matter, 171n9

Black Panther Party (BPP), 108, 109, 170n81

Black Patrol, 110

Black rebellion 109, 113

Brown, John, 1

Bruyneel, Kevin, 86

Bureau of Indian Affairs (BIA), 12, 46, 47, 53, 71, 144

capitalism, 119; American, 76, 120; liberal, 10; racial 3, 27, 28

capitalist, 76, 77; colonial-, 19;

immunity, x. *See also* advantage
imperial/imperialism, 5, 8, 15,
16, 17, 27, 28, 118, 119, 172n17;
conquest, 8; expansion, 117;
practices, 31, 146; space, 16,
28; violence, 18, 31. *See also*
neo-imperialism
incarceration, 1, 95. *See also* jail;
prison
independence, 138, 139
"Indian affairs," 5, 65, 67, 68, 70,
72–74, 80, 81
Indian Patrol, 94, 104, 106, 108,
110, 111, 113, 114
Indian Reorganization Act (IRA),
12, 13
Indians in Minnesota, 70–73
Indigenous: community, 5, 13, 14,
24, 30, 32–34, 45, 47–49, 51, 60,
63, 67, 92, 94, 96, 97, 99, 102,
103, 114, 124, 129, 131, 136,
164n63, 168n63; exclusion, 67,
73; groups, 73, 104; institutions,
48; labor, 23; land, 10, 12, 13, 19,
23, 24, 26, 82; life, 12, 23, 35, 48,
75, 160n56; neighborhood, 14,
25, 30, 33–35, 39, 44, 49, 54–57,
60–63, 110, 150, 160n56; organization, 72, 73, 168n52; presence, 17, 24; relocation, 44, 63,
132; renters, 34, 43, 52, 161n68;
resources, 19; underhousing,
15; urbanites, 50, 51, 71, 72, 83,
93, 94, 95, 97–99, 113; urbanization, 45–47, 62; worlds, 22, 28.
See also non-Indigenous
individualism: liberal, 86; possessive, 77
inequity, vii, ix, 3, 6, 7, 9, 15,
32, 55, 60, 76, 84, 92, 97, 128;
colonial, 3, 5, 21; group-
differentiated, 6, 15, 21, 29, 34,
56, 116; racialized, viii, 4, 27,
33, 66, 67, 77; settler colonial,

15, 34, 35, 46, 66, 86, 156n82;
structured, 129
infrastructural, 56, 152n13
infrastructure, 10, 21, 34, 37, 55,
127
injustice, 3, 11, 69, 72, 76, 81, 83
institutional, 17, 20, 83, 72, 73,
76, 94, 114; exclusions, 14;
knowledge, 75; left, viii; power,
71; practices, 85; reform, 77, 78
integration, 10, 18, 23, 81, 82, 85,
87, 98, 99; integrationist, 79
interstate, 30, 33, 36–39, 43, 61.
See also highway
invasion, 5, 12, 28, 86, 88
Israel, 157n110

jail, 94, 96, 98, 112. *See also* prison
Japanese internment, 46
justice: redistributive, 76;
system, viii, 31, 92, 95, 97, 98,
101, 102, 110, 114, 116, 169n65.
See also injustice

Keeler, Kasey, 23, 24
Kennedy, John F., 80; administration, 73
Kenya, 133, 139
Keynesian, 36, 76
Kipfer, Stefan, 63, 116, 149
Kitagawa, Daisuke, 82
knowledge, 31, 59, 75, 78, 92, 93,
96, 97, 100, 103, 114; production,
27, 29, 31, 66, 67, 78, 92; racialized, 114; racist forms of, 59

labor, 19, 36, 41, 69, 74, 76, 79;
cheap, 42; colonial, 17; Indigenous, 23–25
Lakota, 47
land, 3, 5, 8–12, 60, 62, 69, 130,
135, 136, 143, 144; accumulation, 7; deal, 1; expropriated,
24; Indigenous, 13, 19, 23, 24,

26, 55, 82; theft, 88; use, 135, 156n77
landlord, 14, 43, 51–54, 57–59
land mines, 119, 121, 125, 127, 128
Laos, 131, 137, 138; Laotian, 131, 138
Lardy, Michael, 91, 92
League of Women Voters of Minnesota (LWV), 51, 58, 65–73, 75–88
Leech Lake Reservation, x, 160n54
left, viii, 76, 121; leftist, 139
Lenin, Vladimir, 143, 145
liberal, 5, 66, 75, 76, 77, 79–81, 85, 87, 88, 115; antiracism, 30, 65, 66, 78, 83–85; capitalism, 10
liberalism, 76, 77, 164n63; imagination, 86; individualism, 86; neo-liberalism, 164n63; organizations, 111
Lipsitz, George, 37, 55, 56, 59, 60, 84, 159n17
Little Earth of United Tribes housing complex, xi, 49, 50
Little Mogadishu, 132
Locke, John, 77; Lockean, 156n77
lumber, 2, 136. *See also* timber

"machinery of enforcement," 60, 97, 119, 167n27
Mankato, x, 1; 1862 executions, 1, 2, 11, 55
marginality, 26, 39, 57, 118, 129; Indigenous, 57, 78; infrastructural, 56; urban, 67
Mary Tyler Moore Show, The, 132
Menominee, 70
migration, 9, 11, 37, 46, 47, 97, 130, 132, 133, 135, 136–38. *See also* immigration
military, 16, 118–20, 122, 126–28, 135, 137, 139; antimilitarist,

121, 172n26; geography, 140; militarism, 31, 117, 140, 141
Minneapolis, x, 1, 4, 5, 14; city of, viii, 91; history, 18, 24; police, 8, 9, 31, 91; South, xi, 14, 30, 31, 33, 34, 35, 50, 53–56, 60, 61, 63, 93, 100, 101, 103, 114, 115, 130, 149
Minneapolis American Indian Center, xi, 49
Minneapolis Area Office, 71. *See also* Bureau of Indian Affairs
Minneapolis Department of Civil Rights (MDCR), 52
Minneapolis Police Department (MPD), ix, 31, 91–94, 101, 103–5, 110–13, 144, 166n11; role in murder of George Floyd, vii, 92
Minneapolis Star, 136
Minneapolis Tribune, 14, 15, 57, 65, 68, 71, 82, 83, 106, 111, 132
Minnesota, ix, x, 1, 4, 5, 9; institutions, 2; Minnesotans, 14, 33, 34, 54, 59, 68, 75, 113, 127
Minnesota League of Women Voters, 30, 96, 111, 123
Minnesota River. *See* Mnisota Wakpa
minority, 47, 104; ignored, 68, 70, 80
Mississippi River, x, 11, 39. *See also* Wakpa Tanka
Mitchell, George, 103–4, 105 169n5
Mni Sota, 1, 18
Mni Sota Makoce, 1
Mnisota Wakpa, x, 11
mobility, 47, 63
Mondale, Walter, 71, 79, 162n11
Moscow, 143
Moscow State University, 143, 145
Myer, Dillon, 46

David Hugill is assistant professor of geography and environmental studies at Carleton University in Ottawa, Canada.